SEX ON STAGE

SEX ON STAGE

Performing the Body Politic

Edited by Alison J Carr and Lynn Sally

BLOOMSBURY ACADEMIC
LONDON • NEW YORK • OXFORD • NEW DELHI • SYDNEY

BLOOMSBURY ACADEMIC
Bloomsbury Publishing Plc, 50 Bedford Square, London, WC1B 3DP, UK
Bloomsbury Publishing Inc, 1359 Broadway, 12th Floor, New York, NY 10018, USA
Bloomsbury Publishing Ireland, 29 Earlsfort Terrace, Dublin 2, D02 AY28, Ireland

BLOOMSBURY, BLOOMSBURY ACADEMIC and
the Diana logo are trademarks of Bloomsbury Publishing Plc

First published in Great Britain 2025
Reprinted in 2025

Cover design by Adriana Brioso
Cover images © Adobe Stock

A catalogue record for this book is available from the British Library.

A catalog record for this book is available from the Library of Congress
Names: Carr, Alison J., 1978- editor. | Sally, Lynn, editor.
Title: Sex on stage : performing the body politic / edited by Alison J. Carr and Lynn Sally.
Description: London ; New York : Bloomsbury Academic, 2025. |
Includes bibliographical references and index. |
Summary: "This is the first collection of original essays, articles, and images from authors,
activists, artists, and scholars that grapple with the explicit body and the staging of sex across
multiple spaces - from burlesque to drag, to sex work to celebrity culture. This book uncovers
how gender and sexuality collide on stage in dynamic, dramatic, and thought-provoking
ways. By taking a broad view of sex and the stage, it tracks influences across the underground,
marginalised, and the mainstream, from 'high' contemporary live art to the 'low' of entertainment.
Includes interviews, memoir, photo essays, performance scripts, roundtable discussions, flash
nonfiction, and the traditional essay"– Provided by publisher.
Identifiers: LCCN 2024037852 (print) | LCCN 2024037853 (ebook) |
ISBN 9781350443617 (hardback) | ISBN 9781350443655 (paperback) |
ISBN 9781350443624 (epub) | ISBN 9781350443631 (ebook)
Subjects: LCSH: Sex. | Sex work. | Sex workers. | Gender identity. |
Gender identity in mass media. | Mass media and sex. | Public sex.
Classification: LCC HQ21 .S47225 2025 (print) | LCC HQ21 (ebook) |
DDC 306.7–dc23/eng/20241118
LC record available at https://lccn.loc.gov/2024037852
LC ebook record available at https://lccn.loc.gov/2024037853

ISBN: HB: 978-1-3504-4361-7
          PB: 978-1-3504-4365-5
          ePDF: 978-1-3504-4363-1
          eBook: 978-1-3504-4362-4

Typeset by Integra Software Services Pvt. Ltd.
Printed and bound in Great Britain

For product safety related questions contact productsafety@bloomsbury.com

To find out more about our authors and books visit www.bloomsbury.com
and sign up for our newsletters.

CONTENTS

ACT I
ESSAYS

ACT III
DIALOGUES

FIGURES

ACKNOWLEDGMENTS

The editors would like to thank the many artists, performers, and activists who inspired this collection. We give special thanks to Feona Attwood who was an important contributor to the development of this project. Thanks to our team at Bloomsbury, including our editor, Olivia Dellow.

Ra Malika Imhotep's essay was originally published as "Mama's Marvelous Tar Baby: Black Feminist Experiments in Spillersian Ecdysis," in *The Flesh of the Matter: A Critical Forum on Hortense Spillers* (Vanderbilt University Press, published October 30, 2024).

SETTING THE STAGE: AN INTRODUCTION

by Lynn Sally

This collection has been a long time in the making, both the physical object and the journey to arrive here. For years, we have prepared for opening night. False starts. Failed rehearsals. Delays in production. Throughout we have remained steadfast that, as Carolina Are offers, performances of gender and sexuality are not "inherently un-feminist." Moreover, we believe shining a spotlight on these bodies will illuminate what makes us human, what drives us to create, what moves us to attend live performance tingling with anticipation that we will leave slightly altered from how we arrived.

When we first envisioned a collection of writing on the things we love—live performance that pushes against the decorum of respectability—we wanted to develop an umbrella framework that could incorporate drag, burlesque, performance art, and other performance that celebrates the explicit body. We came up with the title, *Sex on Stage*, partially to be provocative but also because it provided that framework.

Sex on Stage presents original writings and images by artists, activists, performers, and academics—many of whom occupy several of those categories simultaneously—engaging with the themes of sex, gender, and live performance. From burlesque to sex work to traditional theater, the staging of sex pushes against norms of respectability, instead flaunting the body to shock, entertain, tell stories, and display a new kind of gender expression. By taking a broad view of sex and the stage, this book tracks influences across the underground, marginalized, and the mainstream, from "high" contemporary live art to the "low" of nightlife.

The contributors included in this collection—and the performers they discuss—inhabit their bodies in self-authored ways. These are not understudies. Rather, this book is filled with stars of the show. Though each journey offered here is as unique

Thanks to Alison J Carr who provided editorial feedback and writing for this introduction. This chapter, and the collection overall, would not be possible without her, and the many conversations we have had over the years as we developed the scope of this project.

as a fingerprint, what they share is plain: smart people saying interesting things about performances of gender and sexuality.

Though there's nothing about sex that should be shameful, the truth remains, it's not neutral. Sex is multifaceted and complex. Sex makes and conflates meaning simultaneously, and it can—and does—change over time. We turn to Marissa Vigneault's definition of sex in Act 1 to help frame our approach: "Here, I use the term sex in reference to what Amia Srinivasan calls both 'a cultural thing posing as a natural one … gender in disguise' and 'a thing we do with our sexed bodies.'" The multiple meanings of sex are evident throughout the texts here. As Rose Wood puts it in their interview by Joe E. Jeffreys, "There's a prevailing belief that if sex is shown onstage it's for the purpose of titillation. Sex though has other inferences." This project seeks to unpack those "other inferences" for "how we stage intimacy matters," according to Yarit Dor in her interview with Alexander Millington.

Taking a private act and making it a public performance, as we and the contributors explore in this collection, can be a radical act. As Marissa Vigneault offers, "Putting sex on stage has immense potential to disrupt exploitation and rethink sexual labor." Furthermore, sex is part of the human condition. As Dor frames it, "through art we educate others about life and therefore about sex, love, toxic relationships, care, passion, harm and obsession. I think how intimacy is portrayed is connected to how humanity is portrayed." Denying certain bodies pleasure can be dehumanizing, for, as Dor offers, intimacy and sex "should not be owned by a white body, or a slim, muscular body or an able body or a tall body or a young body." Sex is universal and yet it is not universally experienced nor expressed. The contributors here—and the art and artists they discuss—all shed a spotlight on the staging of sex, sexuality, and gender.

Gender Matters

Gender is, as Selena the Stripper puts it, "a nebulous thing." Queer bodies have known for some time that gender is not as straightforward as we have been led to believe. "This is part of the complication of genderqueer identities, their refusal to fit into either side of the binary," Ella-Gabriel Mason offers through their framing of gender performance as "gender auditioning," "gender rehearsal," and "gender bundling." Mason continues: "Nonbinary and genderqueer people unbundle the attributes that the binary so rigidly assigns to masculine and feminine, and that unbundling can look chaotic and illegible from the outside." This collection is committed to this unbundling as it begins from the assumption that gender is not a biological imperative but instead is a social construction.

And yet gender still matters. We continue to struggle with how to describe the material reality of people's experiences without resorting to essentialism or reinscribing a gender binary. As Ella-Gabriel Mason explains, "gender expressions are performances—series of behaviors that are practised with enough diligence over time that the resulting expressions appear authentic." In these pages, we engage with terms like "men" and "women" knowing that they are limited—and limiting—constructs. And yet we are still interested in unpacking their meaning and real-world consequences. As we challenge a static gender binary here, we acknowledge gender continues to carry within it power imbalances. In short, we continue to grapple with how to challenge a static gender binary while also acknowledging that gender still matters.

This is a critically feminist position. As Carolina Are puts it, "We need to avoid starting our discussions from the standpoint that sex, and performances of sexuality, are inherently un-feminist and damaging to women (and to women alone)." The feminism found in these pages challenges the assumption that bodies are rendered objects when displayed. Invoking Laura Mulvey, Are questions, "And what is the difference between dancing for the male gaze and dancing for yourself in front of the male gaze?" We contend that the explicit body is more than titillation; it can be used as a tool to inform, entertain, and move spectators to action.

We offer the radical position that exhibitionism can be a critical component of subjecthood, a position tackled in this collection on the level of praxis. The authors here bear witness to what these bodies do and say—both literally and symbolically—as they boldly insist their right to self-express and challenge rigid norms around gender and sexuality. This collection offers exhibitionism and the staging of sex as a form of activism.

Our contributors understand this first-hand as they come from a range of gender identities and backgrounds. The majority of our contributors are AFAB (assigned female at birth) and/or identify as women. Some of our contributors identify as genderqueer, trans, and nonbinary. Many contributors—and the folks they write about—inhabit multiple marginalized subject positions simultaneously. An intersectional approach is required to shine light on these webs of interconnectivity. Together, these perspectives offer a more nuanced representation than a binary model of gender suggests.

Several of our contributors self-identify as sex workers, openly or covertly. This is not a neutral designation. Sex workers are vilified and policed in the real world, and increasingly on social media as "SW" and other abbreviations are increasingly used to avoid the tyranny of violating "community standards." Though the majority of sex workers chose their occupation, it marginalizes them in traditional society. As a result, sex workers have had to advocate for the value of their labor, their identities, and this fight is ongoing. Denying sex workers—or anybody who puts their explicit body on display—language to describe what they do denies them of their subjecthood. It is censorship. And dehumanizing. And it was one of our goals with this collection to hear directly from those marginalized voices.

With a theme as broad as "sex on stage," there are admittedly numerous omissions in this collection. There is little representation of pornography or live sex acts, or content that grapples with live cam and device screens as stages. New media plays a significant role in the representations of live performance and the explicit body—especially post-Covid—and that is not fully explored in these pages. These omissions should not be read as a dismissal of their importance; rather, we hope this collection is the first of many that takes sex on stage as a significant and legitimate field of study.

This Book's Organization: The Page as Stage

We have extended the metaphor of the stage to the organization of this book. We structured this book around three Acts separated by two Intermissions. Act I features Essays while Act II turns to Monologues (shorthand for one person speaking about their experiences). Act III brings Dialogues (or two people speaking via interviews) into the conversation. In between the three Acts, we offer two Intermissions featuring photo essays that explore sex on stage through images and text. In this way, the book is intended to be experienced, much like the live performance which is the subject explored in these pages.

In our original call for submissions, we encouraged authors to explore a range of styles from traditional essays to creative writing to conversations to photo essays, and what we include here represents the rich range of modalities we received. This is important. So often in the academe, academically trained voices are valorized over lived experience. Academics, who may also be artists and/or activists, are often discouraged from exploring their ideas and experiences in ways that are accessible to a broader audience. Creativity often gets sacrificed for the sake of disciplinary rigor. On the flipside, those not academically trained are rarely given a seat at the table. They are subjects studied, not necessarily those granted permission to speak and produce meaning. Here we do not make a distinction between academic and practitioner, or elevate one type of voice above another. Instead, each contributor is given their moment to shine on stage.

The distinction between the traditional "essay" in Act I and "monologues" in Act II is about writing style, not academic training. In Act I, what the essays have in common is writers and thinkers using secondary materials, as well as personal reflection, to produce meaning. Here several of our academically trained contributors have experimented with style and form, including Ra Malika Imhotep, who weaves excerpts from they performance throughout their innovative essay, and Marissa Vigneault who experiments with autoethnography in her compelling read of a striptease in a museum. These essays explode academic expectations, as Act II opens up critical discourse that emerges from personal stories.

Act I begins with Carolina Are who braids together critical theory with her own experiences as a researcher and pole dancer to reveal what brought her, finally, to decompartmentalize her identities. Next up is Julia Matias's meticulous and engaging close read of Calamity Chang's "foodlesque" burlesque acts that stage—and seek to subvert—Asian stereotypes; this theme of food returns in Erin Rachel Kaplan's fascinating discussion of performance artist Xandra Ibarra's "fucking whiteness" with a bottle of hot sauce. Between these two essays, we hear from Ash Hudson-Myers about the history of staging queer sex through theatrical plays that deal, head-on, with HIV/AIDS. Next up, Ella-Gabriel Mason explores genderqueer identity in strip clubs, weaving their personal experiences, interviews they conducted with other genderqueer stripclub performers, and critical theory.

We take a break from the show to offer a photo essay in our first Intermission about the Whoopee Club (2003–9), London's pioneering theater-meets-nightclub that offered radical immersive performance experiences. This intermission features photographs by Sarah Ainslie and excerpts from a conversation led by Alison J Carr between Lara Clifton and Tamara Tyrer, Whoopee Club founders, discussing how they brought their fantastical fantasies to reality.

In Act II, we pass the microphone directly to artists and activists as they take to the stage with memoirs, scripts, and stories that describe and reflect on the magic of live performance. Forming the bridge between our essays in Act I and our monologues in Act II is Emily Underwood-Lee's piece about her struggles with cancer that weaves excerpts from her performance script with gender theory. Using her license as an artist, Sharon Kivland intervenes on Émile Zola's novel, *Nana*, appropriating sections of the text by changing the tense or orientation of the speaker, or conflating different descriptions from different characters to present the self-possessed subject, Nana. Kivland sifts through the words to reassemble a real body. This textual artwork creates a historical counterpoint in Act II so that we can see the echoes of earlier theatrical forms that are invoked in the staging of sex today.

The majority of the chapters in Act II are performer memoirs: DawN Crandell describes her journey from a fourteen-year-old club kid to founding Brown Girls Burlesque, Zahra Stardust offers a comical take on the "accidents" that have happened in her career as a stripper. Following Stardust is Toussaint Jeanlouis's depiction of putting his Black queer body on display—and the harm that resulted—in an intimate theater show that staged sensorial experiences for patrons. Next, Anna Brooke reveals her acceptance of her body—and her ongoing process to strip away the restrictions imposed on her that, ultimately, have forced her to address her own privilege—through the art of burlesque. Closing Act II, we present Stacey Clare who unpacks her stripper suitcase, narrating the trauma of losing her entire career of costumes and ephemera she had carefully curated, a loss that inspired her to activism and ultimately to the founding of the East London Stripper Collective (ELSC).

Our second intermission picks up where the final chapter of Act II ends, namely, with the founding of the ELSC. This Intermission features the work of Julie Cook, who has documented members of the ELSC through her stark and beautiful portrait photographs. She then has created "police files" of these performers, which include ephemera, fliers, and social media content.

Our final Act III turns from the monologues of Act II to dialogues, or conversations. These conversations shed light on important topics including harm reduction, sexual violence, and the explicit body on stage as theater. Included here is a discussion between Alexander Millington and Intimacy Director Yarit Dor around the role of harm reduction with the staging of sex in live theater and film. Next up Julia Havard and Jadelynn St Dre discuss the creation of St Dre's moving collaborative project that "engaged queer and transgender survivors of sexual violence in community-building and art-making processes." This chapter opens and closes with "poetic choreographies"—much like previous chapters in this collection that weave performance and textual excerpts, including those by Imhotep, Underwood-Lee, and Kivland—and visual representations of St Dre's exhibition "Choreographies of Disclosure: What the Mind Forgets" (Pro Arts Gallery, Oakland, 2019).

Without further ado, we bring to the stage our final act of the show, a conversation between drag scholar and archivist Joe E. Jeffreys and the "The Queen of Filth" Rose Wood, an innovative theater maker who pushes the boundaries of the body in their performances. We cannot envision a more fitting way to conclude *Sex on Stage* than by passing the microphone to Rose and Jeffreys for this thoughtful, compelling conversation. Besides, Rose Wood is a hard act to follow.

The organization of this book into three Acts with two Intermissions offers a kind of structure, but there's no correct way to read this collection. Instead, this book, like live performance, is intended to be experienced. Sit back and watch the whole show by reading it cover to cover, or dip in for a performance or two, and step away to grab a drink at the bar. Stay until the curtain call, or come back another night. A chapter may lead the reader to the next act, or it may lead to an earlier act. Readers may choose their own adventure, so to speak, thereby putting them in control of their reading journey. Like the live performances described here, the audience—i.e., the reader—is an integral part of the show.

We welcome you to *Sex on Stage*. Buckle up, and prepare yourself for a wild ride. Enjoy the show.

Bibliography

Austin, J. L. *How to Do Things with Words*. Cambridge, MA: Harvard University Press, 1975.

Burana, Lily. "We Were Strippers Once." In *Whorephonia*, edited by Lizzie Borden, 357–95. New York: Seven Stories Press, 2022.

Sally, Lynn. *Neo-Burlesque: Striptease as Transformation*. New Brunswick: Rutgers University Press, 2022.

Selena the Stripper. "Interview with Selena the Stripper by Goddess Cori." In *Whorephobia*, edited by Lizzie Borden, 411–21. New York: Seven Stories Press, 2022.

Act I

ESSAYS

Chapter 1

POLE DANCING ACADEMIC: DECOMPARTMENTALIZING THE PERSONAL, SEXUAL, AND PROFESSIONAL WHILE BLENDING POLE DANCE AND RESEARCH CAREERS

by Carolina Are

"What will your life look like when you start de-compartmentalizing?" asked my ex.

It was the first time I'd heard the word.

"Compartmentalizing" means "to separate something into isolated compartments or categories."[1] So by de-compartmentalizing, I could stop being an academic *and* a pole dancer, and I could become a pole dancing academic. I could stop hiding.

For about three years, I tried to live two different lives. Like Bruce Wayne and Batman, but without the money. I was a hard-working PhD student at a London university, keen to teach undergrads and make a name for myself as a researcher. I was also an up-and-coming pole dance performer and blogger, wearing tiny outfits that I didn't want my students or colleagues to see for fear of trouble or loss of job prospects.

I did not know what to do about the two different lives, and I found maintaining them very stressful. I wanted my blog and my writing to be noticed, but I used a different name when I was being interviewed by the media. I wanted to be a researcher, but my cyber-criminology research on online abuse seemed to clash, in my head, with my performances. I was doing something serious and hard—research—and something apparently frivolous and sexy that I loved—dancing. I could not have it both ways.

This fear, this prejudice, were all of my own making.

I am also sure that the internalized whorephobia—the hatred, disgust, and fear of sex workers—handed down by centuries of patriarchal ruling, and its prevalence within higher education, did not help.[2]

I started pole dancing in August 2016, during a master's degree in Criminology at the University of Sydney. I had uprooted myself from London, where I had completed my BA in Journalism and spent a few years working in PR, where I built a safety net of friends, colleagues, and loved ones, but where I had also ended up in an abusive relationship. I had anxiety, PTSD, depression, and leaving London for the furthest place I could imagine to study the subject I loved as a child seemed like the best choice. On the contrary, in Sydney I struggled to make friends since my course was attended mainly by older criminal justice professionals. The reality of living on the other side of the world by myself was that I was lonely, and that my mental health was no better than when I lived in London. My dream of living the carefree surfer's life wasn't to be.

When a contact invited me to try a pole dance class with her, I didn't think twice. Having enjoyed artistic gymnastics as a child, I missed the danger of being upside down, and I found myself unable to work out on my own due to the post-traumatic mess happening in my head.

Back then, I knew very little about pole. I didn't join with the hope of feeling sexy, or to perform. I just needed company, and to move without being stuck in my head. I was not privy to the debates inflaming the pole industry following some pole dancers' attempts to distance themselves from our art's founders, strippers.[3] Nor was I aware of the critical feminist discourse on pole, which painted recreational pole dance as "raunch culture," and as yet another requirement for women to perform their sexiness through "technologies of sexiness," marketed to them so they could conform to an acceptable ideal of female sexuality.[4]

I was drowning and gasping for breath, and needed to stay afloat.

Slowly but surely, pole dancing became my life.

The physicality, fun, and adrenaline I got from pole helped me stay sane and balance out my research with my human needs as I finished my MA and decided to return to London to start a PhD. At the same time, my perception of my body was changing: it wasn't a thing for others to use, but something strong I could rely on to lift me up and help me enjoy myself. It was something I stopped feeling self-conscious about showing, something I was proud of.

Suddenly, pole dancing and its benefits became something I wanted to write—and, really, shout—about.

In London, I rebranded my lifestyle blog as bloggeronpole.com, started training regularly for about ten hours a week, and creating my first pole and floor routines to submit to dance competitions. Subconsciously, I knew I wanted a career in pole, and that this career mattered to me as much as a career in academia.

But in my head, pole dancing seemed to clash with my "serious" PhD, researching online abuse and conspiracy theories under a cyber-criminological framework. Due to prejudices related to women and sexuality, taking part in an art that exists because of strippers (thank you, stripper goddesses!) seemed too risqué to become a respected academic. So, for most of my PhD, I tried to ensure the search results for my academic persona didn't return pictures of me in a thong by using a stage/blogging name and removing my real surname from anything pole related.

It was during the second year of my doctorate that everything changed. I realized that publishing too much from my thesis would have resulted in endless trolling by the abusive subculture I was observing, mirroring previous academics' experiences. And it was during that same summer of 2019 that Instagram started censoring pole dancers' posts and hashtags, changing the course of my online experience and, in doing so, my research interests.

By the third year of my PhD, I was finding academia increasingly frustrating while my pole dancing and blogging career, as well as my activist profile, were booming. I had become an instructor in a popular London pole studio. Citations of my blog were appearing in media articles, research papers, and theses. I had received direct apologies from Instagram about their censorship of our posts (more on that later). I had created campaigns supported by celebrities and petitions signed by hundreds of thousands of people. Being both a researcher and a pole dancing activist at once wasn't just important to me personally—I was in a unique position to conduct research in a suddenly growing but under-researched area.

But how could I do this, when both "old," white, male, and stale academics *and* feminists seemed to view pole dance as taboo, or yet another patriarchal imposition on frivolous women who took it up for clicks and attention?

Critiquing Feminist Critiques

Navigating my persona as a feminist, abuse survivor, academic, activist, *and* pole dancer was made even more difficult by society and academia's own condemnation of pole as a practice.

Insider research about recreational pole dancing is lacking, so researchers who know very little about pole as a practice produce papers that are judgmental in their "feminism," and find out very little about pole in the process. And yet, online material on the positive effects of pole dancing is everywhere—my blog included!—so these attempts at research are not only lazy. They are, quite frankly, just poor.

Feminists have expressed disquiet about the emergence of recreational pole dancing and its links with empowerment.[5] Pole has been so far called "porno chic" or "raunch culture" by researchers, who described it through reductive, heteronormative, sex-negative, and sex worker exclusive lenses that failed to recognize pole as a complex and evolving practice. According to this view, pole is sex, sex is disempowering, and, therefore, a rejection of feminist ideals.[6]

How boring and reductive.

Ariel Levy wonders why a straight woman would want to see another woman spin around a pole in tiny clothes. For her, post-feminists and their free sexuality are exhibitionists portraying a male-imagined caricature of female sexuality. From here she goes on to define their actions as taking part in "raunch culture," where porn takes over culture, fashion, art, and the like, making overt sexuality a requirement for desirability. For Levy, women who pole dance are objectifying themselves.[7]

Whitehead and Kurz manage to do even worse. In a 2009 article in *Feminism and Psychology*, one of the authors took *three* pole dancing classes to write an article about whether pole is empowering or not.[8] Most pole dancers reading this paper would giggle: in three classes, you can probably just manage to hold a couple beginner moves for a few seconds, and my beginner students could testify sexiness is *not* on their mind when their thighs are burning from friction with the pole. Three classes tell you nothing about pole as a practice or as a culture. Three classes are hardly representative of pole's effects on our mental and physical health, and describing such an insignificant interaction with pole does not shed any light on our world.

Whitehead and Kurz describe pole classes as normal gym classes that reduce fat or improve agility—taking the soul and history away from pole dancing and highlighting techniques that most pole studios are moving away from, like advertising pole as a way to get skinny instead of a way to have fun and get strong.

To make things worse, Whitehead and Kurz interview a few pole dancers who stress their distance from those who have created their sport—strippers. A wider investigation into pole dancing, beyond beginner classes and beyond *three* classes, would have shown them how sex worker and sex positive the pole dancing industry can be, and how problematic this discrimination toward a marginalized group is. Yet, having done nothing of the sort, Whitehead and Kurz conclude that while pole outside strip clubs cannot be fully seen as "pornographic," it is still more performative than other exercises such as running or lifting weights, and therefore bad for feminism and women's freedom. *As if* gym bros showing uninterested women just trying to work out how much they can lift were not performative.

While Whitehead and Kurz's paper pre-dates pole dancing's social media virality and its subsequent discussions of pole as both a sport and a practice with a history, their views are, sadly, not uncommon. They are merely a reflection of outsider descriptions of pole dance, and of the general anti-sex work trend that sees a variety of "feminists" campaign for criminalizing and further marginalizing anything even remotely related to the sex trade, as multiple campaigns to shut down strip clubs in the UK seem to show.[9]

Take the male gaze. If I had a penny for each time researchers and average pole detractors tried to bring up a watered down, uncritical mention of Laura Mulvey's male gaze when talking about pole, by now I would have probably made it rain more than Cardi B on her last night at Sue's. According to this (very limited) worldview, pole dancers dance for the "male gaze," a.k.a. when men watch women as sexual objects to be consumed and controlled.[10] The dancers' relationship with the male gaze is, however, hardly ever questioned.

Stripperphobic pole dancers love a male gazey narrative, also repurposed by the main studio owner interviewed in the Netflix documentary *Strip Down, Rise Up*. For her, pole dance studios "remove" the male gaze by creating safe spaces for us to pole outside of strip clubs. Too bad that it was in those strip clubs that pole was first taught, and that pole dancing is not a prerogative of cis het women: it is a practice performed by LGBTQIA+ dancers, by lesbians and bisexual women, by heterosexual, gay and bisexual men, by trans folx and by nonbinary people, who create new styles, movement, and aesthetics within pole every day. So, while the male gaze does need a mention in the history and practice of pole, to me, it is more interesting to interrogate how a sexual gaze, possibly influenced by mainstream male desire, has been evolving after it has been reclaimed by dancers from all sorts of backgrounds.

Pole dancing can indeed look very sexual: most of our moves are inspired by strippers who gave tricks their names and who first wore platform shoes, dancing in clubs mostly populated by men. But while there is a very "puritan" side of pole that aims to cleanse our practice of its stripping origins, most pole dancers actually acknowledge that strippers popularized pole, and they still dance without incurring immorality dilemmas every time they perform a pole trick.

We desperately need more complex research on pole dancing to address these nuances. Nørholm Just and Sara Muhr make a start toward it, arguing that, when trying pole classes, they simply could not ignore pole instructors' expression and perception of empowerment during teaching.[11] For them, the feminist potential of pole lies in reclaiming, rather than erasing, the tension between sexualization and empowerment. It is by embracing this tension that we can further, instead of stunting, feminist discourse. In Just and Muhr's words:

> Any feminist agenda must, therefore, include the right to active female sexualities while continuously criticizing how such sexualities are understood within a patriarchal and sexist society. […] It is not the actions and interpretations of the pole dance instructors (or other performers of sexualized labour)—and their claim to the right to be sexy—that should catch our critical attention. Instead, their intense emotional labour may help us zoom in on—and call out—the sexist structures within which they are discursively and materially embedded.[12]

Perhaps, to understand the appeal of pole, we need to avoid starting our discussions from the standpoint that sex and performances of sexuality are inherently un-feminist and damaging to women (and to women alone). If women dance for the male gaze, who do male and gender nonconforming dancers dance for? How about those who dance for themselves when no one is watching? And what is the difference between dancing for the male gaze and dancing for yourself *in front of* the male gaze?

These are questions that, consciously or not, pole dancers have been exploring while dancing and while sharing pole online, and that researchers have so far been underestimating or misunderstanding. While I do not have an answer for them, I am grateful for my own experience that allows me to question these narratives as I explore my own subculture.

The Pole Dancing Online Media Subculture

In the eyes of a criminologist like me, pole dancing is a subculture.

Subcultures are groups separate from the main society or culture. They come together because they share the wish to resist mainstream cultural values, as well as a common identity, values, and practices that may derive from prejudice, discrimination, and other conditions.[13] Members of a subculture adopt its beliefs, values, jargon, and behavioral norms; they use its channels of communication, adapting to its dress, gesture, and behavioral styles, and even rely on power figures within those groups.[14] And even though the term "subculture" was initially just used to define deviant, criminal groups, it's now being used to define groups deviating from mainstream culture, even just in a cultural sense.[15]

Those who pole dance are part of a subculture because they spend hours working out half naked together (shared "dress" or *undress* sense); they celebrate bodies and their strength (shared values); use similar language, such as names of moves and activities deriving from stripping (e.g., hello boys, vagina monster, heel clacks, and bangs). Pole dancers also share the same "expert" equipment like poles, liquid chalk, and other grip aids, and stripper shoes. Many of us also use social media to network, find training inspiration, and promote ourselves.

While people who take up pole dancing might sometimes experience negative social judgments after they start, many of us have shared the feeling of becoming "addicted" to pole thanks to its physical and mental health benefits.[16] Pellizzer, Tiggeman, and Clark highlight that while recreational pole dance has been described as a sexually objectifying activity, others—and particularly those who practice it—argue that it is an embodying and empowering activity, like other forms of dance. While speaking with both pole dancers and university students, they found that enjoyment of sexualization was related to embodiment, resulting in more positive perceptions of body image and with less self-objectification.

It is striking that researchers have gone into pole dance classes wearing red-light, "SEX! DEVIANCE! DANGER!"-tinted glasses—especially when a better understanding of pole is only a Google search away (censorship aside).

The learning of pole happens online—with tutorials, blog posts, courses, and discussions—as much as offline, and because of this I like to call pole dancing an online media subculture. It was partly thanks to social media tutorials that pole dance hit the mainstream, with more and more dancers using YouTube and then Instagram to be part of the latest fitness trend.[17] A key aspect of our pole subculture is the use of social media to share our progress and to promote our work, to sell online classes or performances. Social networks have become essential toward the spreading and thriving of new subcultures, with each platform using different tones, memes, and jokes that can only be understood by members of a specific subculture.

Online media subcultures can be similar to a fandom.[18] Like a fandom, members of online subcultures share a common identity and culture with other fans, performing specific online actions that represent their belonging to their chosen subculture. These performances can even include the choice of specific profile or cover images, as argued by Gerbaudo, who explains how selective the choice of a picture can be to attract followers with similar ideological purposes.[19] Say hello to the booming trend of costly but fabulous pole dance photoshoots showcasing our favorite moves!

So fans of pole dancing perform their fandom through specific posting techniques online—and all you have to do is open your Instagram or TikTok under the #poledance hashtag (if it hasn't been censored *again*) to see that pole styles and approaches to pole are incredibly varied. You may see pole dancing ballerinas wearing pointe shoes or performing barefoot flows, and you will think pole dance *is* art because polers can indeed create choreographies, flows of moves, and show-stopping poses like ballet dancers. You may see someone performing a set of flips on the pole and think, "wow, pole dance is fitness, a sport! This shit belongs at the Olympics!" And you would also be right. Pole classes follow a straight-up fitness program, with warm-ups, cool downs, and exercises to build strength and/or stamina. Often, we are required to have fitness qualifications to teach it—I have three at the moment, and I cannot get enough of learning more about the physics, physiology, and science behind our practice. Pole is a very physically taxing activity; we get badly injured while doing it. We sweat when we pole dance, and we get much stronger and bendier. Pole dancers (and strippers) are athletes. But pole dance is also sexy, because it was popularized by strippers and stripping is *still* the biggest influence on pole dancers' movement. Online performances of pole dance highlight the diversity of the pole dancing subculture, something that taking three pole classes for the purpose of research cannot offer.

So if pole dance can be art and fitness, why can it not also be sexy?

It is about time we stopped pathologizing and othering sex and those who enjoy it or work with it. Feminist critiques that condemn pole as a performance for the patriarchy are missing the point, assuming that women (and all pole dancers) cannot enjoy having or performing sex, imposing the same archaic, puritanical views of sexuality that the patriarchy imposes on us—that being a sexual being is morally wrong.

Too many research perspectives on recreational pole dancing have been ahistorical and devoid of nuance. While sexualization of women and marginalized communities is everywhere, often imposed on them in ways that they cannot control by advertising and the media, it is practices like consensual sex work or recreational pole dancing that are accused of bringing feminism back decades.[20] But pole studios and performance spaces offered me the opportunity to portray my sexuality on my own terms, and they have sparked movements and trends that normalize different bodies, identities, and unique understandings of sexuality. These practices helped me re-elaborate and reject sexual shame, and own my own sexual energy. I have a right to express myself this way, and doing so makes me no less employable. It should not force me to compartmentalize my identities.

How I Decompartmentalized

I recently gave a lecture addressing a group of PhD students from an American university, invited by a colleague I had met in London during one of the side research gigs I did during my doctorate. My lecture, entitled "Researching and Performing Nudity on Social Media," was about being a researcher/activist fighting social media censorship to help students find their feet in exploring their online presentation.

In the Q&A, my colleague recalled a moment when he asked me if he could follow me on Instagram, back when my pole dancing self and my academic self were two different entities. "I watched you pause," he said, "like you were thinking, 'Can I do this? Do I do this now?'"

I did do it.

I gave him my Instagram handle.

Slowly, I started doing that more and more, hiding my persona less and less, even with colleagues, even at conferences. At another conference, a fellow researcher I was presenting with came up to me and said, "So you're internet famous?" and, after the initial panic, I realized I was not that hard to find, and that being found did not seem to be a problem.

The thought of joining my personae at the right time started to slowly make its way into my head. Then, the right time came, and it was all thanks (but no thanks) to social media censorship.

In the summer of 2019, Instagram began censoring all pole dancing hashtags, our way to find training inspiration, network, and reach new audiences for our classes and performances. This was to comply with FOSTA/SESTA, or the United States' Allow States and Victims to Fight Online Sex Trafficking Act of 2017. An exception to Section 230 of the US Telecommunications Act, FOSTA/SESTA ruled that platforms would become legally liable if they allowed content that promoted or facilitated sex work. With the intermediary liability safeguard that stopped platforms from being legally liable for what was posted on them effectively gone for sexy posts, social media companies began deleting and censoring an increasing amount of content showing skin for fear of being seen as promoting or facilitating the sex trade.[21] Sex workers became FOSTA/SESTA's first target, but pole dancers followed shortly after: performing an art and sport created by strippers makes it difficult for an algorithm to tell which is which, also raising the issue of censoring work practices that, like stripping, are legal in most countries.

In this strange scenario, suddenly, I felt like I could be both people at once. Being an online moderation researcher, I had the means to contextualize what was happening. But I also had this whole pseudo-secret life with networks of censored users who were not being listened to by platforms or the mainstream media, together with my own direct experiences of censorship. My Instagram profile has been deleted and repeatedly shadowbanned since 2019; my TikTok was deleted three times in just one week in 2021.

This situation turned me into an activist researcher: I managed to speak directly with Instagram press, obtaining an apology for their censorship and a (short-lived but important) reversal of the shadowbanning of our hashtags.[22] I started fronting and co-creating a variety of anti-censorship campaigns like #EveryBODYVisible, which gained the support of burlesque superstar Dita Von Teese and the attention of Instagram. I started speaking with censored users about their experiences, getting a deeper understanding of censorship on the platform. This informed my academic papers as much of my activism, and all of a sudden, my experiences and my pole dancing persona *enriched* my academic persona rather than hindering it.

A lack of lived experience does not guarantee neutrality in research: just look at those researchers who tried three pole classes and then wrote uninformed, judgmental accounts of pole dancing as a practice and you'll see everything but

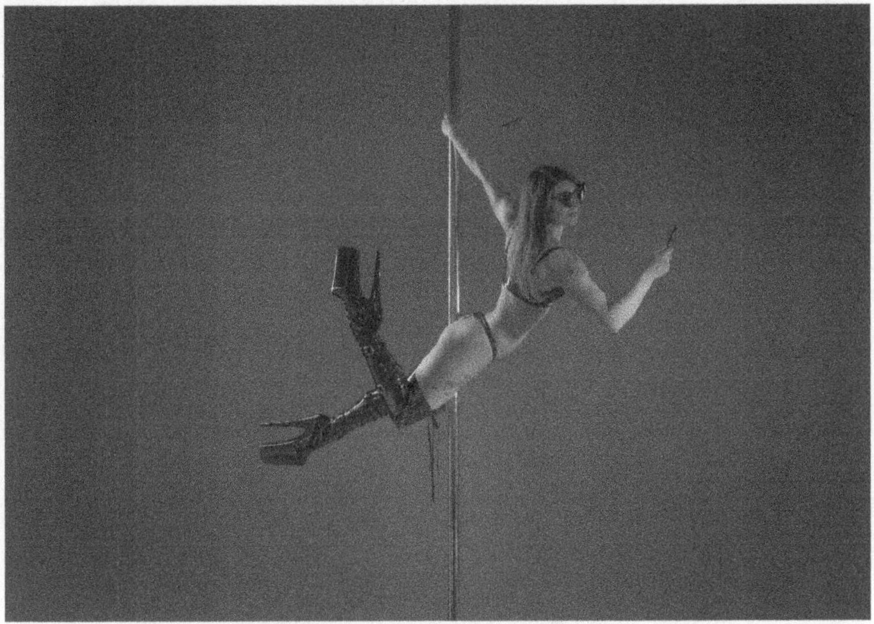

Image 1 Carolina Are, credit Rachel Marshall (@ray.marsh).

neutrality. There is a research benefit in being an active member of the community you are also researching, as long as you keep some perspective.

What matters to me is to help the communities I am part of. By being an "insider" researcher, I can shine a light on the lived experiences of users who post nudity and face censorship, instead of judging them as an outsider. This approach can influence policy that is informed by real-life problems, not by conscious or unconscious biases against nudity and sex.

Eventually, the right time came to make these thoughts, and this "reveal" of both my personae, public to the wider world. On December 16, 2020, the day of my (successful) PhD thesis defense, I came out on Twitter as a pole dancing academic. It was the worst kept secret ever: a lot of my followers and colleagues already knew, and there were a series of articles and video interviews with me where I talked about my work without using my actual surname in anything related to my pole dancing persona. On December 16, 2020, that changed, changing my career's direction in the process. I am not suggesting this was not or is not challenging. It took over a year and a half for me to find a postdoc contract and, to this day, I do not know if I was being rejected because my applications were not up to standards or because my ass is out on the internet. Plus, particularly around those who prefer quantitative research, it can be hard to make the case that ethnography and autoethnography are valid methods to study social media censorship and subcultures—even when the data that platforms publish and share with researchers can offer very few learning points about their moderation

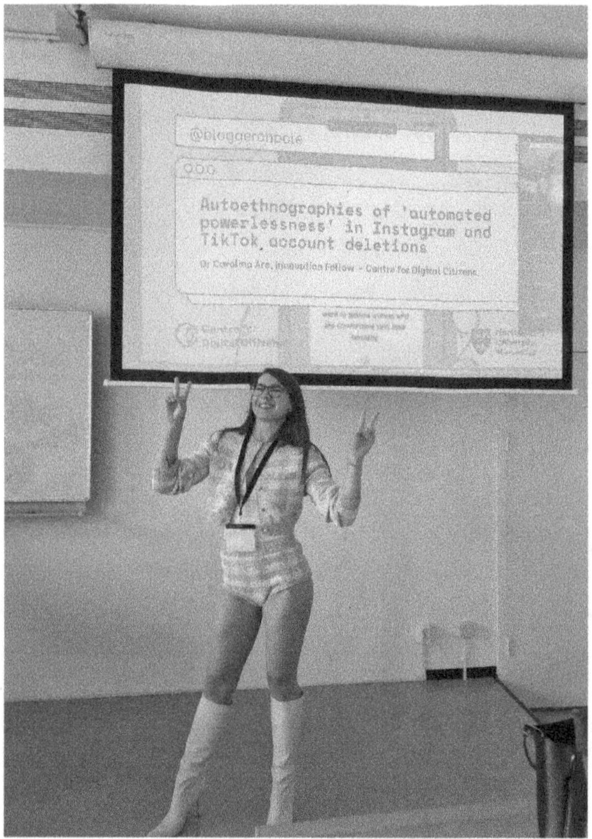

Image 2 Carolina Are, credit Zoe Glatt.

practices. And, of course, inevitably, there are those who assume I am up for it because I am a pole dancer, or because I advocate for sex worker rights. But dickheads are everywhere, not just in academia.

What I am saying is that navigating your different personae takes time. You need to adapt your tactics and how you present yourself depending on your audience: parents, relatives, friends, blogs, mainstream media, social media, academia, and academic journals. It is quite exhausting. But I found blending my research interests with my experiences helpful, particularly because it gives me credibility to manage different stakeholders (e.g., strippers, pole dancers, platforms, journalists, and academic journals) in both fields.

The presence of "insider" researchers with nude online personae or with first-hand experiences in the sex trade in academia is not a threat to research's credibility—it can actually result in better research getting published. The sex worker activist collective Hacking/Hustling, who publish extensive work on social media's censorship of sex work, or the Decoding Stigma Collective, who bridge the gap between sex work, technology, and academia to amplify sex workers' voices, are a case in point. We need more work like this, otherwise whorephobia and fear of sex will never leave academia, and they will inform and promote a reductive, boring, and discriminatory understanding of our world.

I am a researcher *because* I am a pole dancer. I have been pole dancing since the start of my Master's degree in criminology and since my return to academia because pole has kept me sane, active, and curious throughout the lonely and challenging process of getting a PhD.

Notes

1   Merriam-Webster, "Compartmentalize," accessed October 5, 2023, https://www.merriam-webster.com/dictionary/compartmentalize#:~:text=transitive%20verb,Sentences%20Learn%20More%20About%20compartmentalize/.

2   Jessica Simpson, "Whorephobia in Higher Education: A Reflexive Account of Researching Cis Women's Experiences of Stripping while at University," *Higher Education* (2021), https://link.springer.com/article/10.1007/s10734-021-00751-2.

3   Carolina Are, "A History of Modern Pole Dance," *Blogger on Pole*, 2021, https://bloggeronpole.com/2021/07/a-history-of-modern-pole-dance/.

4   Rosalind Gill, "Postfeminist Media Culture," *European Journal of Cultural Studies* 10, no. 2 (2007): 147–66. Also Ariel Levy, *Female Chauvinist Pigs: Women and the Rise of Raunch Culture* (New York: Free Press, 2006).

5   Angela McRobbie, *The Aftermath of Feminism: Gender, Culture and Social Change* (London: Sage, 2009).

6   Levy, *Female Chauvinist Pigs*. Also Rosalind Gill, "Postfeminist Media Culture," *European Journal of Cultural Studies* 10, no. 2 (2007): 147–66.

7   Levy, *Female Chauvinist Pigs*.

8   Kally Whitehead and Tim Kurz, "'Empowerment' and the Pole: A Discursive Investigation of the Reinvention of Pole Dancing as a Recreational Activity," *Feminism & Psychology* 19, no. 2 (2009): 224–44.

9   Dan Barker and Kris Gourlay, "Edinburgh Strip Clubs to Stay Open as Council's Proposed Ban Ruled as 'Unlawful'," *Edinburgh Live*, February 10, 2023, https://www.edinburghlive.co.uk/news/edinburgh-news/edinburgh-strip-clubs-stay-open-26211792.

10 Laura Mulvey, *Visual and Other Pleasures* (Bloomington: Indiana University Press, 1989).

11 Sine Nørholm Just and Sara Louise Muhr, "Holding on to Both ends of a Pole: Empowering Feminine Sexuality and Reclaiming Feminist Emancipation," *Gender, Work & Organisation* 27 (2020): 6–23.

12 Nørholm Just and Muhr, "Holding on to Both Ends of a Pole," 20.

13 Ross Haenfler, *Subcultures: The Basics* (London: Routledge, 2014). Also Michael A. Hogg and Scott A. Reid, "Social Identity, Self-Categorization, and the Communication of Group Norms," *Communication Theory* 16, no. 1 (2006): 7–30.

14 Hans Sebald, "Subculture: Problems of Definition and Measurement," *International Review of Modern Sociology* 5, no. 1(1975): 82–9.

15 Chris Jenks, *Subculture: The Fragmentation of the Social* (Thousand Oaks, CA: Sage, 2004).

16   Joanna C. Nicholas, James A. Dimmock, Cyril J. Donnelly, Jacqueline A. Alderson, and Ben Jackson, "'It's Our Little Secret … an In-Group, Where Everyone's in': Females' Motives for Participation in a Stigmatized Form of Physical Activity," *Psychology of Sport and Exercise* 36 (2018): 104–13.

17   Are, "A History of Modern Pole Dance."

18   Alexis Lothian, "Archival Anarchies: Online Fandom, Subcultural Conservation, and the Transformative Work of Digital Ephemera," *International Journal of Cultural Studies* 16, no. 6 (2012): 541–56.

19   Paolo Gerbaudo, "Protest Avatars as Memetic Signifiers: Political Profile Pictures and the Construction of Collective Identity on Social Media in the 2011 Protest Wave," *Information, Communication & Society* 18, no. 8 (2015): 916–29.

20   Johnny V. Sparks and Annie Lang, "Mechanisms Underlying the Effects of Sexy and Humorous Content in Advertisements," *Communication Monographs* 82, no. 1 (2015): 134–62.

21   Carolina Are and Susanna Paasonen, "Sex in the Shadows of Celebrity," *Porn Studies* 8, no. 1 (2021): 411–19.

22   Carolina Are, "Instagram Apologises to Pole Dancers about the Shadowban," *Blogger on Pole,* 2019b, https://bloggeronpole.com/2019/07/instagram-apologises-to-pole-dancers-about-the-shadowban/.

Bibliography

115th Congress. *H.R.1865—Allow States and Victims to Fight Online Sex Trafficking Act of 2017*. Washington, DC: Congress.gov, 2017–18. https://www.congress.gov/bill/115th-congress/house-bill/1865.

Are, Carolina. "A History of Modern Pole Dance." *Blogger on Pole*. Accessed October 5, 2023. https://bloggeronpole.com/2021/07/a-history-of-modern-pole-dance/.

Are, Carolina. "Instagram Apologises to Pole Dancers about the Shadowban." *Blogger on Pole*. Accessed October 5, 2023. https://bloggeronpole.com/2019/07/instagram-apologises-to-pole-dancers-about-the-shadowban/.

Are, Carolina. "Instagram Censors EveryBODYVisible Campaign against Instagram Censorship—LOL." *Blogger on Pole*. Accessed October 5, 2023. https://bloggeronpole.com/2019/10/everybodyvisible/.

Are, Carolina. "Instagram Denies Censorship of Pole Dancers and Sex Workers." *Blogger on Pole*. Accessed October 5, 2023. https://bloggeronpole.com/2019/07/instagram-denies-censorship-of-pole-dancers-and-sex-workers/.

Are, Carolina and Susanna Paasonen. "Sex in the Shadows of Celebrity." *Porn Studies* 8, no. 4 (2021): 411–19.

Barker, Dan and Kris Gourlay. "Edinburgh Strip Clubs to Stay Open as Council's Proposed Ban Ruled as 'Unlawful.'" *Edinburgh Live*. Accessed February 10, 2023. https://www.edinburghlive.co.uk/news/edinburgh-news/edinburgh-strip-clubs-stay-open-26211792.

Blunt, Danielle, Ariel Wolf, and Emily Coombes. "Posting into the Void—A Community Report by Hacking/Hustling." *Hacking/Hustling*, 2020. https://hackinghustling.org/posting-into-the-void-content-moderation/.

Dale, Joshua Paul. "The Future of Pole Dance." *The Australasian Journal of Popular Culture* 2, no. 3 (2013): 381–96.

Gerbaudo, Paolo. "Protest Avatars as Memetic Signifiers: Political Profile Pictures and the Construction of Collective Identity on Social Media in the 2011 Protest Wave." *Information, Communication & Society* 18, no. 8 (2015): 916–29.

Gill, Rosalind. "Postfeminist Media Culture." *European Journal of Cultural Studies* 10, no. 2 (2007): 147–66.

Haenfler, Ross. *Subcultures: The Basics.* London: Routledge, 2014.

Hogg, Michael A. and Scott A. Reid. "Social Identity, Self-Categorization, and the Communication of Group Norms." *Communication Theory* 16, no. 1 (2006): 7–30.

Jenks, Chris. *Subculture: The Fragmentation of the Social.* London: SAGE, 2004.

Levy, Ariel. *Female Chauvinist Pigs: Women and the Rise of Raunch Culture.* New York: Free Press, 2006.

Lothian, Alexis. "Archival Anarchies: Online Fandom, Subcultural Conservation, and the Transformative Work of Digital Ephemera." *International Journal of Cultural Studies* 16, no. 6 (2012): 541–56.

McRobbie, Angela. *The Aftermath of Feminism: Gender, Culture and Social Change.* London: Sage, 2009.

Merriam-Webster Dictionary. "Compartmentalize." October 5, 2023. https://www. merriam-webster.com/dictionary/compartmentalize.

Mulvey, Laura. *Visual and Other Pleasures.* Bloomington: Indiana University Press, 1989.

Nicholas, Joanna C, James A. Dimmock, Cyril J. Donnelly, Jacqueline A. Alderson, and Ben Jackson. "'It's Our Little Secret … an In-Group, where Everyone's in': Females' Motives for Participation in a Stigmatized Form of Physical Activity." *Psychology of Sport and Exercise* 36 (2018): 104–13.

Nørholm Just, Sine and Sara Louise Muhr. "Holding on to Both Ends of a Pole: Empowering Feminine Sexuality and Reclaiming Feminist Emancipation." *Gender, Work & Organisation* 27 (2020): 6–23.

Pellizzer, Mia, Marika Tiggemann, and Levina Clark. "Enjoyment of Sexualisation and Positive Body Image in Recreational Pole Dancers and University Students." *Sex Roles* 74 (2015): 35–45.

Sebald, Hans. "Subculture Problems of Definition and Measurement." *International Review of Modern Sociology* 5, no. 1 (1975): 82–9.

Simpson, Jessica. "Whorephobia in Higher Education: A Reflexive Account of Researching Cis Women's Experiences of Stripping while at University." *Higher Education* 84 (2021): 17–31.

Sparks, Johnny V. and Annie Lang. "Mechanisms Underlying the Effects of Sexy and Humorous Content in Advertisements." *Communication Monographs* 82, no. 1 (2015): 134–62.

Stardust, Zahra, Gabriella Garcia, and Chibundo Egwuatu. "What Can Tech Learn from Sex Workers? Sexual Ethics, Tech Design & Decoding Stigma." *Berkman Klein Center Collection.* Accessed October 5, 2023. https://medium.com/berkman-klein-center/ what-can-tech-learn-from-sex-workers-8e0100f0b4b9.

Whitehead, Kally and Tim Kurz. "'Empowerment' and the Pole: A Discursive Investigation of the Reinvention of Pole Dancing as a Recreational Activity." *Feminism & Psychology* 19, no. 2 (2009): 224–44.

Chapter 2

"CONSUMING" ASIATIC FEMININITY THROUGH FOODLESQUE: EXPLORING EAST ASIAN EXOTICISM THROUGH CALAMITY CHANG'S *MODEL MI-NORI-TY ROLL*

by Julia Matias

The commodification of Otherness has been so successful because it is offered as a new delight, more intense, more satisfying than normal ways of doing and feeling. Within commodity culture, ethnicity becomes spice, seasoning that can liven up the dull dish that is mainstream white culture.[1]

In neo-burlesque, where striptease is "not solely about *taking off* but is also about *putting on* layers of meaning,"[2] artists like Calamity Chang create work that stages this "seasoning" through performance, literally and figuratively, in her most cherished acts. Broadly, "foodlesque" is a term that burlesque practitioners have adopted to describe food-inspired neo-burlesque acts. While Chang does not claim to have coined the term, she recognizes her role in helping to popularize the genre during the 2000s. She cites "giant food" Halloween costumes she had encountered as her inspiration and acknowledges that she knew of a handful of other performers who had food-based burlesque acts before she started creating her own.[3]

Chang has continued to popularize the genre of foodlesque, especially during Covid-19 lockdowns. Through producing the *Cooking with Calamity*, a foodlesque-specific virtual burlesque showcase series. Foodlesque acts have become a signature part of Chang's repertoire. For Chang, foodlesque acts are defined not by the presence of food in a burlesque act, but by striptease which stages *being, becoming, or un-becoming* food. As a result, foodlesque stages the "consumption" of bodies within a sexualized performance practice. Both food and sex are experiences based on sensory pleasure that have been systematically feminized and commodified through Western colonization. Chang's work operates at what Mary Louise Pratt calls colonial "contact zones," a "social space where disparate cultures meet, clash, and grapple with each other, often in highly asymmetrical relations of domination and subordination—like colonialism, slavery, or their aftermaths as they are lived out across the globe today."[4]

Chang's present foodlesque repertoire consists of acts in which she dresses up and strips out of costumes that resemble various giant food items, which Chang refers to as "popular Asian culinary icons." To date, these include a sriracha bottle (*Sriracha Hawt Sauce*), a cup of noodles (*Cup O'Calamity*), a sushi hand roll (*Model Mi-nori-ty Roll*), and, mostly recently, a take-out cup of boba tea. Chang describes these acts as her personal tribute to the impact of Asian cultural achievements on Western culture: "Everyone recognizes sriracha as a trademark, everyone knows what cup noodles look like. So, for me, it's like a celebration of iconic Asian food images that have permeated and penetrated Western culture and global culture. Food unifies."[5] For Chang, these acts represent her most "sophisticated" approach to tackling the topic of exoticism through the medium of burlesque, though she asserts that they developed out of her more confrontational early work. In these performances, Chang highlights the literal and figurative consumption of East Asian cultures and their bodies by the Western market, explicit even in her titles of the acts such as *Model Mi-nori-ty Roll*. By focusing her practice specifically on Asiatic culinary achievements that have had a prominent crossover into the Western market, Chang's foodlesque acts call to the forefront what Ku, Manalansan, and Mannur refer to as "the slippage between personhood and food" of interest to Asian American food studies. Through a case study based on a scene in *Sex and the City* which draws unsettling comparisons to ordering Chinese take-out and adopting a Chinese child, they elaborate: "Race has become embedded in our everyday orchestration of bodies, meanings, and food. Not merely a descriptive category for people and nation, China—or things 'Chinese'— is also regarded as a commodity to be bought, possessed, and ingested."[6] In *Chop Suey, USA*, Yong Chen describes the United States as an "empire of consumption": "Consumption is the end of empires, simply put. Needless to say, the privileged got fed extremely well in private homes and public events, sometimes with exotic foods from faraway areas that only an extraordinary empire could reach."[7]

All of Chang's foodlesque acts follow a recognizable formula. Chang typically enters the space, fully dressed as a food item, and cleverly strips out of the costume to slowly reveal her body. Usually, as the striptease progresses, more and more pieces of costuming from within the popular lexicon of neo-burlesque performance are revealed. Due to the similarity in the structure of her foodlesque acts, I will provide a close reading of only one of these acts, her punily titled *Model Mi-nori-ty Roll*, in which she dresses up as a Japanese hand roll, which serves as an exemplary representation of Chang's foodlesque format. Often referred to as her "sushi" act, this performance offers a fertile ground for studying how Chang employs her signature foodlesque structure to deconstruct the consumption of East Asian commodities (and bodies) through striptease. Notably, the act showcases some of Chang's most intricate costume reveals and choreography. This transformation is executed creatively, captivatingly, and humorously, aligning with the fundamental principles of neo-burlesque performance.

Model Mi-nori-ty Roll relies more heavily on the musicality of the backing tracks than Chang's other foodlesque acts. In our first interview, Chang spoke at length about the difficulty she found in finding her "forever song" for some of the acts and suggested that the music she used *Model Mi-nori-ty Roll* could eventually change. However, the dramaturgy of the act clearly informed the songs she selected to date. The opening track is "Gion Kouta" by The Peanuts, a Japanese kayokyoku (vintage pop) twin duo popular in the 1960s. Chang said that choosing the opening song for the act took a tremendous amount of research. In *Model Mi-nori-ty Roll*, Chang's goal was to move from a vintage-sounding, grandiose, sweeping song for the act's opening to a fast, upbeat track in the second half of the number. Though Chang is Taiwanese American, it was important to her that the opening song reflected authentic Japanese culture in order to acknowledge the origins of sushi at the beginning of the piece, rather than a Western song like "Turning Japanese" by The Vapors, an English band. When discussing *Model Mi-nori-ty Roll*, she shared: "Yeah, I think [cultural] appropriation is only an issue when it's a power problem. It's like when, oh, you rape and kill all these people, or you give polio blankets to these people, now you're going to put on their classic costumes without acknowledging where it's from, *that's* when it's an issue."[8] However, Chang's choice to limit her entire foodlesque repertoire to East Asian cuisine from different nations sends a more complex message by employing colonial pastiche. I would argue that by employing culinary icons from varying East Asian cultures, Chang works to comment on the ways that all Asian cultures are typically conflated and largely robbed of cultural specificity through the Western gaze and global neoliberal expansion. In doing so, Chang poses a dare to her Western audiences; will they even *notice* her appropriation of other East Asian cultures? Or will they assume and accept these representations are "natural," "innate," or "authentic" to all Asian American Pacific Islander (AAPI) people, even as those images are presented in a highly theatrical style, divorced from a naturalist sense of reality?

Being, Becoming, or Un-Becoming *the Hand Roll*

As the lights come up, we see Calamity Chang at center stage with her back turned, as a sweeping orchestral melody plays evocative of mid-century popular forms. Like in many of Chang's foodlesque acts, the audience sees that she is already comically dressed fully as the food item of this act's basis. She floats her arms from side to side and begins spinning around as the music picks up, gently showing off all the details of her intricate costume. Chang described that her initial inspiration for the act was stumbling across a photo of a child dressed up in a sushi roll costume, which she wanted to recreate as a burlesque act. Chang further developed the act concept in collaboration with MsTickle, a popular neo-burlesque performer and designer known for her inventive costume design and exceptional attention to detail. The act was adapted away from the initial maki roll costume inspiration and into a hand roll, which could be stuffed with layers of costuming and props in order to include more exciting reveals during the act.

Chang's torso is covered in the costume's main "hand roll" area, made from a heavy green brocade textile. Peeking from beneath it is a robe based loosely on a kimono design. However, the gulf at the top of the hand roll tracing around Chang's face, neck, and shoulders are stuffed with large props that resemble a plushie shrimp, carrot shavings, a cucumber slice, and grains of rice with a spattering of caviar. Chang's smiling face emerges from the clever foliage which recreates the detailing and ingredients of a typical hand roll. The entire garment is fastened around her torso with a belt designed to resemble a kimono obi. The detailing in the costume is reminiscent of popular aesthetic tropes in kimono design, such as embroidered flowers and brocade, which are integrated throughout the costume pieces, elevating each garment's overall appearance with rich detailing. The outer wrap of the hand roll is made of a fabric that is speckled in a shiny green material accented with sequins, giving the garment a texture that mimics seaweed. Its border is lined with large crystal rhinestones that help establish its shape's perimeter and emphasize its silhouette under stage lights. *Model Mi-nority Roll* features one of Chang's most spectacular and elaborate costumes.[9]

On a final tambourine hit, Chang takes a pose center stage, emphasizing this moment by taking her hands, which have been gracefully floating around her until this point, and snapping them outward in a sharp motion. She takes two paces stage left, extending one of her legs and holding out her arms to create graceful lines with her body. Softly swiveling her arms, she struts to the other side of the stage, taking a pose on the next subtle cymbal crash of the song before drawing her hands to trace the shape of the sushi roll around her body in a delicate movement before sharply again emphasizing the sound of the cymbals with a motion of her fingers.

Here, Chang's choreography is built around the "strut and pose" repertoire best exemplified by mid-century burlesque performers. Strut and pose choreography,

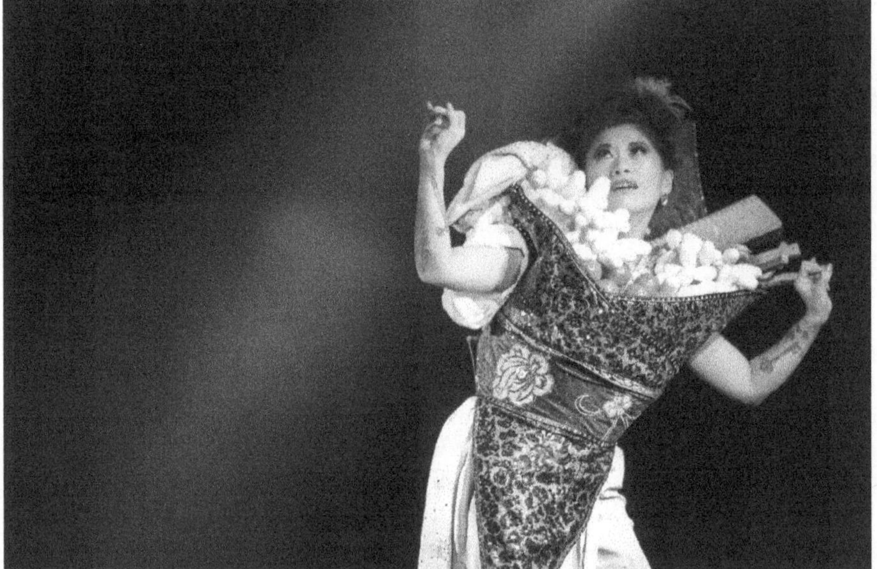

Image 3 Calamity Chang, Sushi Pose, credit Eric Usinger.

often referred to as the "parade," is employed early in a classic burlesque act to show off the opulence and elegance of the performer's costume. Typically, classic burlesque performers are dressed in a glove and gown, boudoir robe, or other large costuming piece which portrays class, luxury, and femininity. This element of classic burlesque costuming can be considered parodic, as it calls back to earlier iterations of the form in the late nineteenth and early twentieth centuries. During this period, women working in burlesque from working-class origins imitated those of wealth and status on the burlesque stage. In her foodlesque acts, Chang subverts this strut and pose tradition, creating a comedic dissonance between the repertoire and the costume piece itself by celebrating the hand-roll garment as if it were a luxurious, glamorous piece akin to a traditional evening gown.

In time with the music, Chang reaches behind her head into the hand roll and pulls out the large plush shrimp prop ornamented with rhinestones. She keeps her arm outstretched upward, allowing the shrimp to sparkle in the stage lights. This first reveal shows that the hand roll is not just one piece but literally *stuffed* with individual props, fashioned to resemble the ingredients the audience sees peeking through its opening. Chang slowly lowers the plush shrimp down, her face now reflecting an expression of awe, before swinging upward in time with the bells of the music to hold the shrimp up with one hand. As she holds it up, she begins to spin around with an expression of wonder painted on her face. As she turns, the shrimp continues to glitter enchantingly under the stage lights. Chang shared that this prolonged emphasis on the shrimp was not part of her initial choreography:

> You know you can rehearse something at home. It's like "oh right," then we do it live and people respond to things you didn't think they would … I don't know why but the first time I performed it and I took the shrimp out everyone just started screaming! Right, it's the first [food plushie prop to be pulled out] … It's the reveal of that. I actually think people don't think it's removable … So then I was like, okay, I'm gonna spend a little bit more time with this shrimp![10]

Chang's commentary points to a dramaturgical process common in both historic striptease and neo-burlesque performance, where audience reactions dictate which elements of a routine become emphasized in performance. As burlesque acts are built to be repeated many times and in many different contexts, they are not subject to a creation structure like a traditional theatrical performance, with rehearsal, previews, and a show run. Rather, most performers with signature acts note how they evolve over time through a reciprocal development process that is collaboratively achieved with the piece's spectators. In short, what works sticks, often becoming further emphasized or embellished, while other elements that do not elicit a positive response are often canned.

In a quick motion, Chang drops the shrimp in time with the bang of a tambourine. Immediately, she grabs for the carrot shavings, pulling them out to reveal that the plush shredded carrot pieces are bound together at their base, which functions to provide a handle for her to grasp. Chang holds it firmly with an iron grip. She reaches behind her back to pull out the remaining veggie, a cucumber slice, as if

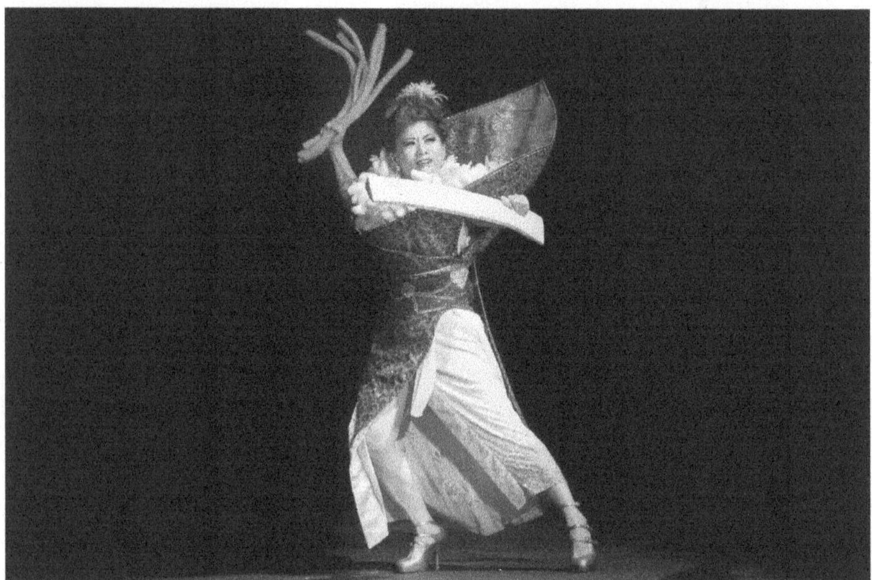

Image 4 Calamity Chang, Sushi Fight Pose, credit Eric Usinger.

reaching to pull a sword from a scabbard's harness. She crosses the two veggies against each other and then takes a series of poses brandishing the veggie pieces like weapons, one horizontally at shoulder-level and the other behind her head. These images are comically evocative of the movement and pose vocabulary common in martial arts and Samurai films that would have also been popular in the 1960s and 1970s. These poses provoke a loud uproarious laugh on the part of the audience in the video. Here Chang uses humor to parody exoticist troupes recognizable from a Western popular culture framework. By utilizing "awareishness"—what Maria Elena Buszek describes as "performing the acknowledgment and flaunting of your capacity for agency and pleasure, both professionally and sexually"—in all her acts, Chang proves that she is "in" on the exoticist joke she is presenting onstage, in effect cheekily disarming her viewer in order to provoke a level of critical engagement with the material she presents in her acts.[11] Chang's foodlesque acts take a fun, lighthearted approach to this material. This dramaturgical decision is partly based on the simple delight and pleasure Chang takes in her source material. When asked about what inspired her acts, she simply smiled and said "I just love food … And I just think it would be funny to be a giant piece of food. So, for me, those acts came from an idea, and then the songs will come later."[12] For Chang, elements of fun, play, and the celebration of Asian cultural achievements are just as important as communicating a hard-hitting political message. Chang has also performed the act at the Asian Burlesque Festival, an annual showcase she co-produces, which she stated has always had many Asian Americans in attendance. As such, Chang noted how her humor also elicits a response from other members of the Asian diaspora who are in on the joke.

Chang continues to emphasize this fight sequence with a high-leg kick and karate chop motions with the prop veggies, blurring the lines between the kung fu and Samurai action movie genres. She swings around the veggies several times before casting them to each side. Caressing her body and the plush rice grains peeking out through the seaweed roll, Chang effectively points to what she plans to do next. She slides her hands down her body to her obi-style belt, untying it while gliding to turn around so that her back is toward the audience. Here, Chang employs a common technique in burlesque performance, which involves teasing the audience by prolonging the expected reveal, building up the viewers' anticipation as they wait for her to *show* them what was behind the costuming piece she is now removing. Drawing from the repertoire of classic burlesque tease here privileges elements of play and the anticipation of the revelation of the body more than it does the naked body itself. Or, as I have argued before, "A unique and personal approach to tease is at the core of classic burlesque—perhaps the central tool that it tries to preserve from the historical tradition."[13]

Turning up the Tease

In time with a crescendo of the music, the tall, pointed shape of the seaweed piece drops to reveal the length of Calamity's silken robe. We now get a full view of the delicate detailing of the white robe, which MsTickle hand-painted an ombre green watercolor effect along the bottom half of the robe. The piece is speckled with floral detailing and rhinestones that begin to catch the light as Chang swings back to face the audience. The rhinestones work to emphasize Calamity Chang's legs, steps, and motions as she moves through space. As she turns, the song changes. Now, the audience hears "Up from the South" by The Budos Band, an instrumental group based in Staten Island, New York. Unlike the first song by The Peanuts, this track has an upbeat, groovy energy evocative of 1970s funk and exploitation films, both periods associated with nightlife and the tail end of twentieth-century burlesque striptease. Chang turns to face us, and we see the plushy rice pieces were constructed as a boa, sewn around a long fabric base with small ostrich feathers woven throughout, the orange caviar pieces accenting each end.

As the costume comes closer to representing popular twentieth-century conventions in burlesque, so too does the music, creating an atmosphere that would feel more familiar to burlesque audiences and heightening the act's energy. Typically, burlesque routines often follow this performance arc, where the act's overall energy escalates in the second half of the number. This usually accompanies revealing the body while the choreography grows more explicitly risqué in nature. In recent years, many acts traditionally feature a floorwork portion in this component, allowing performers to change stage levels while dialing up the raunch factor. Many community members, mentors, and neo-burlesque teachers liken this trajectory to a sexual act, describing that numbers are often designed to build to a climactic ending as more and more of the body is revealed. Chang incorporates this structure into the second half of the piece.

As the horn wails, Chang plants herself mid-stage, grabbing each end of the rice boa and casting her arms open to dramatically emphasize its size. Turning to stand in profile, she slides the boa off one shoulder so that most of its length is grazing her back. She begins seductively tugging it upward to cross over her body. In doing so, Chang employs a common convention in boa choreography drawn from the lexicon of recognizable mid-century burlesque prop usage common in classic burlesque striptease. Unlike more highly codified performance forms, burlesque performers and teachers do not have one specific name for these common movement sequences. However, boa teases like the one exemplified by Chang are commonly taught in many "Intro to Burlesque" courses, which typically include lessons on common props like feather boas. By utilizing this kind of choreography, Chang further plays up the comic dissonance in performing the conventions of classic burlesque striptease while dressed as food. She draws the boa in front of her body, increasing the tension of her grip in time with the accents of the music. Casting down the boa in front of her in a straight line, Chang continues to respond to the hits of the song with her arm motions. In doing so, she also draws the viewer's gaze to the rectangular sleeves of her silk robe, unobstructed for the first time. On another beat of the track, she flicks her head forward, quickly ripping out the feathered pin that was once holding her hair in a neat chignon. Flipping her head backward to send her long black hair cascading behind her, Chang establishes a total shift in her character that matches the changing mood of the act. No longer gentle, elegant, and docile, Chang's characterization shifts to a ferocious huntress as she draws her movement vocabulary more heavily from recognizable stripteasers of the bump and grind era.

Unlike earlier decades in the twentieth century, 1970s burlesque dancers worked during a period when burlesque performance was transitioning into contemporary strip club striptease and often performed burlesque in a more sexually aggressive style. With the sleeves of her garment finally free, Chang uses the fluidity of the sleeve's diaphanous fabric in her choreography by swinging her arms, allowing the lightweight silk sleeves to trail behind her making interesting shapes through the air. Outstretching one arm in front of her, she casts the opposite sleeve over it to face the audience, pulling backward to trail the garment across the surface. This sequence in Chang's choreography works to emphasize and celebrate her costuming choices. She slowly drags the ends of the embellished, colorful robe across the blank canvas of her upper body in order to draw the audience's attention to this custom detailing. Chang creates further visual intrigue in this sequence by rolling her hips in time with the song's upbeat rhythm. Chang pulls back her upstage arm and holds it taut, using the long square sleeves of the robe to act as a curtain to conceal her frame. In a quick motion, she unties and throws away her second, smaller obi-styled belt that matches her robe. The robe is undone, but Chang's outstretched sleeve is held up to delay the reveal of her body. Quickly, Chang swivels around to face backstage, using her downstage arm to cover her flesh. On a quick percussive hit, Chang finally drops her robe and casts it to one side.

Laying Labor Bare

At this point, we see Chang wearing a thong bodysuit; her rear is exposed for the first time. The top of the body suit that crosses Chang's back is made of a mesh close to the color of Chang's skin, creating a nude illusion. However, its lower half is ornamented in a vibrant blue design resembling moving water. The waves are embellished with sparkling rhinestones, creating the visual effect of the waves rippling in the light. She spotlights this big reveal by standing in this pose for a few counts with her arms outstretched above her head. Chang swivels to face the audience. We can now see that this is Chang's final costume layer. At first, she has an arm across her chest, delaying her final reveal until she juts it out on a musical beat. The audience now sees that the front of the body suit is embroidered in a water and koi fish design, a recognizable staple in Japanese art, which appears to be "swimming" through the nude illusion bodysuit. The suit is designed so that blue water waves collect around Chang's groin, with the largest koi fish diving in that direction. This design functions to cover her pubic area while also implying a gushing, wet and humorously "fishy" pelvic region. As she laughingly explained, "the whole thing's I want it to be like a koi fish underneath. You know, like ... on your cooch."[14] The suit features built-in wire cups that emphasize Chang's chest shape. Her glittering silver pasties are cut in a simple round shape, creating a cohesive color palette with the rhinestones elsewhere on the garment. She leans forward to trace one of her hands up her downstage leg, up her torso, and into her loose tresses of hair, further working to emphasize the final full reveal of her body as her eyes roll back in ecstatic delight.

As in all of Chang's foodlesque acts, the unobstructed revelation of the body of an East Asian woman concealed within an Asian food product provokes critical analysis, centralizing not only the sexualization of East Asian women for Western "consumption" but gestures to early-AAPI labor history deeply tied to the food service industry. After the Chinese Exclusion Act expired in 1892, the United States continued to enforce Chinese Exclusion Laws until 1943. Restaurant work was one of the few ways Chinese immigrants could enter the United States during this period.[15] As Calamity Chang strips out each of her costume food items, she reveals that wrapped up inside them is the body of an East Asian woman who is centrally responsible for their production. In doing so, Chang foregrounds the cultural process by which these figures are consumed and draws attention to the invisible labor and bodies behind the production of these food items.

Peeling off the "Model Minority" Myth

Chang reaches down, touching both her arms to the floor on one hit of the music before athletically slamming the rest of her body down on the boa beneath. When she lands, her legs are bent behind her in a traditional pin-up-like pose. "Riding" the boa prop is a common convention in burlesque striptease, allowing performers to return to the prop and reanimate it. Seated on the boa, Chang outstretches her arm and points her fingers before getting up again and sassily pointing one of her arms to the side on the next beat. Crossing her legs in front of one another, she raises both arms and clasps them above her head while playfully gyrating her hips in time with the funky horns in the track. Jutting her arms out to each side, she proudly and furiously plays up the last few chords of the song. Chang takes a dramatic pose center-stage with her arms outstretched above her head in a "come and get me" style. The final beat hits, and the audience begins to roar. Compared to the demure character she portrays at the beginning of the act, Chang's final reveal leaves her triumphant, self-possessed, powerful, and unrestrained.

The trajectory of *Model Mi-nori-ty Roll* deconstructs the Model Minority myth of its namesake, popularized after the Second World War to suggest that Japanese Americans, and subsequently, other Asian Americans, were able to buy into North American society through their supposed "innate" strong work ethic, attention to detail, and subservient demeanor. These biases were notably anti-Black in nature. Researchers, like William Petersen in his 1966 *New York Times* article, popularized the idea that it was a lack of work ethic as exemplified by the Japanese Americans, and not a confluence of other social factors, that barred Black Americans from transcending their social conditions.[16] By literally shedding away the artifice of a "model mi-nori-ty" role, Chang reveals a different kind of Asiatic corporal figure free from such imposed constraints. Through wielding "exotic" displays of Asiatic femininity, Chang helps playfully provoke audiences to question what Western biases they are "fed" daily. By literally shedding away the artifice of a "model mi-nori-ty" role, Chang reveals a different kind of Asiatic corporal figure that does not play by the rules or confine herself to any expectations of playing the law-abiding, courteous role assigned to her.

Notes

1   bell hooks, "Eating the Other: Desire and Resistance," in *Black Looks: Race and Representation* (New York: Routledge, 2015), 21.

2   Lynn Sally, *Neo-Burlesque: Striptease as Transformation* (New Brunswick, NJ: Rutgers University Press, 2021), 74.

3   Interview with Calamity Chang. Interviewed by Julia Matias. Zoom, November 14, 2019.

4   Mary Louise Pratt, *Imperial Eyes: Travel Writing and Transculturation* (London: Routledge, 2007), 7.

5   Interview with Chang, 2019.

6   Robert Ji-Song Ku, Martin F Manalansan, and Anita Mannur, *Eating Asian America: A Food Studies Reader* (New York: New York University Press, 2013), 3.

7   Yong Chen, *Chop Suey, USA: The Story of Chinese Food in America* (New York: Columbia University Press, 2014), 25.

8   Interview with Chang, 2019.

9   Chang cites LA-based performer Lux LaCroix as the choreographer of this piece, noting that she needed help to avoid the "danger of being upstaged by her costume" (Interview with Chang, 2021).

10 Interview with Chang, 2019.
11 Maria Elena Buszek, *Pin-up grrrls: Feminism, Sexuality, Popular Culture* (Durham, NC: Duke University Press, 200), 43.
12 Interview with Chang, 2019.
13 Julia Matias, "'Working On and Against' Classic Burlesque Conventions in Zyra Lee Vanity's Irie Love," *Canadian Theatre Review* 189 (2022): 27–32, 27.
14 Interview with Chang, 2021
15 Heather R. Lee, "A Life Cooking for Others," in *Eating Asian America* (New York: New York University Press, 2013), 57.
16 Kat Chow, "'Model Minority' Myth again Used as a Racial Wedge between Asians and Blacks," *NPR*, April 19, 2017, sec. Code Switch, https://www.npr.org/sections/codeswitch/2017/04/19/524571669/model-minority-myth-again-used-as-a-racial-wedge-between-asians-and-blacks.

Bibliography

Calamity Chang. "*Model Mi-Nori-Ty*" Sushi Burlesque at 5th Annual Asian Burlesque Extravaganza NYC, 2017. https://www.youtube.com/watch?v=p4qJOlV39ng.

Calamity Chang. Interview with Calamity Chang. Interview by Julia Matias. Zoom, November 14, 2019.

Calamity Chang. Interview with Calamity Chang. Interview by Julia Matias. Zoom, August 6, 2021.

Chen, Yong. *Chop Suey, USA: The Story of Chinese Food in America*. New York: Columbia University Press, 2014.

Chow, Kat. "'Model Minority' Myth again Used as a Racial Wedge between Asians and Blacks." *NPR*. Accessed April 19, 2017, sec. Code Switch. https://www.npr.org/sections/codeswitch/2017/04/19/524571669/model-minority-myth-again-used-as-a-racial-wedge-between-asians-and-blacks.

hooks, bell. "Eating the Other: Desire and Resistance." In *Black Looks: Race and Representation*, 21–39. New York and London: Routledge, 2015.

Ku, Robert Ji-Song, Martin F Manalansan, and Anita Mannur. *Eating Asian America: A Food Studies Reader*. New York: New York University Press, 2013.

Lee, Heather R. "A Life Cooking for Others." In *Eating Asian America*, 53–77. New York: New York University Press, 2013.

Matias, Julia. "'Working On and Against' Classic Burlesque Conventions in Zyra Lee Vanity's Irie Love." *Canadian Theatre Review* 189 (2022): 27–32.

Pratt, Mary Louise. *Imperial Eyes: Travel Writing and Transculturation*. London: Routledge, 2007.

Sally, Lynn. *Neo-Burlesque: Striptease as Transformation*. New Brunswick, NJ: Rutgers University Press, 2022.

Chapter 3

SELLING OUT: ART, STRIPPING, AND DESIRE

by Marissa Vigneault

I have personally heard this reiterated by a number of [Hannah] Wilke's peers who grew tired of the artist disrupting various art events by performatively taking her clothes off. Wilke's performance of beauty—her modeling and foregrounding of the body she inhabited—was in fact a strategy.[1]

I was in Los Angeles in February 2018 when a friend said: "Go see the Tino Sehgal piece at the Hammer." The pleasantly prodding tone of his voice led me to visit *Stories of Almost Everyone*, the exhibition that included Sehgal's work, later that afternoon. In the backseat of a sun-filled Uber on my way to the Hammer's Westwood neighborhood, I Googled "Tino Seghal Hammer Museum UCLA." A few blurry images and a review in the *LA Times* hinted at what I would see: some kind of striptease-cum-artwork in one of the museum's brightly lit white cube galleries. I remember thinking: "What will this do to me?" As if I knew a Barthesian prick was coming.

The plastic veneer of Los Angeles is too slick for me; it doesn't pierce me. I like the grime of New York. It sinks into my skin; an invisible tattoo. I think Hannah Wilke, the artist who has received the bulk of my intellectual attention over the past decade, also felt this way. In the 1970s, while visiting her sister in Los Angeles, she would stay at the Chateau Marmont with her then partner, Claes Oldenburg. But Wilke always returned to *the* city; her city; my city. She only left for good in January 1993, after succumbing to the effects of lymphoma.

Wilke performed her striptease-cum-artwork *Invasion Performance* on November 8, 1975, at the opening reception for Lynda Benglis's *Sculpture* exhibition at the Paula Cooper Gallery in New York.[2] That evening, Wilke, a recognized fixture in the quickly growing SoHo art scene, equally notorious for her beauty and artistic brazenness, sauntered over to Benglis's kitschy, faux-classical columns atop a river of draped blue fabric and began to strip, pulling an opaque top up and over her head. A silver-painted column adapted to become a prop as she moved her body through a series of poses reminiscent of classical statuary and contemporary pin-ups. Fred McDarrah, then staff photographer for *The Village Voice*, took the only known photographs of Wilke's performative intervention.

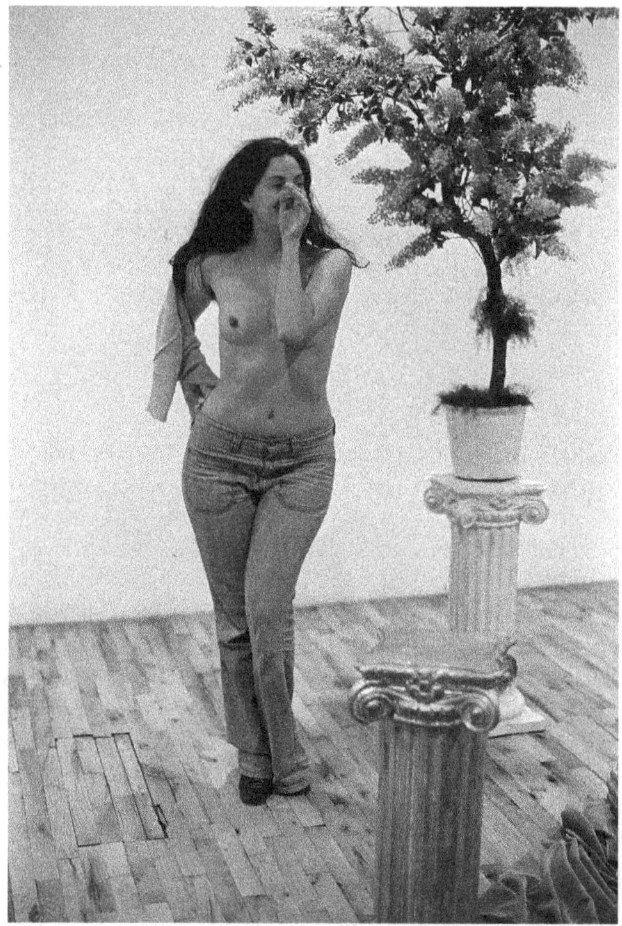

Image 5 Hannah Wilke, *Invasion Performance*, Paula Cooper Gallery, NYC, 1974, credit Fred McDarrah.

In McDarrah's images, Wilke is staged, highlighted against a white gallery wall and framed by branches of a flowering potted tree. The removed shirt is held like a scarf, a teasing twist of fabric that highlights the curves of her exposed torso—the conceal and reveal of the striptease artist. Wilke's facial expressions run the gamut from amused and playful to sexy and empowered. Her gaze is directed toward the camera, and by default the later viewer of the photographs. No other people are visible, and it is only assumed that Wilke equally directs her gestures toward a crowd behind the camera. The effect of McDarrah's cropping of the gallery space is that we feel singular in Wilke's attentive moves, as if the laboring of her body is intended for each of us individually. It is here, in this warped space of time, that I most acutely feel the collapse of distinction between the gallery and the strip club, both sites of spectacle and economic exchange, a point very much intended by Wilke.

Invasion Performance, rarely discussed in scholarship on either Wilke or Benglis, is a work that frustrates me as a removed art historian (the disembodied academic mind) and as a viewer (a very embodied body) after the fact. Wilke's striptease in the art gallery is precisely a historical tease to me, one who will never experience the sensation of occupying the same space as she pulls a shirt over her head and cocks a hip out to enhance her curves. Or weaves a large white cloth around her naked form, as she did for a performance at The Kitchen in New York in November 1974. Or even strips out of a three-piece white suit behind Marcel Duchamp's *Large Glass* (1915–23) at the Philadelphia Museum of Art in 1976. These three acts of artistic stripping purposefully transpired within art world institutional spaces: an experimental performance space, a cutting-edge gallery in SoHo, and an established and relatively traditional temple of art in Philadelphia. Each space functioned as a stage for Wilke to stage her sex. Here, I use the term "sex" in reference to what Amia Srinivasan calls both "a cultural thing posing as a natural one ... gender in disguise" and "a thing we do with our sexed bodies."[3] By bringing the striptease—a performative act popularly associated with the realm of pleasure, kitsch, and darkened clubs—into the space of the museum—traditionally aligned with serious and cerebrally oriented white cubes—Wilke critically collapsed categorical distinctions that have maintained highbrow/lowbrow and avant-garde/kitsch divisions in cultural production and consumption. She also collapsed the bodily and the cerebral, whereby the staging of her embodied sexuality—one that simultaneously proffers the erotic as pleasure and art—operates as a counter to the distanced ideal of modernism, or what Amelia Jones has called the "assumption of 'disinterestedness' behind conventional art history and criticism."[4] Modernism's white cube promotes, if not necessitates, a state of "disinterestedness" in which the viewer is held at a distance; look but do not touch. But what about *feel*? Feeling is a psychic extension of touch, an imaginary projection of a past sensation. Looking at a body touching sensitive flesh as it strips itself bare evokes a visceral response. I feel as phantom touch what my vision takes in. A tactile processing.

My project on Wilke has always been a projection of what I wished I experienced; to know not just the removed visual analysis of what I see in the archive, but the sensation of comfortable discomfort with my body.[5] To know a physical reaction beyond the reach of conceptualization. Would I have been pierced by Wilke, as I was by the performer of Seghal's tauntingly titled *Selling out*?

What do I do with any work of art that pierces me like a Barthesian *punctum*? According to Barthes, what I seek out—what I am culturally interested in—is *studium*: "I invest the field of the *studium* with my sovereign consciousness."[6] But what breaks (punctuates; disturbs) *studium* is *punctum*, an unexpected "element which rises from the scene, shoots out of it like an arrow, and pierces me ... this wound, this prick, this mark ... sting, speck, cut, little hold—and also a cast of the dice ... the accident which pricks me (but also bruises me, is poignant to me)."[7]

I stage *studium*. *Punctum* un-stages me. Why does this poignant prick leave me bruised? Is bruising always bad? What if we think about it as a mark that indicates healing? An internal trauma made visible on our delicate surfaces. Something we can share with the Other. (Is this what the Other desires of us?)

Barthes specifically referenced the photograph in relation to *studium* and *punctum*, and this is often the way I encounter performance art; as archival photographs or internal mindgraphs (mental images resulting from textual descriptions). But encounters with art forms other than photographs may equally produce a *punctum*, what Barthes considered to be an excess beyond what can be observed and is therefore always uncoded and unnameable: "What I name cannot really prick me. The incapacity to name is a good symptom of disturbance."[8]

Performance art in real time is particularly suited to disturbance, for the introduction of a live body into the visual field produces a "this-is-now," in contrast to the "that-has-been" of the photograph. Within this field, I become aware, as Margaret Iversen writes, that "while I look at things, I am looked at. My activity, then, is equally a passivity. Visual perception, tied to the body, is perspectival and partial."[9] Or, as Lacan notes, "I see only from one point, but in my existence I am looked at from all sides."[10] It is recognition of Cartesian misrecognition (the inadequacy of *cogito ergo sum*) that led Lacan to theorize that "in the scopic field, the gaze is outside, I am looked at, that is to say, 'I am a picture.'"[11] Wilke, in staging her subversive stripteases, foregrounded her dual status as conceptual producer and physical material. "I think one can have a body and a mind," she said, as she made herself "into a work of art instead of other people making you into something you might not approve of."[12]

To say "I am a picture" is not the same as saying "I am a work of art," yet both result in a type of seizing or freezing, what Lacan called a "fascinatory effect" that is "one of the dimensions in which the power of the gaze is exercised directly."[13] It is through the gaze—"things look at me, and yet I see them"—that I both desire the Other and the Other desires me.[14] Iversen cites this disparity between "subject of consciousness" (*studium*) and "subject of desire" (*punctum*) to deftly connect the Lacanian gaze to the Barthesian *punctum*, whereby the "subject, which can only be heard in the lacunae of discourse, can only be glimpsed in the gaze."[15] Desire, which in the Lacanian sense is defined by a lack (the *objet petit a*), emerges in the visual field as a disturbance, an unsettling disorganization akin to the *punctum*. Within the external field of the gaze, I am, always, the object of an/Other's desire; that is to say, "I am a picture."

The striptease-cum-artwork is a performative eruption (a disturbance; an unsettling disruption) of sex as fantasied ideal—as desire; impulse; flush; flesh—in the staged setting of the gallery and museum. Such performance disturbs the framed and contained (*studium*) simulations of the body and sex found throughout the history of art. Take, for example, Gustave Courbet's *The Sleepers* (1866). The Petit Palais, Paris, where the painting is housed, describes the painting as: "emblematic of the world of reverie and bliss of the painter who jubilantly celebrated the beauty of the body."[16] But what body? Whose body? An arrangement of flesh-colored paint across the surface of a canvas is hardly a body, although I agree it makes reference to one. And what of the sexual act implied by the two figures blissfully intertwined in silken sheets. Does this de-fanged visualization of "sex" as projected through the hetero-lens of the male artist pierce me? No.

But Wilke's work still does. And so did the performer of Seghal's *Selling out*. Sehgal, a British-born artist based in Berlin with an academic background in dance and economic theory, does not use the word "performance" to describe his work, but rather "sculptures," "installations," "situations," or "pieces," which produce and are produced by active encounters between people.[17] Such encounters can be direct or oblique, but are always positioned toward the intimate, as actions and conversations usually deemed private are disclosed in public spaces. Such is seen, for example, in *Kiss* (2003), an endurance piece (or what MOMA refers to as a "constructed situation"[18]) where two trained dancers entangle themselves in poses evocative of work by Auguste Rodin, Constantin Brancusi, Gustave Klimt, and Jeff Koons. Their warm actions in openly visible spaces position the viewer as voyeur who engages both intellectually with the art historical references and pleasurably with the erotic spectacle.

Sehgal has a strict "no photos, no videos" policy of his work, which is nearly impossible to enforce in our cell phone camera era. The images of his work I have viewed online were surreptitiously taken by others without institutional permission. But that is exactly what I like about them: an absence of authoritative context, which allows for distribution of the popular eye. The angle and slightly blurred edge immediately suggest the aesthetic of the cell phone photo, while the lack of direct eye contact by any of the "players" or "interpreters," as Sehgal prefers to call the situation participants, or even the observers reinforces a furtively placed lens. I took no photos of my own encounter with Sehgal's work in the Hammer, not that my lack of action makes it any more meaningful or sacred. Rather, I share my experience of *Selling out* through words filtered by my memory, which is at best a hazy reformation of what I saw, what I heard, and what I felt. In part, I use other people's photos to scaffold my own visualization of the staged museum space: the color of the floors; the brightness of the room; the placement of the pedestals; and slowly wilting flowers from Kapwani Kiwanga's *Flowers for Africa* (2018) installation. But what I remember of the individual interpreter on the afternoon of my visit changes with every retelling of my story (my stories for almost everyone).

Selling out, enacted a handful of times since its creation in 2002, programs a distanced yet intimate triangulation between artist, solitary player, and viewer. In total, seven players of varying gender identity animated *Selling out* on varying schedules during the three-and-a-half month run at the Hammer. Each player, outfitted in a museum security guard uniform, worked a shift, walking around the space of the gallery in a tedious sort of way. Once a visitor entered the room, however, the player made a decision: remain clothed—one might say guarded—or launch into a striptease. On the day I attended the Hammer the player decided to strip for me. I was somewhat primed for this possibility, as Google had offered a digital trigger warning, yet fundamentally it is impossible to be prepared to witness a work of art—a sculpture, an installation, a piece—strip in real time. I walked into the gallery, scanning the space until I saw her—the player that day was burlesquer Diamondback Annie—and she saw me. She smiled and then looked away, took a few steps in her black heels—(Am I remembering this correctly? Or do I just want there to be heels? How influenced is my memory from scrolling through photos of

Annie on Instagram?)—and dropped her guard badge onto the floor, marking the beginning of the act. For the next few minutes she undulated through the space, slowly peeling off her garments while coyly catching my gaze. With the exception of a brief moment when an older man entered the gallery and whiplashed back out, I was the only viewer in the space during the striptease. I felt dually paralyzed and energized, but consistently uncertain of what my "correct" reaction should be. I smiled, I watched, I maintained a proper physical distance; I was overtly polite and respectful of her actions, which concluded with her in a flesh-colored G-string whispering: "Tino Sehgal, Selling out, 2002." I didn't applaud, but I did silently mouth "thank you" before turning on my own heels and exiting the gallery. What I wanted to do was walk back in to see if she would strip for me again. To put down a bit of my academic guard the second time around and take pleasure in the experience. Instead, I walked outside into the open-air courtyard of the Hammer, flicking on my sunglasses in an attempt to retreat back to the "closed system" of exchange Sehgal anticipated between the player and me.[19]

I wonder: where is pleasure located in a "closed system" of exchange? Does the player of Sehgal's situation feel (take) pleasure in the act of stripping for an unknown other? What pleasure do I feel (take) when viewing a seductively undulating body strip away the bulky layers of an official (read: oh so unsexy) museum guard uniform? To return to Barthes, whose assessment of the "pleasure of the text" may equally be read as the "pleasure of the artwork," pleasure is never simple, but "a drift, something both revolutionary and asocial, and it cannot be taken over by any collectivity, any mentality, any ideolect … It is obvious that the pleasure of the text is scandalous: not because it is immoral but because it is *atopic*."[20] Atopic: unusual; without place. Pleasure without place is exactly what makes pleasure so pleasurable. And also what makes it so discomforting (a disturbance) when staged in the sterilized white cube.

The gallery spaces at the Hammer flow between open areas and enclosed rooms, and circle around a three-story courtyard designed in the late 1980s by Edward Larrabee Barnes. The result is a mix of darker, more traditional galleries, which display the gifted collection of Armand Hammer, and light-filled, white cubes intended for contemporary exhibitions, such as *Stories of Almost Everyone*. *Selling out* could have been positioned in any space around the museum—certainly a person wearing a Hammer guard uniform would not seem out of place wandering the breezeways. As art critic Christopher Knight tantalizingly asked, what meanings would be produced if Sehgal's players stripped in front of one of the Hammer's Salomes dancing?[21] But Sehgal and the Hammer curators staged the situation in the white cube, which is partly about control—there was a warning sign about "mature content" as one entered the galleries—and partly about flipping the viewer's expectation of space. One, presumably, doesn't expect to see a live striptease in the purified arena of the art museum. A painted striptease, sure. Our categorical celebration of the nude in art history is deeply embedded, as evidenced by the valuation of Gustave Moreau's Salome paintings, among countless others. But to experience a striptease in Los Angeles one would not typically head to the Hammer. Rather, a site such as Sam's Hofbrau is where you direct the Uber driver.

The interior of Sam's, darkened but with spotlights on the dancer's poles, cues a particular type of behavior, where looking at a stripping body is wholly expected and a bout of pleasurable bodily response the norm.

Controlled darkness, or what Noam Elcott writes of as "artificial darkness," is a result of technological advances notably linked to the initial spaces of cinema.[22] Movie houses of the early twentieth century directed the viewer's eye toward a cone of light projected onto a screen creating a periphery of darkness for obscene (beyond the scene) behaviors. In the margins of darkness bodies could come together in pleasurable encounter. Or they could remain singular and distanced, deriving scopic pleasure from the moving images. Burlesque theaters similarly turned on the spotlighting of moving limbs, in this case in-the-flesh. And as strip clubs swiftly replaced burlesque theaters in the postwar decades, patrons of such spaces adapted their behaviors to further amplify the escapism made possible by 24/7 artificial darkness. For it is in darkness, where I am invisible, that the external gaze is temporarily kept at bay. In darkness, I cannot be *"photo-graphed"* and, therefore, I am *not* a picture.[23]

But the space of the strip club is quite precisely *not* the space of the museum gallery, and Sehgal's purposeful collision of the two exposes this differentiation. An infusion of brightness made the gallery where I saw *Selling out* just so … visible, especially me. Anonymity in a darkened margin was not an option. I looked at Annie and she looked at me, and from the next room a guard looked at me looking at Annie. I was exposed (I was *photo-graphed*)—meaning vulnerable, but also called out—for the pleasure I experienced, a pleasure we are taught to suppress in favor of intellectualizing a work of art, especially conceptual art, which is where we may locate *Selling out*'s artistic siblings.[24]

Reflecting on my experience years later, my most vivid and consistent thought is about how I reacted to the player's actions in the space of the museum: Did my response match institutional expectations? Did I perform correctly? Or did I misstep, even slightly, when my bodily response of pleasure seeped through as if I were a patron in a strip club? Herein lies a driving point of my thinking: how do we define proper conduct when the definition of a space, and more specifically its function, is so blurred? Social cues inform us how to behave in a museum and in a strip club, but those two spaces are typically distanced from one another. And if high art is brought into the artificially darkened arena of the low-brow strip club and stripping is brought into the equally artificially lightened space of the high-brow art gallery the result is a disruption of spatial meaning; something feeling out of place. A collision in the vein of kitsch, which forever occludes a neat division of identities.

Where then may pleasure and bodily enjoyment reside in the curated space of the gallery without being foreclosed by claims of entertainment and escapism, as if these have no critical merit? Charges of forefronting unserious and immoral content are levied by those critical of curatorial incorporations of pleasure, presumably due to pleasure's intractable tie to the bodily rather than the cerebral. Yet, as Dieter Roelstraete writes, such objections to pleasure (sex) in the (staged) museum gallery:

assumes that pleasure itself cannot think—that it is "unthinking" and therefore does not belong to the world of the intellect—and that thinking, conversely, cannot possibly be a source of real, quasi-erotic pleasure. Strange Cartesian dichotomies. Are we to consume art with our logical faculties alone? Check our bodies, trusted seats of "feeling," at the reception desk? Automatically distrust every laugh, smile, or smirk that swims to the surface of our countenance as a perfidious symbol of intellectual bondage, every time we walk through a museum?[25]

It is through my body that my experiences are borne out, eventually lodged as memories in both the sensitive surfaces of my skin (that grimy tattoo of New York) and my hippocampus. I want to experience my body as a pleasurable body in the space of the gallery. I want the flush of uncertainty, the memories of past touch, of something deep in my gut to surface again. I want to trust the coy smirk of the player as she strips for me—only me—before her shift ends and she is, alchemically, converted into non-art.

Dorothy Dubrule, one of the ecdysiast players of Sehgal's piece at the Hammer, wrote of her experience:

> [T]he mechanisms of gallery site and museum audience still bends us into the shape of an art object, depersonalized and reproduced with only slight variations … It is freeing to be an art object; there is no shame, no desire. There are no moods, no pain, and no bad days. There are no expectations that a sculpture will respond to or take responsibility for the social conditions it may evoke or produce simply by being there.[26]

Thinking of oneself as a sculpture is something Sehgal encouraged the players to do, which raises deep ethical questions around the treatment of performance-based labor and the necessity of artistic care. Such issues were similarly highlighted in July 2021, when a small group of women-identified and nonbinary musicians staged Ragnar Kjartansson's *Romantic Songs of the Patriarchy* (2018) at the Guggenheim Museum in New York. For seven hours a day, four days straight, the performers individually repeated the same song—"some songs are ambiguous, some songs are violent, and some are just beautiful love songs"—to the point of rupture of the song's narrative, and, potentially, of the performer's themselves.[27] Fittingly, Kjartansson referred to the piece as an "open wound" with no resolution. Kate Dwyer described it as an unwitting "manifestation of the patriarchy itself: it is a white man's artwork that requires women and nonbinary people to do physically draining and emotionally devastating labor."[28] This is what led musician Miriam Elhajli to back out of the Guggenheim iteration: "I didn't want to spend a lot of emotional labor helping a man understand his place within the patriarchy," she said.[29]

The toll of emotional and physical labor on the sensate body, even (especially) in the name of Art, must be considered in relation to the objectification of the performer for hire. Does paying an hourly wage justify the exploitative misuse of another's labor, as capitalist claims so often assert? How does one determine a fair wage for turning oneself into an object, staged for another's pleasure? In 2011, performance artist Yvonne Rainer penned a letter to Jeffrey Deitch, then director of the Museum of Contemporary Art, Los Angeles, in vociferous objection to Marina Abramović's planned "entertainment" at their annual donor gala. The letter, additionally signed by a number of art world heavies, slammed the artist and the institution for "subjecting her [Abramović's] performers to possible public humiliation and bodily injury."[30] And while the performers were paid $150 for their three hours of artistic labor, such a low wage coupled with high stakes suggests, as Rainer wrote, a "cheerful voluntarism" that "says something about the pervasive desperation and cynicism of the art world such that young people must become abject table ornaments and clichéd living symbols of mortality in order to assume a novitiate role in the temple of art."[31]

Dubrule, who received $33 an hour to perform *Selling out* at the Hammer, noted the physical toll on her body: "At the end of my first shift, my body feels like it has fallen down a rocky hill. My knees are swollen from crawling and sliding on the concrete gallery floor. My hips are sore from gyrating, my lower back aches from standing in heels."[32] I wonder if the male performers in their flat orthopedic shoes experienced the same bodily discomfort; fashion does tend to pain the female body. But what also of psychic pain, produced from the disconnect between knowing oneself as a subject (the "subject of consciousness") and experiencing oneself as an object (the "subject of desire"). For Dubrule, it was uniqueness (her subjectivity) that came under siege: "*Am I just the product of a design? What would my rebellion look like? Apathy? Anger? Am I angry that I am earnestly doing the work of inviting my own objectification, or was my doing it always intended to be an exotic tantrum inside gallery walls, crafted to titillate museum patrons?*"[33] Dubrule's self-reflection reveals her as simultaneously thinking subject and visual object, which precisely complicates the idea of performer as art object; a disruptive split is inevitable when someone else stages you as a sexual object, even if you staged yourself first.[34]

"Every porn scene is a record of people at work," writes Heather Berg, situated "at the intersection of life and work, pleasure and tedium, entrepreneurial hustles and waged labor."[35] Berg's statement may equally be applied to the players who realize *Selling out*; every strip in the gallery is a gesture of their bodily labor in pursuit of art, both pleasurable and tedious. Yet there is a type of privilege in stripping in the relative safety of the brightly lit art gallery watched over by actual guards, a point noted by Dubrule:

> I am a pretend sex worker in a high-end simulation. I do not face anything like the social stigma, precarity, or abuse people in the actual sex work industry do. My performance does not reveal to its patrons pervasive and debilitating systemic inequality, the direct connection between the wage gap and the sex work industry, the statistics on violence suffered by sex workers, and the faulty public policy which holds sex workers accountable for their own safety.[36]

I do think *Selling out* has the potential to reveal everything Dubrule highlights, if we open up space to bring these supposedly taboo subjects out of artificial darkness and into the light. We can and should think of the gallery as a stage where systemic inequality, the wage gap, sexual violence, and failed public policy are addressed via consenting bodies. Putting sex on stage has immense potential to disrupt exploitation and rethink sexual labor, as suggested by Cecilia Gentili, whose activism actively counters sex work as immoral and/or degrading: "Sex work is a service industry. We often help people with social anxiety, disabilities, those who are figuring out their sexualities or gender identities."[37]

I wonder about my own position as one who experiences pleasure at the expense of another's labor. Was it fair of me to take more than I paid (which was nothing) to watch Annie strip? Or is the intellectual cost of thinking through and writing about my experience on these pages enough to reach a zero balance? Patriarchal capitalism, per Berg, assumes that "sex should be private and free."[38] And as Amia Srinivasan has addressed in depth, sex is "said to be a natural thing, a thing that exists outside politics. Feminism shows that ... sex, which we think of as the most private of acts, is in reality a public thing."[39] *Selling out* is, ultimately, neither private nor free, a subversive riposte to closed-door systems that maintain inequities via sex-based discrimination.

But Hannah Wilke already recognized this decades before the first player stripped in animation of *Selling out*. Dubrule, in a reflection somewhat akin to Lacan's assertion that "there always was a gaze behind," had a historical eye on Wilke when she wrote[40]:

> I think a lot lately about the lineage of feminist performance artists who authorized their bodies in their artworks as I pace around the gallery ... *Back when they made those seminal works, is this what they had in mind for the future? A job market where artists could take their clothes off and get verbally abused in a museum for hours at a time and pay their taxes with the proceeds? I feel complicit in a dangerous fantasy.*[41]

Feminist artists have been staging sex as subversive labor—"sex as a political phenomenon, as something squarely within the bounds of social critique"[42]—since the 1970s; earlier, if we remove the temporal bracket around the production of "Feminist Art." But the heavy intellectual weight of their actions—Wilke's striptease performances; Marina Abramović's *Role Exchange* (1975); Andrea Fraser's *Untitled* (2003)—has been lifted by critics who cannot or will not see pleasure as intellectual. As Wilke recalled: "It's okay for Vito Acconci to do his sex thing under the floorboards—that's called conceptual art. But when I wanted to do a conceptual piece—a massage parlor with me being massaged by men—my dealer just smiled and said, "Hannah, why don't you just come up to my hotel instead?'"[43] How humorously unfunny.

Lauren Fournier writes: "the history of feminism is, in a sense, a history of autotheory—one that actively seeks to bridge theory and practice and upholds tenets like 'the personal is political.' As an impulse, autotheory can be traced through early feminist conceptual art, video art, performance, and body art … "[44] Autotheory, as an "impulse," connects me to Wilke. But the "personal-theoretical, incidental, gut-centered nature of autotheoretical research" also grounds me in my own body.[45] So what does it mean that I am a pleasurable viewer, or at least a viewer susceptible to pleasure? I enjoyed *Selling out* from a disembodied perspective as work of art in the lineage of conceptualism. But I also enjoyed the striptease as an embodied observer taking pleasure in the exposure of flesh in the real. I personify the confusion of space and of art, which is itself a disruptable category, as its demands are always scattered around the viewers' desires. I, too, desire something of Sehgal's work. Intimacy is perhaps the right word. But not intimacy in the romantic sense. Rather, intimacy in the form of close knowledge, something private, and personal, and secretive. (I guess I want to see the bruises.) This is the seduction of Sehgal's work; the promise of intimacy that blossoms only as a promise. It is, of course, an intimacy that can never be secured. So where I am left—and where I leave you—is in the mire of unanswerability. The space between absolutes, a grayzone that is neither fully visible nor invisible, akin to a desired memory where I walked back into the gallery and Annie stripped for me again.

Notes

1   Connie Butler, "Needed Erase Her? Don't. Hannah Wilke's Female Image," in *Hannah Wilke: Art for Life's Sake*, eds. Tamara H. Schenkenberg and Donna Wingate (St. Louis: Pulitzer Arts Foundation, in association with Princeton University Press, 2021), 67.

2   On *Invasion Performance*, Wilke said: "I did it because I felt, in a way, her [Benglis] using her body was sexually negative, very macho … it didn't really have anything to do with real feminism; and, I really don't even know if it had anything to do with her art, per se … It was very funny, 'cause I knew I was being bad; it is interesting that people should not upset other people's art shows, yet, people can upset other people's lives." "Artist Hannah Wilke Talks with Ernst," *Oasis de Neon* (1978): n.p. Quoted in Nancy Princenthal, *Hannah Wilke* (Munich, Berlin, London, and New York: Prestel, 2010), 61.

3   Amia Srinivasan, *The Right to Sex: Feminism in the Twenty-First Century* (New York: Farrah, Straus and Giroux, 2021), xii.

4   Amelia Jones, *Body Art/Performing the Subject* (Minneapolis: University of Minnesota Press, 1998), 5. Jones has also aligned modernism's "refusal of pleasure" with "denial of female agency." Amelia Jones, "Postfeminism, Feminist Pleasures, and Embodied Theories of Art," in *New Feminist Criticism: Art, Identity, Action*, ed. by Joanna Frueh, Cassandra L. Langer, and Arlene Raven (New York: Harper Collins, 1994), 28.

5   "But the unconscious also sees, throwing onto a screen its projected desires, fantasies and fears." Margaret Iversen, "What Is a Photograph?," *Art History* 17, no. 3 (September 1994): 459.

6   Roland Barthes, *Camera Lucida* (New York: Hill and Wang, 1980), 26.

7   Barthes, *Camera,* 26–7.

8   Barthes, *Camera,* 51.

9   Iversen, "What Is a Photograph?," 456.

10 Jacques Lacan, "The Split between the Eye and the Gaze," in *The Four Fundamental Concepts of Psychoanalysis*, ed. Jacques-Alain Miller, trans. Alan Sheridan (New York and London: W.W. Norton & Company, 1978), 72.

11 Jacques Lacan, "What Is a Picture?," in *The Four Fundamental Concepts of Psychoanalysis*, ed. Jacques-Alain Miller, trans. Alan Sheridan (New York and London: W.W. Norton & Company, 1978), 106.

12 Quoted in "Artist Hannah Wilke Talks with Ernst," n.p.

13 Lacan, "What Is a Picture?," 118.

14 Lacan, "What Is a Picture?," 109.

15 Iversen, "What Is a Photograph?," 457.

16 "The Sleepers," *Petit Palais Musée des Beaux-Arts de la Ville de Paris*, accessed October 27, 2023, https://www.petitpalais.paris.fr/en/oeuvre/sleepers.

17 Claire Bishop, "No Pictures, Please: Claire Bishop on the Art of Tino Sehgal," *Artforum* 43, no. 9 (May 2005): 215–17.

18 "Tino Sehgal, The Kiss, 2003," *The Museum of Modern Art*, accessed October 27, 2023, https://www.moma.org/collection/works/1117525.

19 Bishop, "No Pictures, Please."

20 Roland Barthes, *Les Plaisir du Texte* (New York: Hill and Wang, 1975), 23.

21 Christopher Knight, "It Takes a Striptease to Enliven 'Stories of Almost Everyone' at the Hammer Museum," *Los Angeles Times*, February 6, 2018, https://www.latimes.com/entertainment/arts/la-et-cm-stories-hammer-review-20180206-htmlstory.html.

22 Noam M. Elcott, *Artificial Darkness: An Obscure History of Modern Art and Media* (Chicago and London: University of Chicago Press, 2016).

23 "It is through the gaze that I enter light and it is from the gaze that I receive its effects. Hence it comes about that the gaze is the instrument through which light is embodied and through which … I am *photo-graphed*." Lacan, "What Is a Picture?," 106.

24 I think here of the rhizomatic structure of siblings and cousins as discussed by Helen Molesworth in "How to Install Art as a Feminist," in *Modern Women: Women Artists at the Museum of Modern Art*, eds. Cornelia Butler and Alexandra Schwartz (New York: MoMA, 2010), 499–513.

25 Dieter Roelstraete, "How about Pleasure?" in *Ten Fundamental Questions of Curating*, ed. Jens Hoffmann (Milan: Mousse Publishing, 2013), 142.

26 Dorothy Dubrule, "What I'm Doing When I'm Selling Out," *SFMOMA Open Space*, April 25, 2019, accessed October 27, 2023, https://openspace.sfmoma.org/2019/04/what-im-doing-when-im-selling-out/.

27 Adam Iscoe, "The Guggenheim's Marathon of Misogynist Music," *The New Yorker*, August 16, 2021, https://www.newyorker.com/magazine/2021/08/23/the-guggenheims-marathon-of-misogynist-music.

28 Kate Dwyer, "At the Guggenheim, a Performance Piece Raises Questions of Feminist Art and Emotional Labor," *W Magazine*, July 2, 2021, https://www.wmagazine.com/culture/ragnar-kjartansson-romantic-songs-patriarchy-guggenheim-performance.

29 Iscoe, "The Guggenheim's Marathon of Misogynist Music."

30 Yvonne Rainer, et al., "Final Letter to Jeffrey Deitch and MOCA Regarding Annual Gala," *Artforum*, November 12, 2011, https://www.artforum.com/news/final-letter-to-jeffrey-deitch-and-moca-regarding-annual-gala-29378.

31 Rainer, et al., "Final Letter to Jeffrey Deitch." Performers were paid $150 and a year membership to MOCA for rehearsal time plus the three-hour performance. Performers re-performing Abramović's iconic endurance pieces during MoMA's 2010 exhibition *The Artist Is Present* were paid "$50 for a two and a half hour shift,

without paid rehearsal time, paid breaks or workers' compensation." See: E. C. Feiss, "Endurance Performance: Post-2008," *Afterall*, May 23, 2012, https://www.afterall.org/article/endurance-performance-post-2008.

32 Dubrule, "What I'm Doing When I'm Selling Out."

33 Dubrule, "What I'm Doing When I'm Selling Out."

34 According to Lacan, "there is something that establishes a fracture, a bi-partition, a splitting of the being to which the being accommodates itself, even in the natural world … both in sexual union and in the struggle to the death … the being breaks up, in an extraordinary way, between its being and its semblance, between itself and that paper tiger it shows to the other." Lacan, "What Is a Picture?," 106–7.

35 Heather Berg, *Porn Work: Sex, Labor, and Late Capitalism* (Chapel Hill, NC: The University of North Carolina Press, 2021), 1.

36 Dubrule, "What I'm Doing When I'm Selling Out."

37 Cecilia Gentili, "This Is What Will Make Sex Work in New York Safer," *New York Times*, October 17, 2021, https://www.nytimes.com/2021/10/17/opinion/decriminalize-sex-work-new-york.html?referringSource=articleShare.

38 Berg, *Porn Work*, 6.

39 Srinivasan, *The Right to Sex*, xii.

40 Lacan, "What Is a Picture?," 113.

41 Dubrule, "What I'm Doing When I'm Selling Out."

42 Dubrule, "What I'm Doing When I'm Selling Out," xiii.

43 Hannah Wilke, quoted in Dorothy Sieberling, "The Female View of Erotica," *New York Magazine* 7, no. 6 (February 11, 1974): 58.

44 Lauren Fournier, *Autotheory as Feminist Practice in Art, Writing, and Criticism* (Cambridge, MA and London: The MIT Press, 2021), 8.

45 Fournier, *Autotheory*, 5.

Bibliography

Albu, Christina. *Mirror Affect: Seeing Self, Observing Others in Contemporary Art.* Minneapolis: University of Minnesota Press, 2016.

Barthes, Roland. *Les Plaisir du texte.* New York: Hill and Wang, 1975.

Barthes, Roland. *Camera Lucida.* New York: Hill and Wang, 1980.

Berg, Heather. *Porn Work: Sex, Labor, and Late Capitalism.* Chapel Hill: The University of North Carolina Press, 2021.

Bishop, Claire. "No Pictures, Please: Claire Bishop on the Art of Tino Sehgal." *Artforum* 43, no. 9 (May 2005): 215–17.

Buszek, Maria Elena. *Pin-Up Grrrls: Feminism, Sexuality, Popular Culture.* Durham: Duke University Press, 2006.

Carr, Alison J. "The Stripper." In *The Routledge Companion to Media, Sex and Sexuality*, edited by Clarissa Smith, Feona Attwood, and Brian McNair, 362–70. New York: Routledge, 2017.

Dubrule, Dorothy. "What I'm Doing When I'm Selling Out." *SFMOMA Open Space.* April 25, 2019.

Dwyer, Kate. "At the Guggenheim, a Performance Piece Raises Questions of Feminist Art and Emotional Labor." *W Magazine.* July 2, 2021.

Elcott, Noam M. *Artificial Darkness: An Obscure History of Modern Art and Media.* Chicago and London: University of Chicago Press, 2016.

Ernst. "Artist Hannah Wilke Talks with Ernst." *Oasis de Neon*, Part 1 (1978): n.p.

Fournier, Lauren. *Autotheory as Feminist Practice in Art, Writing, and Criticism.* Cambridge, MA and London: The MIT Press, 2021.

Gentili, Cecilia. "This Is What Will Make Sex Work in New York Safer." *New York Times.* October 17, 2021.

Iscoe, Adam. "The Guggenheim's Marathon of Misogynist Music." *The New Yorker.* August 16, 2021.

Iversen, Margaret. "What Is a Photograph?" *Art History* 17, no. 3 (September 1994): 450–64.

Jones, Amelia. *Body Art/Performing the Subject.* Minneapolis: University of Minnesota Press, 1998.

Knight, Christopher. "It Takes a Striptease to Enliven 'Stories of Almost Everyone' at the Hammer Museum." *Los Angeles Times.* February 6, 2018.

Lacan, Jacques. *The Four Fundamental Concepts of Psychoanalysis*, edited by Jacques-Alain Miller, translated by Alan Sheridan. New York and London: W.W. Norton & Company, 1978.

Princenthal, Nancy. *Hannah Wilke.* Munich, Berlin, London, and New York: Prestel, 2010.

Rainer, Yvonne, et al., "Final Letter to Jeffrey Deitch and MOCA Regarding Annual Gala." *Artforum.* November 12, 2011.

Roelstraete, Dieter. "How about Pleasure?" In *Ten Fundamental Questions of Curating*, edited by Jens Hoffmann, 137–44. Milan: Mousse Publishing, 2013.

Sally, Lynn. "'It Is the Ugly That Is so Beautiful': Performing the Monster/Beauty Continuum in American Neo-Burlesque." *Journal of American Drama and Theatre* 21, no. 3 (Fall 2009): 5–23.

Sally, Lynn. "Performing the Burlesque Body: The Explicit Female Body as Palimpsest." In *Popular Performance*, edited by Adam Ainsworth, Oliver Double, and Louise Peacock, 161–77. London: Bloomsbury, 2015.

Schweitzer, Dahlia. "Striptease: The Art of Spectacle and Transgression." *The Journal of Popular Culture* 34, no. 1 (Summer 2000): 65–75.

Sieberling, Dorothy. "The Female View of Erotica." *New York Magazine* 7, no. 6 (February 11, 1974): 58.

Srinivasan, Amia. *The Right to Sex: Feminism in the Twenty-First Century.* New York: Farrah, Straus and Giroux, 2021.

Chapter 4

"THE AUDIENCE IS MY SOURCE OF HATE": XANDRA IBARRA AND FUCKING WHITENESS

by Erin Rachel Kaplan

As a native Texan who grew up on the US-Mexico border as a brown-skinned femme woman, Xandra Ibarra knew that the politics of that border were already being played out on her body. As a performance artist, Ibarra has used her body as the stage to enact the tensions between the United States and Mexico, between whiteness and brownness, between masculine and feminine, between queerness and heteronormativity. Ibarra had an interest in performance at a young age, but it was her exploration of sex work shortly after college that reignited this passion. Working as a Dom, Ibarra found that she had to use her "body as material to be able to withstand pain or to perform pain on others."[1] In essence she came to the realization that her work as a Dom was fundamentally a performance—one in which she was constantly negotiating her role in collaboration with her client (the other "performer"). Her body became a vehicle for the pain/pleasure of another which she felt was, at once, performative, powerful, and empowering.

From her early work in the BDSM (bondage, domination, submission, masochism) community Ibarra found herself drawn to the more public stage in the form of burlesque, beginning her career by taking on the moniker *La Chica Boom*. When I interviewed her in 2018, she told me that in choosing the name she was "'ground[ing it] in the form of burlesque; even the name itself is a burlesquing of [her] racialized sexuality.'" Ibarra wanted to be able to "'make fun of [her] own raciality'" and felt that the burlesque stage offered that space.[2] She began by creating short pieces that took on issues such as the hypersexualized notions of *Latinidad*, queerness, race, and sexuality. Over the course of ten years, Ibarra created over one hundred of these short burlesque pieces which she titled *Spictacles*, again as a parody of the derogatory term, "spic"—that is levied upon Latinx people. Ibarra's *Spictacles* were created with the purpose of using camp and disidentification to critique majoritarian views of queer, brown-skinned, women.

However, after ten years of ejaculating hot sauce, fisting *piñatas*, masturbating at the Statue of Liberty, stripping in a *luchador* mask and more, Ibarra felt that her work had ultimately "failed."[3] Ibarra spoke at length in our interview about how in the end she was performing for mostly white audiences who just "didn't get it." It was as if Ibarra *was La Chica Boom,* both on and off the stage. Audience members practiced their elementary Spanish with her off stage and hollered things like "*Mamacita!*" and "Hot Tamale!" at her. Even her fellow performers on the burlesque circuit did not know how to separate the character of *La Chica Boom* from the person of Xandra Ibarra. Instead of challenging the racialized stereotypes of a hypersexualized *Latinidad,* her work seemed to *reify* those notions for her audience and her fellow performers.

She told me "I wasn't trying to teach—it wasn't didactic; it was jacking off with humor. But I still wanted to deconstruct all those things."[4] What Ibarra realized after ten years as *La Chica Boom* was that her work "was reifying; I don't think I was deconstructing. I didn't understand what was going to happen when you reify racial tropes and then use comedy and then on top of that use sex."[5] For Ibarra, who kept confronting her audience with her own racialized sexuality, aggressively, assertively, and unapologetically asking them to see the violence that occurs when your body is marked as brown, as femme, and as queer, she had to ask herself, "what is this thing I created?!" as she realized the deep chasm between what she was "trying to do with what was actually happening," she acknowledged that much of her work was, in her words, a "failure."[6] Her "failure" to convince the audience to do the work of reading her performances as she intended them to be read is something Ibarra talks about at great length and with a deep and profound acceptance of the reality that her audiences kept failing, and that she kept failing to communicate to them why they failed.

In an effort to confront her self-perceived failures and to "'deal with the toxic relationship that [she] either imagined or had with white audiences,'" Ibarra chose to create a new piece called *F*ck My Life (FML)* in which she kills *La Chica Boom* once and for all and is reborn as *La Cucarachica.*[7] "In Spanish a *cucaracha* is a cockroach; here Ibarra genders the cockroach as a *cucarachica* reminding us that part of *La* Chica *Boom,* will always be there, in that hard, reviled casing of a cockroach."[8]

This chapter begins by looking at Ibarra's more recent work post-*La Chica Boom* in which she directly challenges and fucks (and fucks with) white womanhood, white femininity, and whiteness itself. Focusing on her 2013 collaboration, *Untitled Fucking* with feminist performance artist Amber Hawk Swanson, as well as her works, *La Corrida, Training for Exhaustion,* and her series of menstrual prints, *She's on the Rag,* this chapter will argue that in enacting her confrontational model of audience engagement, Ibarra has found new and explosive ways to fuck—and fuck with her audience.[9] Finding a kind of joy and generative process in the discomfort and fear of her spectators, Ibarra creates a safe space for brown, femme, queer bodies, desires, and sexualities.

"The Audience Was My Source of Hate … "

In speaking of her time as *La Chica Boom* and the ultimate death and then rebirth-as-cockroach of the character in *FML,* Ibarra told me that "the audience was my source of hate. I don't think the audience liked the show. I don't think the audience was supposed to. I have the white audience I was critiquing *at* the show."[10] In several of her following works, Ibarra actively and aggressively performs that "hate" and dislike for her audiences by creating works that they/we (as I too am a white cisgendered spectator of her work) are not meant to simply enjoy. Ibarra wants us to be as uncomfortable with our racism, sexism, and homophobic ideologies and ethics as she is having been victimized by them, and in a way is seeking revenge for injuries collectively done to her by the white supremacist cis-hetero-patriarchy of which we are all a part.

After *FML,* Ibarra chooses to avoid being in the co-presence of her spectators, engaging in what Christina León terms an "opaque aesthetic" in which she can continue to use her raced, sexed, gendered body as a stage for the performance of her own intersecting identities, but without her audiences in the same physical space.[11] Creating photographic exhibits, films, and interactive videos, Ibarra has transcended the title of burlesque or even performance artist—becoming more of a multimedia, multimodal, art-maker, while bringing with her the most salient and semiotic imagery from her days as *La Chica Boom.*[12]

Recuperating the Tapatia Bottle Strap-On made famous in her 2004 burlesque *Spictacle, La Tortillera,* as well as the emblem of a cockroach, Ibarra cedes the control and interpretation of her work to audiences she cannot necessarily see or speak back to in her performance, but no longer must suffer the "burden of liveness" that comes with real-time presence of spectators.[13] In Ibarra's own words, her more recent work "traces this difficult mode of existence through a variety of media—namely, performance, photography, objects, and video" working to "capture the ways of being that comprise a fucked life: the material realities of living

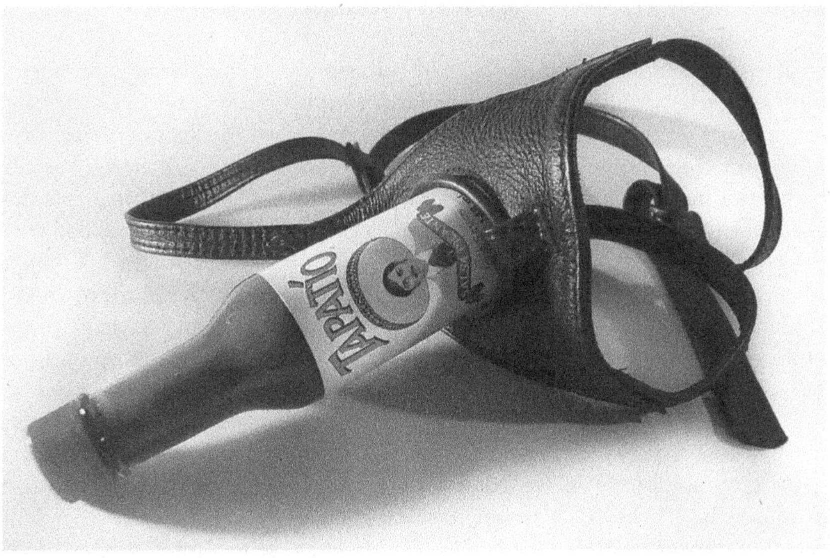

Image 6 *Tapatío Cock,* 2004, Xandra Ibarra.

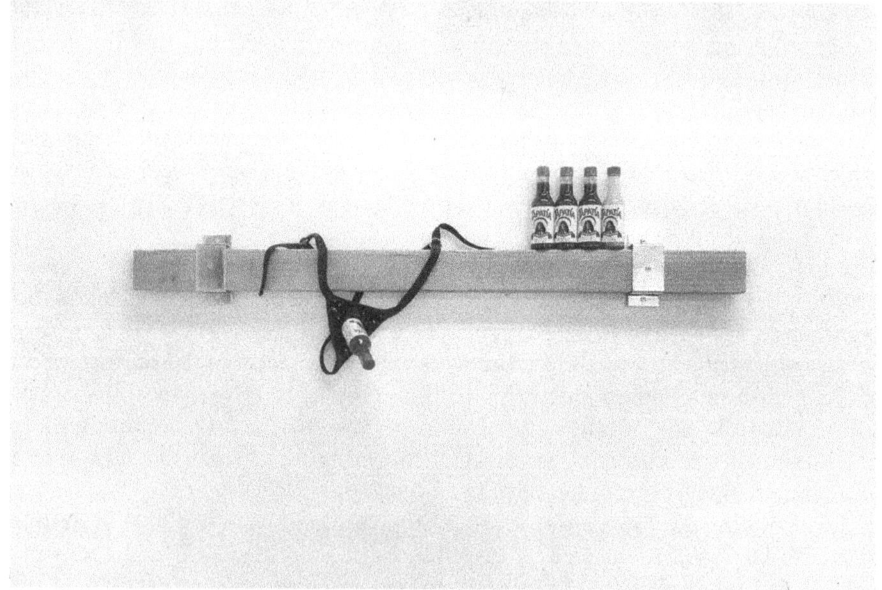

Image 7 *Tapatío Cock and Spic Jouissance Bottles* (Installation View), Xandra Ibarra.

in degradation as a minoritarian subject without rushing to produce narratives of overcoming or celebrating negativity."[14]

Untitled Fucking

One of the first of these multimedia installations was her collaboration with fellow multimedia artist Amber Hawk Swanson in *Untitled Fucking* (2013). One of the most sexually explicit of her works, Ibarra and Hawk Swanson's piece treads the line of being at once performance and also pornography. Ibarra herself has said that this piece "is both pornography and art. There are a lot of things that don't make it porn, but also a lot of things that don't make it art."[15] The filmed encounter consists of Ibarra wearing *cucaracha* (cockroach) pasties and stilettos "fucking a bent over, equally feminine and sultry, Hawk Swanson, first with a bottle of *Tapatío*, and then with her hand," while Hawk Swanson repeats over and over the phrase, "Feminism? That's deep. I think I need a minute to think about that so … I don't know" in a valley-girl accent Image 8.[16] One significant element of this piece that challenges the provocation, "isn't this just porn?" is that the camera is positioned in such a way that we don't actually "see anything" graphic in the film. In the bottom left of the frame we see Hawk Swanson's face while her body is bent on all fours on the bed. Behind her we see Ibarra, but we don't actually *see* the "fucking." This piece is not filmed from the "man's"—or in this case the "top's"—point of view (in homosexual relationships the top is generally the partner who "gives" whereas the "bottom" is the partner who "receives"). It does not situate itself as "girl-on-girl porn" for the male or hetero-sexist gaze.

Hawk Swanson's pale, fair skin, and bright red lips dressed in a black bustier, thigh-highs, and shiny black heels, with her long dark hair and cropped short bangs, evoke the image of Betty Paige, queen of the 1950s pin-up models, a specific version and interpretation of a white feminine ideal. Ibarra in contrast is behind her, wearing her cockroach pasties and a dark smoky eye with a look of intensity and seriousness on her face. Her project is one of pleasure and the joy of queer sex and she is determined and focused in her task. While this scene *is* about giving pleasure to Hawk Swanson, she does not climax until after Ibarra ejaculates hot sauce all over her backside, reminding us that her spiciness cannot be contained. Iván Ramos writes about this moment in his 2016 article, "Spic(y) Appropriations: The Gustatory Aesthetics of Xandra Ibarra," noting that once the hot sauce has covered Hawk Swanson and the bed upon which the performance takes place that this mess reminds us that "unlike any other flavor, spiciness demands stamina and commitment to the gustatory as an almost sadomasochistic experience, one that *Untitled Fucking* unites most explicitly to the act of lesbian sex."[17]

There *is* an element of the sadomasochistic taking place here. The encounter is consensual, but the danger that comes with "playing" with hot sauce is real. Ramos reminds us that "a hand that has touched a hot chili or a seed that has smuggled its way beyond the plate will transmit the burning sensation to the skin," so one could only imagine what might happen were the bottle to break open inside of Hawk Swanson.[18] The film plays with this fear, the fear of injury, the fear of danger, and the fear of hotness and spiciness to make a point. Hawk Swanson might *enjoy* the fucking in *Untitled Fucking,* but it is Ibarra who, for once, gets to enact *her* aggression on the (willing) white body of another—she literally screws the very white womanhood she can never hope to embody.

Ibarra and Hawk Swanson did not plan or rehearse this encounter. Ibarra said that each artist admired each other's work and they decided to collaborate, "'So we're fucking?' 'Yeah' 'So I'll see you at 6 o'clock.'"[19] The project was also part of Hawk Swanson's "The Feminism? Project" which consisted of ten scripted videos edited from "interviews with a variety of women. Their original responses to the topic of feminism range from naïve surprise to composed discourse but become flip one-liners and ironic ramblings when voiced by Hawk Swanson in valley-girl intonation and enacted in provocatively sexual contexts."[20]

Ibarra confessed that while they didn't know exactly what would happen when they met, they had planned to have Hawk Swanson return to her valley-girl accent and repeat lines of text—so they simply set up their camera and began to film. Ibarra was going to occasionally interject, "colonialism, that's deep … I need to think about that so … I don't know" echoing Hawk Swanson's phrase but decided it was too didactic. They wanted to allow the film to speak for itself.[21]

I had the opportunity to view the piece, along with the aforementioned Tapatía bottle and strap-on at the exhibit, at *On Our Backs: The Revolutionary Art of Queer Sex Work* at the Leslie Lohman Museum of Art in New York City in 2019. As I

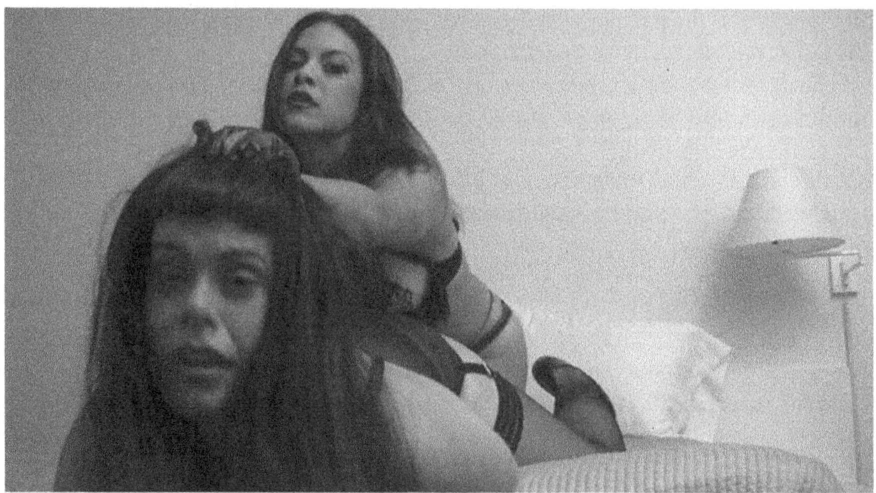

Image 8 *Untitled Fucking*, video still, Xandra Ibarra and Amber Hawk Swanson.

moved around the exhibition surrounded by the works of a plethora of explicit body artists, I turned a corner to find a row of small cabins, painted in a vibrant red which stood out against the clean white walls of the museum interior. Inside the first cabin were a small, black stool, a pair of headphones, and a small screen playing *Untitled Fucking* on repeat.

I entered the cabin in the last few minutes of the performance and watched as Hawk Swanson breathlessly and with eyes closed repeat her line again and again. At times, she would lose her line as she was given over to moaning with pleasure and would slip further down the bed and out of frame. Each time Ibarra would pull her hair upwards to bring her face back into view and Hawk Swanson would again find her text. After Hawk Swanson's climax, Ibarra kisses Hawk Swanson's bottom and slaps her playfully on the ass and gets off the bed. And the video begins again.

To watch the film from the beginning after seeing the end was a relief. I knew how it ended and thus did not have to worry (as I would have if seeing it from beginning to end) that Ibarra's Tapatío bottle might shatter, and I could only imagine what that would be like for Hawk Swanson. With this anxiety allayed, I was able to appreciate and critically engage with the film, watching Hawk Swanson move from discomfort, to awkwardness, to pleasure, to ecstasy. About three-quarters of the way through the video, Ibarra "cums" with her hot sauce onto Hawk Swanson's back which is then covered and dripping with the bright red sauce. By this point Hawk Swanson is more or less rendered speechless, and then Ibarra fists her into orgasm.

Iván Ramos writes of this "cum shot" as

the ultimate unleashing of Ibarra's project. Her cum-shot releases the substance that in this context offers a reframing of racialized queer politics. Spiciness is in equal parts alluring and dangerous, and perhaps out of all culinary experiences expands in and beyond the mouth, often exposing the very boundaries between inside and outside. After all, sweetness may be cloying, bitterness distasteful, saltiness annoying; but spiciness expands, takes over one's body, brings tears to one's eyes.[22]

What Ramos is getting at here is that Ibarra's project, from *Tortillera* to *Untitled Fucking* and beyond, is a project which lays bare white Americans' fear that the spiciness of "spic-hood" could travel north of the US-Mexico Border and "contaminate" white American bodies, particularly white American *female* bodies, while simultaneously acknowledging that Americans are also drawn to the sensations that this spiciness has to offer. We are at once attracted to and repelled by the "heat" that Ibarra and others like her bring to the table. Amber Jamilla Musser notes that "[s]piciness indexes not only the simultaneous fear of and desire for difference on the part of white normative culture, but also Ibarra's rejection of assimilation. Ibarra wields power through this hot sauce. She makes her racialization visible *and* desirable."[23]

There is much to unpack in this piece, from the performances themselves to the objects featured in the video. Ibarra, wearing her signature *cucaracha* pasties, echoes her (de)evolution into *la cucarachica,* and the Tapatío strap-on serves to once again remind viewers of her inherent "Mexi-sexiness" and the spiciness of her "spic-hood." In many ways, these artists are still engaging in a disidentifying performative, staging the dominant culture's greatest fears, a Mexican body "topping" the body of a white woman, who not only isn't objecting, but is thrown into orgasmic pleasure from that penetration. In doing so, Ibarra is fucking whiteness and the abuse she has suffered at the hands of a majoritarian, cis-heterosexist, white culture. Moreover, the piece, in many ways, is engaging critically with issues endemic to the topic of feminism. In her review of the film, Juana María Rodríguez notes that "being compelled to talk about feminism, as she is getting pounded from behind with a bottle of Mexican hot sauce, registers the ongoing difficulty of feminist discourse to reconcile the complexities implicated in political (and sexual) postures organized around pleasure, power and difference."[24] In this film, Ibarra has the power as she "tops" Hawk Swanson, but there is no sense of her taking advantage of it. Ibarra is enjoying the act of pleasuring Hawk Swanson and while we might fear for Hawk Swanson's safety (will the bottle break inside her?), Ibarra is clearly taking care of her partner, as is evidenced when Hawk Swanson requests "another finger please."[25] The idea that this is a consensual act might make it all the most fearsome to a viewer who might ask, "who *wants* someone to do this to them?" For viewers to see a white woman being "topped" in such a manner is a direct confrontation to white femininity and to white feminism and it is meant to provoke those who choose to watch.

In Ibarra and Hawk Swanson's artist's note, they state:

Through queer sexual vocabulary of topping, bottoming, and "bottoming out," Ibarra and Hawk Swanson's collaboration stages the deep and complicated interplay between the performance of white feminism and the feminisms of color that whiteness excludes. The piece also poses a collective challenge to the systems of representation that discipline the notion of political "voice." Working in the erotic interplay between saying and doing, Hawk Swanson and Ibarra rehearse the queer and feminist contradictions that arise when explicit sex and performance collide, directing us towards the untitled and yet to be articulated horizons of political possibility.[26]

Musser argues that in this "'conversation' about feminism, power and penetration act as fulcrums for pleasure, and we gain a new language for thinking about brown jouissance."[27] Thinking through the works of Julia Kristeva, she posits that maybe brown jouissance "can be found in this understanding of the body as object and abject" as bodies of color can "become objects of art" though their performances of self as abjection turns into "agency."[28]

Ironically, Ibarra's Tapatía bottle, a performing object from her work ten years earlier, speaks not of brown jouissance, but instead what Ibarra calls "spic-jouissance." The bottle features a photo of Ibarra with her green wig and signature *La Chica Boom* smile/grimace and includes on its ingredient list: "armargura, commodified negation, dedicated invader subjectivity, toilet water, Las 3 lupes, and alternity, cucharacha logic as a preservative." Its nutritional categories are: "libidinal investment, repulsion, and aborted melancholia" and above those is the statement, "Es Una Puta … Bien Jota" ("a very queer whore").[29]

Like the bottle, which is by its very nature "spic-y," Ibarra's racialized body cannot be separated from itself; it is a visually Latina body and thus has inscribed upon it all of the fears, desires, and eroticism of what Rodríguez calls the "sexual archives flavored by attachments and memory."[30]

As such, Ibarra and Hawk Swanson are not only confronting spectators with the eroticization of race and interracial sex, but rather, as Rodríguez argues, the performance "rejects the liberal demands of color blindness in our most intimate encounters and insists on a more color-conscious consideration of sexual relations. Importantly, the interpretive possibilities of this racially embodied erotic performance are not predetermined."[31] Thus Ibarra and Hawk Swanson are not teaching us a lesson, so to speak, they are providing viewers a visual and semiotic text that we might interrogate our own desires, fears, and maybe even sexual proclivities and hang ups.

For some, this performance, this sexual improvisation, is simply too perverse to be art—much less feminism, but as Juana María Rodríguez compellingly argues, if feminists allow the "politics of respectability to set the terms of what might constitute a feminist agenda, we vacate the space of public discourse on sex to others who will not hesitate to assign meaning to our psychic and corporeal practices."[32] This argument, that it is *precisely* the "perversion" portrayed in *Untitled Fucking* that makes it powerful, is a compelling and persuasive one, because not only are Ibarra and Hawk Swanson refusing the polite politics of white feminism, they are creating and embodying representations of queer sexuality for audiences of all kinds. Thus, they confront their audiences with these perversions and in doing so normalize them. In her article, "Queer Sociality and Other Sexual Fantasies," Rodríguez's calls for a recognition of and reckoning with queer desire, or as she terms it, "queer sociality" which she defines as "a utopian space that both performs a critique of existing social relations of difference and enacts a commitment to the creative critical work of imagining collective possibilities."[33] In my personal opinion as a viewer, there is something profoundly utopian *and* feminist in what Ibarra and Hawk Swanson performed in that both participants receive pleasure without any regard for the usual trappings of the culturally accepted motivations for female sexuality (procreation and/or the pleasure and gratification of the male body, gaze, or desire). Hawk Swanson's pleasure is clear in her bright and full-volume orgasm, and Ibarra's pleasure is written into the smile on her face as Hawk Swanson cums and she playfully slaps and then kisses Hawk Swanson's bottom. Indeed, the staging of queer female desire is a deeply political act. In order to be considered acceptable in what Rodríguez calls "the fold of collectivity," even a collectivity of feminism "we must first be liberated of our sexual deviance, our politically incorrect desires."[34] What *Untitled Fucking* makes abundantly clear is that these desires are only as "incorrect" as is our limited ability to accept queer representations of female sexuality, which are inextricably tied to a "consideration of race, gender, and embodiment that needs to be unpacked."[35] When we take these considerations into account in the viewing of this film there is no doubt that Ibarra and Hawk Swanson are confronting the politics of pleasure, queer sociality; and the fears of abjection, *Latinidad*, and infestation (vis-à-vis Ibarra's *cucaracha*) of brownness into whiteness.

Rodríguez argues that it is the "touch of sex" that can offer potential moments of the recognition of desires that exist outside of the "constraints of the quotidian" and that in trying to create moments of recognition there is always a risk of unintelligibility and failure.[36] She goes on to argue, however:

> [T]hrough our real and imagined sexual encounters, queers enact the possibility of disentangling bodies and acts from preassigned meanings, of creating meaning and pleasure anew from the recycled scraps of dominant cultures. Through eroticization and pleasure, we are thus presented with the possibility of remarking and remaking the pain and refusal of social intelligibility that constitute our daily lives, and sometimes the promise is enough.[37]

I argue here that what Ibarra and Hawk Swanson are working toward in *Untitled Fucking* is opening up that promise of creating meaning. Ibarra has stated that she doesn't want the piece to be immediately intelligible to audiences, for as much as Ibarra works to create art, to fuck herself and Hawk Swanson into legibility, she wants the audience to work for it, too. She aims to blur the lines between sex and sexuality, between desire and abjection, between performance and pornography, "into a mess where it's difficult for the audience to make sense of them. When I do that, that's when I feel like I made a successful work of art," even when an audience fails to read it as she intends it to be read.[38] In doing so, Ibarra puts the onus on her audiences to figure out her work and the ways that they are implicated in it, either implicitly or explicitly so. She refuses to be easily legible, asking her spectators to "do the work" that comes with unpacking the ever-challenging structures of race, sex, gender, sexuality, abjection, and embodiment. In this way, *Untitled Fucking* serves as a kind of jumping off point for audiences to interrogate their own perceptions, privileges, and maybe even perversions.

In this piece, Ibarra wanted to explore queer desire and her own racial and sexual identity. She wanted to explore her "desire to dive into hyperbole. It was connected to [her] racial identity and [her] sexual identity." When she was reborn as *la cucarachica,* she gave herself over to the abject, to the "disgust, invisibility, hypervisibility, and infestation, along with its state of presumed metamorphosis."[39] While Ibarra can be *La Chica Boom* in all her various disguises and iterations she is still who she was the very first time she stepped onto the stage and into the spotlight to be seen by her (predominantly) white audiences. Ibarra writes of her transformations:

When a cockroach changes during adolescence through ecdysis, it removes its exterior casing to fashion a new self that only ends up resembling the old. Aren't Latinidad and spichood similarly fucked—the fuckedness of always already being the same or of resemblance in repetition? Even when I attempt to reassemble new skin, sick of my spic casings, I remain destined to be crucified through them. I can only discard and abandon the carcass; I'm stuck. My new being through ecdysis remains within "the order of the same."[40]

In Tina Takemoto's analysis, this work speaks to "the debilitating impact of failure, especially for queer artists of color."[41] Takemoto concludes her essay, "Queer Art/ Queer Failure" asking that "as we continue to explore the artistic potentialities of queer failure and learn new ways to fail better, we must also remain vigilant in reminding ourselves that it certainly does matter who and what is being done (or undone) when we endeavor to queer failure and fail as queers."[42] One can interpret Ibarra's works, beginning with *Untitled Fucking* and continuing to the present, to be actively confronting her "failures." Her failures to be white, to be hetero-, to be male—and using them to "fuck" her audience as much as she feels that she has been "fucked" by them.

Sick and Tired of Being Sick and Tired

Since 2013 Ibarra has continued to expand her work in various modes and through multiple mediums of performance. In *La Corrida,* the audience is invited to run (virtually) along the US-Mexico Border.[43] Ibarra places a treadmill in this installation and when a spectator runs on it, the film of Ibarra, running in combat boots, booty-shorts, and her signature cockroach pasties, plays, taking the viewer across the "Rio Grande/Rio Bravo and various locations in the Chihuahuan desert between the United States and Mexico on the border of El Paso/Juarez."[44] If you want to see the half-naked Ibarra running, and running, and running—the blazing hot desert sun beating down on her as she momentarily collapses on the dusty ground before pulling herself up and running again—you have to run too. There is an implicit request within the piece; if you want to "enjoy" watching Ibarra suffer, you must consent to some degree of discomfort in partnership with her. She is no longer allowing her audience to be passive spectators; she asks us to do more than just the work of critical thinking (as she has little faith in us to do so), as she needs us to put our bodies into the work as well.

In *Training for Exhaustion* (2015) Ibarra plays with what Amelia Jones calls, "queer feminist durationality" which Jones defines as "the potential for doing something with artwork through interpretation that … reactivates [the artist] by returning them to process and embodiment—linking the interpreting body of the present with the bodies referenced or performed in the past as the work of art."[45] In this piece, Ibarra takes on the character of a trainer, who will lead sixteen complete strangers on a "performance jog" through Oakland, California. Ibarra requires that they wear face masks (which she calls *cucaracha* lenses) and grow cockroach skeletons through hypnosis. Ibarra's goal was "to build stamina to be sick and tired of being sick and tired" in some small way making her audience feel as tired of her raciality, her "spic-casings," her "fuckedness" as she is.[46]

Ibarra's confrontational paradigm extends even to her Etsy store where she sold Rorschach inkblots made of her own menstrual blood in *She's on the Rag* from 2013–20. At the 2017 Association for Theatre in Higher Education (ATHE) conference, Ibarra gave a talk about her oeuvre, from her early days as *La Chica Boom* to the present. In her discussion of *She's on the Rag,* Ibarra admitted that choosing Etsy as a platform for selling the $130 prints was deeply intentional, as she has a very specific notion of *who* spends their time shopping on Etsy—upper-middle-class white women. The very kind of person Ibarra has repeatedly and will continue to "fail" to be, but who she will nevertheless want to confront and, at times, to "fuck with." At her store she offers the following "Announcement" to her shoppers:

> What do you see? This menstrual rorschach test gauges a person's personality and emotional logic; It can even detect underlying psychological disorders like light-weight racism. Tell me what YOU see, smell, taste and feel & I will read you in English AND Spanish. Video consultations/readings provided upon request with an additional charge for each purchase.[47]

The shopper eager to learn from Ibarra just what their reading means and willing to pay the additional fee will receive a kaleidoscopic video of menstrual Rorschach images with a Spanish voice over and English subtitles which makes little sense and is intended, in my opinion, to confuse, confront, and even offend the viewer. For example, the video available on her website begins by telling the viewer:

> Bats, moths, and paper airplanes are generally safe responses. They are also common answers for sexual deviants. These responses suggest you suffer from a fetish for flying. You often ask yourself: Why can't I fucking fly? The pressure of

the expectations to fly makes you feel as if you were stuck between two fags on coke looking for exterior organs in a small foul smelling and damp bathroom. You give the impression that you don't care about flying and you do your best to avoid conversation about it. This makes you prone to anxiety, however it inspires you to masturbate often about your mother. Yes, your fucking mother.[48]

It goes on. Ibarra is not interested in interpreting what people see in her menstrual blood. Christina León reads these prints as an "opaque form of camp" wherein she plays with "the form of that which is conventionally understood to be formless, abject, or raw material: menstrual blood."[49] I don't disagree with León in her analysis of these prints, but I believe that there is something inherently confrontational in the work as well. Ibarra asks the (upper-middle-class white) women who buy things on Etsy to spend their money on her grotesque and abject gesture, and then insults them with her interpretations of what they see. As she said in an interview on the pieces with *Hyperallergic*:

All consultations will be excessive, campy, absurd, and explore the psychic interiority of all the identitarian things we love to hate, womanhood and raciality. [...] I am always already in the process of selling myself because of my fucked condition as a racialized and gendered "other." As a result I am never seen. However, I am sighted as a commodity or as excess. This project allows me to use my blood/my body parts without being sighted. Instead I share discarded parts of my body (uterine lining) with you. I am asking you to see me without me. I am asking that you acknowledge that fucked subjects bleed. I am still sharing my body with you but prohibiting you from seeing me—instead I parody Western practices of psychological assessment to pathologize and "read" you via video consultations.[50]

It is a confrontation, a "fuck you!" to the receiver. A kind of "topping" in which Ibarra, once again returning to her roots as the Dom, is in complete control. Moreover, it is a reclamation of meaning-making wherein Ibarra tells the spectators what *she* sees in *their* viewing of what is ultimately her monthly (queer) failure to reproduce as a good, heteronormative woman should. León writes, "If this is what the colonialist majority wants to access—the hidden, private interiority of the racialized subject/fetish—then Ibarra provides this aggressively, in literalized form. And yet she provides for another, more positive reading as well: in this form, interiority is habitually shed such that while one may remain stuck, one does indeed endure."[51] Moreover, like the *cucarachica*, she bleeds, but does not die.

Like the immovable object that is met by an unstoppable force, Ibarra keeps confronting us, she keeps saying "fuck you." She incorporates each failure of reception into her next performance and into her pedagogy. If you choose to confront your audience as your enemy and force them to see that which makes them uncomfortable, as a performer failure will sometimes follow. But this confrontational model of explicit body performance sees failures as the generative seeds of future performance. Ibarra's "failures" have something to teach us, and she uses those failures as the fuel for her next exploration, her next idea, her next performance. Moreover, as she grows as an artist, performer, and theorist-of-performance, Ibarra becomes more and more confident telling us to "fuck off," saying "fuck you," and knowing that while we may or may not listen to that request, we might actually hear something that helps us to realize just how awful it really is to be totally and completely fucked.

Notes

1   Xandra Ibarra, Interview with the Author, April 5, 2018.
2   Quoted in Erin Kaplan, "*La Chica Boom* and the Pedagogy of Queer Failure," *Theatre Topics* 30, no. 2 (2020): 86, accessed August 9, 2021, https://doi.org/10.1353/tt.2020.0015.
3   To view these and other *Spictacles* visit: "Spictacle," *Xandra Ibarra*, accessed October 5, 2023, https://www.xandraibarra.com/spictacles.
4   Ibarra, Interview, 2018.
5   Ibarra, Interview, 2018.
6   Ibarra, Interview, 2018.
7   Quoted in Kaplan, "*La Chica Boom*," 90.
8   Kaplan, "*La Chica Boom*," 90.
9   For more on this, see Kaplan, "*La Chica Boom*," 85–97.
10 Quoted in Kaplan, "*La Chica Boom*," 90.
11 Christina A. León, "Forms of Opacity: Roaches, Blood, and Being Stuck in Xandra Ibarra's Corpus," *ASAP/Journal* 2, no. 2 (2017): 377, https://doi.org/10.1353/asa.2017.0037.
12 See her work *Spic Ecdysis* for more: Xandra Ibarra, "Spic Ecdysis" (2014), accessed July 18, 2018, http://www.xandraibarra.com/spic-ecdysis/.
13 Coined by Jose Esteban Muñoz in *Disidentifications: Queers of Color and the Performance of Politics* (Minneapolis: University of Minnesota Press, 1999). Muñoz argues that "[p]erformance, from the positionality of the minoritarian subject, is sometimes nothing short of forced labor" (189) and that minoritarian subjects are often subjected to the "burden of liveness" wherein they are "mandate[d] to 'perform' for the amusement of a dominant power bloc" and that these performances become "encouraged" and are often (more or less) required for queer and minoritarian subjects (187).
14 Xandra Ibarra, "ATHE Conference 2017 Plenary: A Spectacular Balancing Act," in Plenary, eds. Carlos Alexis Cruz, Roy Gomez Cruz, Jane Childs, Xandra Ibarra, Kareem Khubchandani, Chris LaShua, Louis Patrick Leroux, and Chase Waites (Association for Theatre in HIgher Education, Las Vegas, NV).
15 Ibarra, Interview, 2018.
16 Juana María Rodríguez, "From the Square," *Untitled Feminism* (blog), March 19, 2014, https://www.fromthesquare.org/untitled-feminism/#.W1JQ49hKg0o.
17 Iván A. Ramos, "Spic(y) Appropriations: The Gustatory Aesthetics of Xandra Ibarra (Aka La Chica Boom)," *ARARA- Art and Architecture of the Americas*, no. 12 (2016): 17.
18 Ramos, "Spic(y) Appropriations," 17.
19 Ibarra, Interview, 2018.

20 Kendra Greene, "Ten Videos from the 'Feminism?' Project," *MoCP: Museum of Contemporary Photography*, accessed July 23, 2018, http://www.mocp.org/detail.php?type=related&kv=12779&t=objects.

21 Ibarra, Interview, 2018.

22 Ramos, "Spic(y) Appropriations," 17.

23 Amber Jamilla Musser, *Sensual Excess: Queer Femininity and Brown Jouissance* (New York: New York University Press, 2019), 70.

24 Rodríguez, "From the Square," 2014.

25 Xandra Ibarra and Amber Hawk Swanson, *Untitled Fucking*, Video, ON OUR BACKS: The Revolutionary Art of Queer Sex Work, Leslie-Lohman Museum of Art, December 2019.

26 Amber Hawk Swanson, "The Feminism Project," accessed August 9, 2021, https://amberhawkswanson.com/The-Feminism-Project.

27 Musser, *Sensual Excess*, 72.

28 Musser, *Sensual Excess*, 87.

29 Xandra Ibarra, "Strap-On Harnesses, Tapatío Cock, Spic Jouissance Bottle and Boxes," accessed August 6, 2021, https://www.xandraibarra.com/tapatio-cock/.

30 Juana María Rodríguez, *Sexual Futures* (New York: New York University Press, 2014), 131.

31 Rodríguez, "From the Square," 2014.

32 Rodríguez, "From the Square," 2014.

33 Juana María Rodriguez, "Queer Sociality and Other Sexual Fantasies," *GLQ: A Journal of Lesbian and Gay Studies* 17, no. 2–3 (January 1, 2011): 332, https://doi.org/10.1215/10642684-1163427.

34 Rodriguez, "Queer Sociality and Other Sexual Fantasies," 336.

35 Rodriguez, "Queer Sociality and Other Sexual Fantasies," 334.

36 Rodriguez, "Queer Sociality and Other Sexual Fantasies," 338.

37 Rodriguez, "Queer Sociality and Other Sexual Fantasies," 338.

38 Ibarra, Interview, 2018.

39 Xandra Ibarra, "Ecdysis: The Molting of A Cucarachica (2015)," *Women & Performance: A Journal of Feminist Theory* 25, no. 3 (September 2, 2015): 355. https://doi.org/10.1080/0740770X.2015.1136480.

40 Ibarra, "Ecdysis," 355.

41 Tina Takemoto, "Queer Art / Queer Failure," *Art Journal* 75, no. 1 (January 2, 2016): 87, https://doi.org/10.1080/00043249.2016.1171547.

42 Takemoto, "Queer Art," 88.

43 Xandra Ibarra, "La Corrida," accessed September 20, 2018, https://www.xandraibarra.com/la-corrida/.

44 Xandra Ibarra, "La Corrida Interactive Treadmill Video Installation (2012)," 2012. http://www.xandraibarra.com/la-corrida-installation/.

45 Amelia Jones, *Seeing Differently* (London: Routledge, 2012), 174.

46 Xandra Ibarra, "Training for Exhaustion (2015)," *QED: A Journal in GLBTQ Worldmaking* 4, no. 2 (2017): 76. https://doi.org/10.14321/qed.4.2.0076.

47 Xandra Ibarra, "She's on the Rag: Menstrual Rorschach Tests," *Etsy*, 2018. https://www.etsy.com/shop/ShesontheRag?ref=search_shop_redirect.

48 Xandra Ibarra, "She's on the Rag: Menstrual Rorschach Tests," 2016. http://www.xandraibarra.com/shes-on-the-rag/.

49 León, "Forms of Opacity," 383.

50 Dorothy Santos, "Reading Menstrual Rags Like Rorschach Tests," *Hyperallergic*, November 11, 2015, https://hyperallergic.com/252940/reading-menstrual-rags-like-rorschach-tests/.

51 Santos, "Reading Menstrual Rags," 385.

Bibliography

Greene, Kendra. "Ten Videos from the 'Feminism?' Project." *MoCP: Museum of Contemporary Photography.* n.d. Accessed July 23, 2018. http://www.mocp.org/detail.php?type=related&kv=12779&t=objects.

Hawk Swanson, Amber. "The Feminism Project." August 9, 2021. https://amberhawkswanson.com/The-Feminism-Project.

Ibarra, Xandra. "La Corrida Interactive Treadmill Video Installation (2012)." 2012. http://www.xandraibarra.com/la-corrida-installation.

Ibarra, Xandra. "Ecdysis: The Molting of a Cucarachica (2015)." *Women & Performance: A Journal of Feminist Theory* 25, no. 3 (2015): 354–6. https://doi.org/10.1080/0740770X.2015.1136480.

Ibarra, Xandra. "She's on the Rag: Menstrual Rorschach Test." 2016. http://www.xandraibarra.com/shes-on-the-rag/.

Ibarra, Xandra. "Training for Exhaustion (2015)." *QED: A Journal in GLBTQ Worldmaking* 4, no. 2 (Summer 2017a): 76. https://doi.org/10.14321/qed.4.2.0076.

Ibarra, Xandra. "ATHE Conference 2017 Plenary: A Spectacular Balancing Act." Carlos Alexis Cruz, Roy Gomez Cruz, Jane Childs, Xandra Ibarra, Kareem Khubchandani, Chris LaShua, Louis Patrick Leroux, and Chase Waites. In *Plenary*. Las Vegas, NV: Association for Theatre in Higher Education, 2017b.

Ibarra, Xandra. Interview with the author. 2018.

Ibarra, Xandra. *Strap-On Harnesses, Tapatío Cock, Spic Jouissance Bottle and Boxes.* 2021. https://www.xandraibarra.com/tapatio-cock/.

Ibarra, Xandra. "La Corrida." n.d. https://www.xandraibarra.com/la-corrida/.

Ibarra, Xandra. "She's on the Rag: Menstrual Rorschach Tests." *Etsy.* n.d. https://www.etsy.com/shop/ShesontheRag?ref=search_shop_redirect.

Ibarra, Xandra. "Spic Ecdysis." n.d. Accessed July 18, 2018. http://www.xandraibarra.com/spic-ecdysis/.

Ibarra, Xandra. "Spictacles." n.d. Accessed June 20, 2018. http://www.xandraibarra.com/spictacles/.

Ibarra, Xandra and Amber Hawk Swanson. *Untitled Fucking.* Video. ON OUR BACKS: The Revolutionary Art of Queer Sex Work, Leslie-Lohman Museum of Art. 2019.

Jones, Amelia. *Seeing Differently: A History and Theory of Identification and the Visual Arts.* London: Routledge, 2012.

Kaplan, Erin Rachel. "La Chica Boom and the Pedagogy of Queer Failure." *Theatre Topics* 30, no. 2 (2021): 85–97.

León, Christina A. "Forms of Opacity: Roaches, Blood, and Being Stuck in Xandra Ibarra's Corpus." *ASAP/Journal* 2, no. 2 (2017): 369–94. https://doi.org/10.1353/asa.2017.0037.

Muñoz, José Esteban. *Disidentifications: Queers of Color and the Performance of Politics.* Minneapolis: University of Minnesota Press, 1999.

Musser, Amber Jamilla. *Sensual Excess: Queer Femininity and Brown Jouissance.* New York: New York University Press, 2019.

Ramos, Iván A. "Spic(y) Appropriations: The Gustatory Aesthetics of Xandra Ibarra (Aka La Chica Boom)." *ARARA- Art and Architecture of the Americas*, no. 12 (2016): 1–18.

Rodriguez, Juana Maria. "Queer Sociality and Other Sexual Fantasies." *GLQ: A Journal of Lesbian and Gay Studies* 17, no. 2–3 (2011): 331–48. https://doi.org/10.1215/10642684-1163427.

Rodriguez, Juana Maria. *Sexual Futures*. New York: New York University Press, 2014a.

Rodriguez, Juana Maria. "From The Square." *Untitled Feminism* (blog). March 19, 2014b. https://www.fromthesquare.org/untitled-feminism/#.W1JQ49hKg0o.

Santos, Dorothy. "Reading Menstrual Rags Like Rorschach Tests." *Hyperallergic*. November 11, 2015. https://hyperallergic.com/252940/reading-menstrual-rags-like-rorschach-tests/.

Takemoto, Tina. "Queer Art / Queer Failure." *Art Journal* 75, no. 1 (2016): 85–8. https://doi.org/10.1080/00043249.2016.1171547.

Chapter 5

THE INHERITANCE: QUEER SEX IN THE THEATER OF HIV/AIDS

by Ash Hudson-Myers

Mickey, why didn't you guys fight for the right to get married instead of the right to legitimise promiscuity?

—Larry Kramer, *The Normal Heart*[1]

In an article discussing the success of *The Inheritance* on Broadway, Virginia Anderson wrote of her concerns that contemporary staged narratives of HIV and AIDS were replicating narrative tropes and representational beats taken straight from theater of the late 1980s and early 1990s. Anderson's concern was "that *The Inheritance* will continue to reinforce a history that relegates conversations about the history and future of HIV to the 1980s, to New York City, even to white gay men. Surely, this history is vitally important, but it's not the only history of the AIDS epidemic and it's not the only present and future."[2]

The Inheritance is a sprawling two-part epic based on E.M. Forster's *Howards End*. The play primarily takes place in New York and a small homestead a few hours' drive outside of the city during the final years of the 2010s. It explores the ways in which queer histories are entwined, suggesting that time is not necessarily linear, but rather the past, present, and future are in continuous conversation with one another. Morgan (E.M. Forster) refers to his own work within the play itself to highlight this queer temporal dialogism; rather than evoking *Howards End*, he evokes *Maurice*. Morgan comments that the novella *Maurice* "was then, as you are now, a link in this chain of gay men teaching one another, loving one another, hurting one another, understanding one another. This inheritance of history, of community, and of self."[3] The present must contend with not only the past, but also look toward the future.

During the play's first part, a group of financially comfortable gay New Yorkers discuss what the queer community should be working toward as a community now that their societal needs have been met during "the Obama years."[4] Tristan, the only character who is specified to be a Black man responds, "Let's talk about addiction, about the resurgence of HIV among gay men of color."[5] While Tristan is a Black man living with HIV, the play does not talk about his condition. The second part of the play explores Leo's seroconversion. During the play's premier, West End transfer, and Broadway transfer, Leo was played by Samuel H. Levine. As such, Leo is a character that is coded as white. As Anderson highlights above, the history of mainstream HIV/AIDS theater is typified by the foregrounding of ailing white bodies.[6] Historically, mainstream plays exploring HIV/AIDS have had to contend with the question of sex, either through didacticism of "safer" sexual practices, or through the eroticization of alternative forms of sexual union. Often these plays—either intentionally or unintentionally—moralize about certain sexual practices. During the early years of the AIDS crisis, the intent for doing so is clear. However, in *The Inheritance* Lopez seems to continue this tradition of placing good (safe) and bad (dangerous) sexual practices on a binary. It is not the practice itself that makes a sexual act good or bad, but the context in which a particular act is played.

The Inheritance was first performed in 2018, a year after NAM (national AIDS manual) the British information-sharing HIV/AIDS charity endorsed the U=U consensus statement.[7] U=U stands for Undetectable Equals Untransmittable; simply put, the acronym draws attention to the fact that people with HIV who have a viral load that cannot be detected within the bloodstream, and who are also on a course of effective medication, cannot pass HIV on to seronegative sexual partners. This includes through condomless sex, be it oral, vaginal, or anal. Along with effective HIV treatment, in the UK, preventative medication is available on the NHS in England, Wales, Scotland, and Northern Ireland. These preventative medications are known as PrEP (Pre-Exposure Prophylaxis) and PEP (Post-Exposure Prophylaxis). While these medications are widely available in the Global North, that should not suggest that there exists medicative justice in these countries, nor in the Global South. For the gay urbanities of *The Inheritance*, however, these medications would not only be known about, but would also play a role in the way these sexual agents conducted their sex lives. In 1996, the Vancouver AIDS Conference demonstrated the ways in which combination therapies could help combat HIV/AIDS, leading the illness to become chronic rather than fatal. Commentators such as Andrew Sullivan suggested that these combination therapies heralded the end of HIV/AIDS.[8] We are closer today to ending the ongoing HIV/AIDS crises than we were in 1996, yet certain sexual scenarios within *The Inheritance* are still framed as dangerous. If we consider representations of sex rather than plot, *The Inheritance* could have been written at the same time as Tony Kushner's *Angels in America*.

I was not the first to draw parallels between *The Inheritance* and *Angels in America*, and I certainly will not be the last. Michael Billington subtitled his review of *The Inheritance* "Angels in America meets Howards End."[9] The influence of *Howards End* is embedded within Lopez's play: theater programs and printed texts all feature the line "inspired by the novel *Howards End* by E.M. Forster."[10] As I will show, intertextual references to *Angels in America* do exist within Lopez's play, though Lopez does not draw attention to this in the same way he does to Forster's work. *The Inheritance* is in some ways a play that contends with Kushner's earlier epic. Eric Glass's "The world will spin without me" echoes Belize and Prior Walters's words: "The world only spins forwards."[11] The final line of dialogue in *The Inheritance* is "You do what they could not … You live."[12] This offers more than just a passing resemblance to Prior's blessing of "More Life" at the end of *Angels*; Lopez's play inherits dialogic messaging from a play that has come before.[13] *The Inheritance*, while focusing on the lives of New Yorkers, exists transnationally and transculturally. Lopez's two main sources of inspiration seem to be a British author and an American playwright.

Matthew Lopez is an American playwright, writing a play based in New York, exploring an American lineage of history, yet the play premiered in London's Old Vic theater, and seemed to be hailed as a modern classic thanks to its transfer to the West End's Noël Coward Theatre. When the play transferred to Broadway it was a British export. Often HIV/AIDS plays from the United States find success in the West End, while the opposite is rarely the case. In keeping with this tradition, the Broadway transfer of *The Inheritance* received a lukewarm response. Alan Sinfield wrote in 1999 the ways in which the success of American HIV/AIDS narratives in the UK led to queer British communities conflating the British experience of HIV/AIDS with that of the United States "Because the fiction and drama of AIDS have drawn British gays vicariously and powerfully, into North American experience, we may be tempted to believe that we have passed through the crisis."[14] The impact that AIDS had upon the queer community is undeniable; however, queer Brits did not experience AIDS in the same way as their American counterparts, much in the same way that queer North Americans could not experience the exact same trauma caused by the passing of Section 28 in the UK. Queer experiences in the Global North, particularly the United States and UK, may be analogous, but they are not exact. US theater audiences seem to be less convinced, moved, or impacted by British portrayals of HIV/AIDS than are British audiences watching US theatrical productions. Even within shared country borders there are a multiplicity of queer communities, yet *The Inheritance* posits that there may only be a single queer community, as such, the morals at the heart of *The Inheritance* are implied to be the correct way of existing as a queer person.

Eric Glass, the primary protagonist of *The Inheritance* asks: "How else can we teach the next generation who they are and how they got here? Human culture from time immemorial has been transmitted through stories, right?"[15] Lopez's use of the word "transmit" here holds double meaning, and this double meaning seems to complicate Eric's relationship with stories. When referring to HIV/AIDS, transmission is negative; it is to be avoided. Yet the transmission of stories seems to be framed positively. As I will discuss, the sex Eric has is framed as being safe due to the context in which he engages in sexual activity. I would argue that while it seems that Eric's words have a double meaning, this is to demonstrate that Eric is aware that he exists in a historical moment in which seroconversion still exists, but he himself is not at risk from such a possibility. Eric has sex in a context that is framed by the play as safe, as such all he can and will transmit is stories.

In *Mainstream AIDS Theatre*, Jacob Juntunen writes:

> Ultimately, mainstream theatre in the U.S. at the end of the twentieth century was able to use capitalism to incorporate, package, and sell ideas that began as radical but became palatable to a large, hegemonic audience. In so doing, mainstream theatre supported the emergent ideology of gay civil rights, helped incorporate it into the dominant ideology, and gave LGBT citizens, particularly gay men, a new place in the U.S. nation.[16]

However, incorporation involves conforming or assimilating to existing power structures. This frames a binary of minoritized subjects that exist within these structures: those who are willing to assimilate and those who are not. Those who are willing to participate in existing networks of power and control are reinforced by the self-same structures as being a "good" minority, while those who do not wish to engage with these structures are framed as "bad" minorities. In *The Inheritance* there are "good" sexual contexts and "bad" sexual contexts. While wider access to PrEP and PEP have to some degree taken the risk out of risk behaviors, that does not mean that all condomless sex is presented equally. Within Lopez's play the safety of such practices are dependent on the participants' position to normative cultural practices.

Eric Glass is a financially comfortable, middle-class white New Yorker, who, due to familial inheritance, finds himself occupying a large flat overlooking New York's Central Park. Eric exists in the Pantheon of HIV/AIDS theater protagonists who live comfortably despite their career not being a crux of their character; the work of the characters around them is much more often in focus. Eric works in a nonprofit while *Angels in America*'s Prior lives modestly off a trust fund, though his character description suggests he works freelance as an interior decorator. The same can be said for Ned Weeks from Larry Kramer's *The Normal Heart*. Weeks, a staged version of Kramer himself, lives comfortably off the earnings he makes bouncing between projects. It should be noted that Prior is the only one of these three characters who contracts HIV. Despite being a play about HIV/AIDS, the difficulties which Eric encounters involve losing property and the end of his relationship. Eric's views are that of a contemporary liberal: he wants what is best for his community, but he is not prepared to rock the boat to achieve it. This is exemplified in his willingness to date and marry the Republican Henry Wilcox. However, at the beginning of the play Eric is dating Toby Darling, an author and playwright.

Early in the play Eric and Toby have sex. The scene is played for comedy rather than arousal. Both actors are fully dressed, though they speak of the encounter as if they were naked. Despite this, the dialogue between the couple makes it explicit that the sex being had is condomless. During the sex, Eric asks Toby to marry him, and the encounter ends with Toby ejaculating inside Eric, who exclaims post-coitally: "Holy shit! I've got your cum inside my ass and we just got engaged."[17] The dialogue reinforces the comedy of the scene. By making the sex between Eric and Toby comical, it becomes safe. The scene is absurd and abstract, as such there can be no real consequences from the sex itself. Another way in which the sex is framed as having no consequences is its positioning as resembling heterosexual sex. Toby has cum in Eric; Eric has been bred. The marriage proposal comes at the moment in which Eric has been impregnated by Toby.[18] That this sexual act is framed as occurring within a homonormative familial context the act becomes ahistoricized from earlier acts of breeding which the receptive partner would become a host (impregnated) by a virus. At no point is there any fear that Eric may become seroconverted: the family setting acts as inoculation from the dangers of HIV.

Later in the play Eric invites his group of friends around, and they are discussing the state of the queer community. A character despairs that his entire personality is based on his sexuality, to which his husband responds, "But being gay isn't all you are, baby. You're a lawyer, you're married, you're about to become a father."[19] Rather than being identified based on his potential for queerness, this person is encouraged to celebrate his successes through a heteronormative lens: marriage, parenthood, and career.

At the end of the play, the audience is told of the ways in which the lives of these characters go once the curtain falls. This temporal trick merges death and life to form a theatrical liminal space in which the future of these characters has occurred, will occur, and is occurring. Eric ends his days living in a farmhouse in upstate New York, the play's equivalent to Howards End. We are told that "Eric's three children, seven grandchildren and fourteen great-grandchildren inherited the house, which they maintain to this day as a cherished family home."[20] The history of Eric's farmhouse is that of a haven for the ill and dying during the height of the AIDS crisis. By the play's end the house has been transformed from a community home to a family home. The queer ghosts that haunt the home are exorcized, and a shared community safe space becomes private property. The tree at the center of the estate which is said to cure all ailments has become privatized. The inheritance of the play's title is no longer community-based; it is individualistic.

The Inheritance is not the only play exploring the impact of HIV/AIDS to end in the marriage of the play's primary character. *The Normal Heart* also ends in a marriage: the marriage of Ned Weeks to his lover Felix. Describing this scene, which occurs on Felix's deathbed, John M. Clum notes:

> Kramer gives Felix a death scene that Dumas or Giuseppe Verdi would have admired. After Felix dispenses some final bits of wisdom and advice, he and Ned are married by a doctor in the presence of Ned's now-apologetic brother. There can be no loving relationship, only a deathbed marriage. Gay men are once again doomed to be alone.[21]

Even if ending in tragedy is inevitable, marriage in this scenario acts as a form of confession, a renunciation of the promiscuity that Kramer typified as stereotypical within the gay community, as can be seen in *The Normal Heart* and his early novel *Faggots*.[22] Eric Glass's sex is safe because he engages with a lifestyle that can be described as homonormative. In Lopez's play, sex that exists in contexts that are not based on these ideals is presented as being dangerous.

In his essay "Mourning and Militancy" Douglas Crimp despairs that the emergence of AIDS hindered the radical queer potential of divergent sexual practices:

> Alongside the dismal toll of death, what many of us have lost is a culture of sexual possibility: back rooms, tea rooms, bookstores, movie houses, and baths; the trucks, the pier, the ramble, the dunes. Sex was everywhere for us, and everything we wanted to venture: golden showers and water sports, cocksucking and rimming, fucking and fist fucking. Now our untamed impulses are either proscribed once again or shielded from us by latex.[23]

Sexual acts were culturally coded as being either correct or incorrect way for queer people to engage in sex. Any sex that had the potential to continue the spread of AIDS was considered unsafe and potentially immoral; the queer community were both the jailers and jailed within a self-formed sexual panopticon. In Kushner's *Angels in America*, sex was separated into oral and anal, with anal sex being practiced by the morally dubious and downright evil. *The Inheritance* continues this legacy of coding certain sexual practices as good or bad. While anal sex does not specifically signify safe or dangerous sexualities, the location and context in which the sex takes place alters whether sex can be deemed safe or not.

Clum concisely described the mathematics of AIDS into six simple equations:

AIDS = homosexuality
AIDS = disease
Homosexuality = disease
Homosexuality = AIDS
Nonmarital, uncontrolled sex = disease
Transgression of family values = disease[24]

However, I would argue that these equations become easier to discern in mainstream HIV/AIDS theater the more contemporary the play. This is because there has been a wider shift in medicalized interventions. In *The Normal Heart*, Weeks disparages promiscuity, arguing that "more sex isn't more liberating. And having so much sex makes finding love impossible."[25] The argument presented by Weeks is reminiscent of earlier gay plays such as Mart Crowley's *The Boys in the Band* in which homosexuality itself was pathologized. While it is impossible to argue that Larry Kramer was a forthright and active HIV/AIDS activist, it is difficult not to read *The Normal Heart* as a justification or an "I told you so" for his portrayal of gay male life in his 1970 novel *Faggots*.

William M. Hoffman's 1985 play *As Is* serves almost as an antithesis of Kramer's play. Here queer sex is celebrated, and Hoffman, through his characters, actually provides a counter to Kramer's queer pessimism: "Saul. God, I used to love promiscuous sex. / Rich. Not 'promiscuous,' Saul, nondirective, noncommitted, nonauthoritarian."[26] By the play's end it is the couple that is bolstered as the strongest queer relationship. While this is similar to the way in which Lopez frames the couple—both plays are pro-sex after all—Hoffman wrote *As Is* during a time in which all gay sex was regarded as being potentially life-threatening. Thirty years later Hoffman's messaging is no longer radical. Both *The Inheritance* and *As Is* present sex and relationships similarly, yet the historical contexts in which both plays were written and first performed show the ways in which certain ways of thinking about gay sex in the context of HIV/AIDS have become outdated.

In the early 1990s, the transmission routes of HIV and AIDS were better understood, and yet we see in Kushner's *Angels* a reluctance to include anal sex in a way that is not moralized. Anal sex is only mentioned in relation to two characters: Louis and Roy Cohn. The sexual practices of other characters (that the audience is informed about) are purely oral. Despite wanting a baby with her husband Joe, the first sexual advance Harper makes is telling Joe she listened to a show on the radio that taught her how to give a blowjob. Meanwhile, Prior quips to his partner Louis: "If I hadn't spent the last four years fellating you I'd swear you were straight."[27] When Prior discusses his difficulties gaining and holding an erection, Belize comments, "My jaw aches at the memory."[28] Though the transmission of HIV through oral sex is possible, the risk of contraction is much lower than through anal sex whether with or without a condom. Oral sex is the safer sexual practice and therefore the better (gooder) sexual practice.

If *Angels in America* has a villain, it is undoubtedly Roy Cohn. Kushner's Cohn is based on real-world lawyer Roy Cohn. Both the real-world Cohn and his theatrical counterpart die from complications due to AIDS. Cohn is explicitly stated as having engaged in anal sex multiple times. Cohn's doctor alludes to Cohn's sexual practices, highlighting that he has treated Cohn for everything including "syphilis to venereal warts. In your rectum. Which you may have gotten from a whore in Dallas, but it wasn't a female whore."[29] Roy Cohn has been a receptive partner for anal sex on more than one occasion and this has led to him contracting AIDS. The second example of anal sex being presented within Kushner's epic is after Louis leaves Prior. Louis is unable to deal with his partner's diagnosis and the symptoms that emerge. Louis goes cruising in The Ramble in Central Park to engage in anonymous sex. At first Louis is extremely conscientious about condom usage, almost walking off when an anonymous man says he does not use rubbers; however, as the act continues the prospect of transmission is almost treated as divine punishment for Louis's sins against Prior:

Man: It … [the condom]
Louis: What?
Man: I think it must've … It broke, or slipped off, you didn't put it on right,
    or—You want me to keep going? Pull out? Should I-
Louis: Keep going.
Infect me.
I don't care. I don't care.[30]

Louis continues to meditate on AIDS as divine punishment when he says that "I fucked around a lot more than he [Prior] did. No justice."[31] Sex in early HIV/AIDS theater does not exist amorally. While contemporary HIV/AIDS theater often attempts destigmatization through the celebration of sex's amorality, this is not the case in Lopez's play.

Above I mentioned that a key narrative beat of *The Inheritance* is Leo's seroconversion. Samuel H. Levine who plays Leo also plays the role of Adam, a character who also has a history of experiencing seroconversion. Adam tells Toby about the time he was briefly HIV-positive due to bottoming during a gangbang in a Prague bathhouse. Adam asks how "an experience that transcendent [could] yield consequences so terrifying?"[32] Unlike the sex scene between Eric and Toby, this scene is not played for comedy, though the sex is also not simulated on stage. Adam describes his encounter in detail, purposefully eroticizing the encounter. The telling of the story serves a dual purpose. Within the narrative of the play, Adam is trying to arouse Toby. As a playwright, Lopez is also trying to arouse the audience. When the realities of HIV are made explicit within the story, there is a Pavlovian impact: both Toby and the audience are framed as being complicit in this act of transmission; our arousal is a clear indicator of our guilt. While it is later implied that Adam falsified this story, the context in which the sex occurred is not redeemed as safe or good. It remains dangerous: a bathhouse is a site of unrestrained sexual freedom, and therefore sexual danger.

Leo's seroconversion is much more important to the structure of the play than Adam's story. The transmission occurs on Fire Island, a location well-known within the gay community as a queer utopia in which sex and drug consumption are the norms. Leo, a sex worker, is taken to Fire Island by Toby. Here Toby uses Leo as a commodity "trading Leo's body away for access, for drugs."[33] During their time on Fire Island both Toby and Leo begin experimenting with injectable narcotics. While the sharing of hypodermic needles is another transmission route for HIV, when Leo learns of his status, he immediately connects HIV with Fire Island, and more specifically, his sexual encounters: "Which of the nameless strangers had it been? Leo thought of the chain of infection that had passed down along the years."[34] Once learning of his transmission, Leo fully embraces his role as a dangerous sexual body:

> The money Eric had given him was all that he had until he could hustle up some—but no: his diagnosis, his … virulence. That would be irresponsible. But what of the man who had given it to me? What had been his responsibility to me? Leo's stomach growled and he thought: fuck it. And he went out in search of another trick.[35]

However, through befriending Eric, Leo becomes a redeemable ailing body. Leo is returned to health—though not cured—due to his distance from Toby (framed as a dangerous sexual agent) and his new proximity to Eric.

Toby refuses this proximity to Eric; while he does not contract HIV, he is still representative of dangerous sexuality. His refusal to embrace homonormativity means he has no place in Lopez's world. Toby ends the play by committing suicide. My choice of phrasing here is intentional; I am fully aware that to speak of "committing" suicide is archaic. However, it is the phrase that best suits Toby's death. Toward the end of the play Toby is faced with the decision to "heal or burn."[36] Lopez suggests that healing consists of Toby making amends with his ex, while burning would involve Toby continuing his life of drug use and sexual promiscuity. Finally willing to confront his childhood in an attempt to heal, Toby comes to the conclusion that he "can never heal, that he was only built to destroy." The scene of Toby's death is narrated by Young Man 1 (once more, Samuel H. Levine):

> A single care, upside down in flames. And inside of it, Toby Darling, who could not heal. Burned alive by the fire that consumed him long before help was called, a lifetime before help arrived.[37]

I decided upon the phrase committed suicide because it holds an ironic and moralizing linguistic bent in relation to Toby's death. This is the first action to which Toby commits; this is most starkly contrasted with his inability/unwillingness to commit to his relationship with Eric. Describing the scene of Toby's death, Lopez's writing seems to suggest that Toby would not have been able to heal had he wanted to. The metaphorical fire that consumes Toby sets him apart as a "bad" gay in Lopez's narrative. There is no room for "bad" gays in the finale of Lopez's work, and it is for this reason that Toby must die: he is irredeemable.

In recent years, particularly in the UK, access to PrEP has accelerated. It is now available through the NHS in England, Wales, Scotland, and Northern Ireland. With such swift progress in both medical intervention and social and community messaging regarding ongoing HIV and AIDS crises, how can contemporary theater respond and hold contemporary theatrical interventions? Can we learn from the past to construct a new future in which sex is neither pathologized nor moralized upon, or must we forget what has come before and focus only on what comes next? Christopher Castiglia and Christopher Reed argue that the promises of the past can help us consider and reshape the ways in which we narrativize the present and future. If we are "urged never to cast our eyes back, never to turn from a dubious vision of normativity-as-progress glimmering beyond a perpetually receding horizon" how do we begin instead to perform "strategic remembering?"[38] Two examples of strategic remembering appear in solo performances; first is Nathaniel J. Hall's *First Time* and second is Jack Holden's *Cruise*. *First Time* draws on the messaging of U=U to create a piece of educational theater. Hall uses solo performance as a way of reinforcing his sexual agency despite his serostatus. Hall draws attention to his own attractiveness and his sexual availability. As Hall is on effective treatment and is undetectable, he cannot pass on HIV to his sexual partners, as such he can perform the incredible feat of destigmatizing HIV by eroticizing the body with HIV: "That's right, in terms of people in this room, where HIV is concerned, I'm the safest person you could be having sex with."[39]

Jack Holden on the other hand uses his experience volunteering with the UK's LGBTQ+ Switchboard to tell the story of a person living with HIV who contracted the virus in the mid-80s in which life expectancy was roughly forty-eight months. Holden as actor, writer, and character highlights his own sexual naiveté during the 2010s:

> Another of the rules is that we can't tell people where to go cruising.
> I'm so vanilla back then
> I wouldn't even know to recommend Hampstead Heath.[40]

This is then contrasted with the sexual adventurousness of Mickey during the 1980s:

> With the sexual confidence of the person whose story he is recounting:
> You actually … wait … you went cottaging?
> "Cottaging, cruising, dogging, saunas. You name it.
> That's how I met Fat Sandy!"
> "Wasn't it … dangerous?"
> "Yes, That's kind of the point."[41]

This exchange both subverts and reinforces examples of dangerous sexuality which I have highlighted above. Though sexual geographies outside the realm of the family home are framed as dangerous, this danger is not negative. The danger involved is erotic and joyful. The use of the word "dangerous" could have multiple potential meanings. It is never specified whether these dangers are sexual, as demonstrated in *The Inheritance*, or if the dangers posed are from outside influences such as police looking to entrap gay men, or the danger of fag bashing. It is possible that the danger encompasses all the above. On the day that Mickey expects to succumb to AIDS he has "harmless fun" with "two perfect strangers."[42] Through framing sexual encounters in nonnormative sexual geographies as thrilling during a period in which AIDS was in a wider state of crisis, it allows audiences to frame sexual encounters in those same geographies but in a later temporal context as erotically charged. This sex is not dangerous; it is simply sex. Holden's play demonstrates that it is possible to look back to the early history of HIV/AIDS and discuss sex in a way that does not borrow the same sexual mores of that period.

The year 2021 could be considered the fortieth anniversary of AIDS. The year saw the release of Russell T. Davies' *It's a Sin*, proving that there is still demand for narratives regarding HIV/AIDS. Larry Kramer passed in 2020; a year later the National Theatre also produced a revival of his play *The Normal Heart*. In 2020 *Faggots* also received a reprint. The National Theatre revival of *The Normal* Heart, much like the National Theatre revival of *Angels in America*, suggests the ways in which British responses and understandings of HIV/AIDS are still linked with the US experience and the temporal experience of the period of AIDS as crisis. *The Normal Heart's* politics were contentious when it was first performed in 1985;

to have its message repeated uncritically thirty-six years later by a government-subsidized national theater demonstrates that more theater that celebrates the amorality of sex needs to be written, produced, and performed. Future HIV/AIDS theater can leave the moralizing behind when it excites the heart, and the head, and the genitals.

Notes

1   Larry Kramer, "The Normal Heart," in *The Normal Heart and the Destiny of Me* (New York: Grove Press, 2000), 78.

2   Virginia Anderson, "Selective Memory and Other Perils of Representing AIDS on the Twenty-first-century Broadway Stage," *Somatechnics* 10, no. 2 (2020): 259.

3   Matthew Lopez, *The Inheritance* (London: Faber & Faber, 2018), 230.

4   Lopez, *The Inheritance*, 85.

5   Lopez, *The Inheritance*, 85.

6   See Ash Hudson-Myers, *"Well, Close the Fucking Curtain!": The Ailing White Body and the Disposability of Minoritised Medical Professionals in the Theatre of HIV/AIDS*, https://ashpernpapers.substack.com/p/well-close-the-fucking-curtain-the.

7   "NAM Endorses Undetectable Equals Untransmittable (U=U) Consensus Statement," *NAM aidsmap*, February 9, 2017, https://www.aidsmap.com/news/feb-2017/nam-endorses-undetectable-equals-untransmittable-uu-consensus-statement.

8   Andrew Sullivan, "When Plagues End," *New York Times Magazine*, November 10, 1996, https://www.nytimes.com/1996/11/10/magazine/when-plagues-end.html.

9   Michael Billington, "The Inheritance Review—Angels in America Meets Howards End," *The Guardian*, March 29, 2018, https://www.theguardian.com/stage/2018/mar/29/the-inheritance-review-stephen-daldry.

10 Lopez, *The Inheritance*.

11 Lopez, *The Inheritance*, 135; Tony Kushner, *Angels in America: A Gay Fantasia on National Themes* (New York: Theatre Communications Group, Inc., 2013), 290.

12 Lopez, *The Inheritance*, 300.

13 Kushner, *Angels in America*, 290.

14 Alan Sinfield, *Out on Stage: Lesbian and Gay Theatre in the Twentieth Century* (New Haven: Yale University Press, 1999), 329.

15 Lopez, *The Inheritance*, 86.

16 Jacob Juntunen, *Mainstream AIDS Theatre, the Media, and Gay Civil Rights* (New York: Routledge, 2016), 26.

17 Lopez, *The Inheritance*, 34.

18 Breeding is a sexual practice in which the penetrative partner ejaculates into the rectum of the receptive partner. The term derives from outdated sexual politics that suggest that penetrative partners are the masculine while receptive partners are the feminine. While this definition is basic, and can be complicated by various sexual agents such as power bottoms, femme tops, and cumdumps, *The Inheritance* engages with this binary divide.

19 Lopez, *The Inheritance*, 82.

20 Lopez, *The Inheritance*, 294.

21 John M. Clum, *Still Acting Gay: Male Homosexuality in Modern Drama* (New York: St. Martin's Press, 2000), 63.

22 "Ned: Do you realize that you are talking about millions of men who have singled out promiscuity to be their principal political agenda, that one thing they'd die before abandoning. How do you deal with that?" Kramer, *The Normal Heart*, 26.
23 Douglas Crimp, "Mourning and Militancy," in *Melancholia and Moralism* (Cambridge, MA: The MIT Press, 2002), 140.
24 Clum, *Still Acting Gay*, 40.
25 Kramer, *The Normal Heart*, 51.
26 William M. Hoffman, *As Is* (New York: Dramatists Play Service, Inc., 1990), 28.
27 Kushner, *Angels*, 20.
28 Kushner, *Angels*, 64.
29 Kushner, *Angels*, 45.
30 Kushner, *Angels*, 60.
31 Kushner, *Angels*, 201.
32 Lopez, *The Inheritance*, 75–6.
33 Lopez, *The Inheritance*, 203.
34 Lopez, *The Inheritance*, 242.
35 Lopez, *The Inheritance*, 247.
36 Lopez, *The Inheritance*, 272.
37 Lopez, *The Inheritance*, 290.
38 Christopher Castiglia and Christopher Reed, *If Memory Serves: Gay Men, AIDS, and the Promise of the Queer Past* (Minneapolis: University of Minnesota Press, 2012), 10.
39 Nathaniel J. Hall, *First Time* (London: Nick Hern Books, 2020), 41.
40 Jack Holden, *Cruise* (London: Methuen Drama, 2021), 4–5.
41 Holden, *Cruise*, 21.
42 Holden, *Cruise*, 56.

Bibliography

Anderson, Virginia. "Selective Memory and Other Perils of Representing AIDS on the Twenty-first-century Broadway Stage." *Somatechnics* 10, no. 2 (2020): 254–61.
Billington, Michael. "The Inheritance Review—Angels in America Meets Howards End." *The Guardian*. March 29, 2018. https://www.theguardian.com/stage/2018/mar/29/the-inheritance-review-stephen-daldry.
Castiglia, Christopher and Christopher Reed. *If Memory Serves: Gay Men, AIDS, and the Promise of the Queer Past*. Minneapolis: University of Minnesota Press, 2012.
Clum, John M. *Still Acting Gay: Male Homosexuality in Modern Drama*. New York: St. Martin's Press, 2000.
Crimp, Douglas. "Mourning and Militancy." In *Melancholia and Moralism*, 129–49. Cambridge, MA: The MIT Press, 2002.
Hall, Nathaniel J. *First Time*. London: Nick Hern Books, 2020.
Hoffman, William M. *As Is*. New York: Dramatists Play Service, 1990.
Holden, Jack. *Cruise*. London: Methuen Drama, 2021.
Hudson-Myers, Ash. *"Well, Close the Fucking Curtain!": The Ailing White Body and the Disposability of Minoritised Medical Professionals in the Theatre of HIV/AIDS*. https://ashpernpapers.substack.com/p/well-close-the-fucking-curtain-the.
Juntunen, Jacob. *Mainstream AIDS Theatre, the Media, and Gay Civil Rights*. New York: Routledge, 2016.

Kramer, Larry. "The Normal Heart." In *The Normal Heart and the Destiny of Me*, 1–118. New York: Grove Press, 2000.

Kramer, Larry. *Faggots*. New York: Grove Atlantic, 2020.

Kushner, Tony. *Angels in America: A Gay Fantasia on National Themes*. New York: Theatre Communications Group, 2013.

Lopez, Matthew. *The Inheritance*. London: Faber & Faber, 2018.

NAM aidsmap. "NAM Endorses Undetectable Equals Untransmittable (U=U) Consensus Statement." February 9, 2017. https://www.aidsmap.com/news/feb-2017/nam-endorses-undetectable-equals-untransmittable-uu-consensus-statement.

Sinfield, Alan. *Out on Stage, Lesbian and Gay Theatre in the Twentieth Century*. New Haven: Yale University Press, 1999.

Sullivan, Andrew. "When Plagues End." *New York Times Magazine*. November 10, 1996. https://www.nytimes.com/1996/11/10/magazine/when-plagues-end.html.

Chapter 6

THE ONLY WAY OUT IS THROUGH VIP: DISCOVERING GENDERQUEER IDENTITIES THROUGH HIGH FEMME STRIP CLUB PERFORMANCES

by Ella-Gabriel Mason

It's a humid summer day. I feel a fat drop of sweat beading beneath my right breast, slowly rolling down my ribcage beneath my loose muscle tank. I am sipping coffee from a cup labeled "Gabriel." I am wondering what to make of the pleasure I feel when the cute barista addresses me that way. Or rather the way I feel when the cute barista calls the name of my great-grandfather into the air, and I stride forward in response. Choosing to be recognized in this way. The barista's back is already turned. The drama of the moment is for my heart alone.

Sweating in the coffeeshop, I try once again to work my way through Judith Butler's *Gender Trouble*. This is the work in which she articulates the theory of gender performativity—the idea that gender is not innate, but rather the consequence of our repeated behaviors. Noting the distinctions between biological sex and social expression of gender Butler says:

> If sex does not limit gender, then perhaps there are genders, ways of culturally interpreting the sexed body, that are in no way restricted by the apparent duality of sex. Consider the further consequence that if gender is something that one becomes—but can never be—then gender is itself a kind of becoming or activity, and that gender ought not to be conceived as a noun or a substantial thing or a static cultural marker, but rather as an incessant and repeated action of some sort.[1]

Gender is an active performance, not a biological imperative. I've heard this theory referenced in dozens of articles, books, and lectures. It's become critical to how I think about identity. But flipping through the first chapters I find myself in a morass of references to French philosophers I've never heard of before. I close the book in frustration, realizing that what I really want is reassurance.

I'm reading Butler but I'm craving a nonbinary Brené Brown. I want a queer academic to tell me that I'm not crazy or childish for experimenting with new names. I want someone older to tell me that the strange mix of dysphoria and euphoria I float between is just information, and not a sign that anything is wrong. I want someone with professional credibility far beyond my own to tell me, "Yes, you can change your name to Ella-Gabriel and still be taken seriously."

In this chapter, I will trace how coming into a genderqueer, genderfluid, or nonbinary identity can be wrapped up in the gender performances practiced by strippers. A former stripper, I began noticing that whenever I got together with friends from the industry, an increasing number of us were beginning to identify as something beyond the binary we were raised with. I do not intend to make a simple causal claim; working in the sex industry doesn't turn someone genderqueer. However, the heightened gender performances enacted by myself, my coworkers, and our customers did help to denaturalize the gender binary, opening up new ways of identifying, practicing, and performing my gender outside of the strip club.

My analysis is built around my personal experiences—drawing on memory, photos, and journals from my years in the industry—and from interviews with three other current and former strippers who identify as genderqueer or nonbinary. All three interviewees—Chris, Henri, and Lala—responded to an inquiry I distributed through the Sex Workers' Outreach Project national email listserve. I am identifying each interviewee solely by first name and/or a stage name to preserve anonymity. This continues to be a necessity because of the discrimination against current and former sex workers. I and all three interviewees are white. While the raced and classed nature of how gender is performed in the strip clubs was commented upon by all of my interviewees, first-hand accounts from nonbinary Black and POC strippers, as well as a more intentional look at class and educational backgrounds, is needed.

My tracing begins with a personal narrative, outlining how I learned the skills of high femme performance in the strip club. I then turn to an experience of what I call **gender auditioning** described by Chris, using their story to unpack ideas of authenticity and practice. Chris's gender audition story moves me to a consideration of how convincing gender performances require a period of **gender rehearsal**. In the binary gender system, human attributes are designated masculine and feminine. This **gendered bundling** of characteristics is critical to the process of gender auditioning, gender rehearsal and to the way corporate strip clubs regulate performances of femininity. I then turn to stories from Henri and Lala about how they have been able to maintain alternative and subversive performances of femininity by pursuing jobs at working-class and independent clubs.

These stories highlight the ways in which the heightened gender performances that take place in strip clubs can serve to denaturalize both femininity and masculinity. Both I and my interviewees reflect on ways in which that denaturalization allowed us to break apart the bundling of attributes that occurs in the binary gender system and discover modes of gender expression that feel more "authentic" and desirable.

I conclude that if gender is a performance, then it is time to consider the actions that make up gender auditions and gender rehearsals. Genderqueer, genderfluid, and nonbinary strippers have a unique vantage point as our professional lives depend on our ability to create convincing performances of genders we do not entirely align with, and our personal well-being requires an ability to disassemble the bundled attributes curated by the binary gender system.

Stripping forced me to develop skills of high femme performance I had refused to learn as an adolescent, first out of disinterest and later out of shame. High femme is a term originally used to describe lesbian women who dress in hyper-feminine styles—dresses, high heels, makeup, long hair, long nails. I designate the skills of stripper performance as high femme because they embody these same hyper-feminine codes of dress and behavior. Additionally, I am attempting to create some separation between performances of femininity and assumed heterosexuality. High femme aesthetics have been practiced by queer people of multiple genders for generations. So much so that when I wanted to learn how to contour, a coworker told me the best way to learn was to watch drag queen tutorials.

Though my club, like many, had a "house mom" who ran the dressing room and offered to do the dancers' makeup, her style was stuck in the years of her youth, the 1980s. I had no choice but to learn how to do my own face. In addition to contouring there was the application of eyeshadow, eyeliner, brow gel, mascara, and lipstick. I learned to curl and style my naturally lank hair. I developed strong opinions about lingerie (yes to lace, straps, and harnesses; no to fake snakeskin, pink, and neons) and high heels (yes to boots and peep-toe pleasers; no to platform mary-janes). Every shift I strode out of the dressing room in my platform shoes and my evening gown—a plunging gold bodice and black skirt with slits on either side that came up to the tops of my thighs, feeling like a powerful, fierce femme fatale.

This high femme performance was not only limited to costuming, it was also a matter of how I danced onstage. As Jessica Berson explores in her study of strip clubs, not all dancing is "sexy dancing."[2] I practiced languid, fluid movements circling the pole and crawling across the stage. I punctuated the sense of flow with rhythmic movements to shake the flesh of my buttocks and thighs—shimmies, shakes, and twerking. Occasional sharp and athletic movements could be used to draw attention: a drop from the pole into a split or a sudden straddle in a headstand, platformed heels smacking on the floor on either side of the face. But these were to be used sparingly. From my observations and experience, it didn't pay to demonstrate my athleticism more than that. It was important to remain approachable and easy to tip. It's difficult to tuck a bill into the garter of a fast-moving target.

Even offstage, strolling around the club floor, the gestural performance continued. I exaggerated the sway of my hips as I walked. I perched on bar stools, holding my core muscles tight, keeping my neck long, tilting my head in conversation. Each movement served as an advertisement as I tried to sell a lap dance or time with me in a private room.

Learning how to perform this iteration of high femme began to heal the shame from my teenage years. There was nothing so mysterious or inaccessible about doing makeup or dressing pretty after all. It was all a skill I could learn and practice and perform, just as Butler's theory of performativity suggested. I could feel ownership over this presentation. Even with the changes in clothing and makeup, even with the dim, colored lights of the club, I was not fully transformed. I was still recognizable, both to myself in the mirror and, on one horrifying occasion, to the coach of my childhood little league team. In fact, I could still recognize the same person, the same body, that was derided as an overly masculine dyke. What had changed was that I signaled my femininity with my costuming, and I was framed by the expectations of the strip club. Customers came to my club to see conventionally "hot" women strip. I was stripping there, ergo I was a hot woman. How profoundly arbitrary and ridiculous it seemed to me!

✳✳✳

When I spoke with Chris, a former stripper and one of the interviewees, they described a similar steep learning curve with the art of high femme performance. Chris came of age during the grunge era when "even the cool kids were wearing beat up jeans and flannels," and so they "escaped some performative gender stuff just by virtue of being into Nirvana." They were a nerdy kid, neurodivergent, and coming out of a painful and traumatic childhood. They told me that stripping gave them a sense of power and healing from those childhood experiences; it felt good to "perform being a badass and watching you all play along." At the same time the kind of high femme they were allowed to perform was sharply regulated by the management at the club:

> This was one of the first times I had to perform gender and I wanted to perform a more edgy gender. I wanted a different vibe. I said "I want my stage name to be Jesse," and they're like "No, you're a Tiffany, you're so girl-next-door." I'm like, "I don't want to be girl-next-door. I want to take a whip and crack it on the stage and make people scared of me." And they're like, "No, you need to look like the babysitter next door that all the dads are hot for."[3]

It wasn't the case that no one at Chris's club was allowed to perform a more dominating form of femininity, but Chris was told, both by management and by coworkers, that they in particular were not able to perform that version of high femme convincingly. They were not even allowed to try. Their audition for the strip club was also a **gender audition**; the managers looked at Chris and decided on the form of femininity they thought would be believable. The results of this gender audition carried through Chris's years of stripping. They were not given the opportunity to rehearse a more aggressive or dominant femme performance within the club and so the results of the audition became a self-fulfilling prophecy.

When a few of the other queer dancers from the club formed a lesbian burlesque troupe to perform at the gay clubs they told Chris "We're only putting you in one of our routines, because you're not the kind that all the queers go for." This denial of Chris's ability to perform their queerness and a version of femininity that felt attractive and authentic for them was incredibly frustrating:

> There was this denial of my ability to perform anything other than playboy-lingerie-girl-next-door look. And so I was being denied an edginess as well as a gender neutrality. It was like getting excited that you get to play dress up and then someone's like "not like that."[4]

Chris craved an "edgy" expression of femininity because it felt more authentic to them. It aligned more closely with how they experienced themselves as a nonbinary person, even before they had that language to describe themselves. Yet the managers were not convinced that the audience would believe this expression. This raises two contradictory models of authenticity: interior authenticity and performed authenticity.

When I feel authentic, I sense an alignment between my expression and my interiority—an interior authenticity. When I describe someone else as authentic, their behavior is in line with what I believe their interiority to be—a successfully performed authenticity. It is entirely possible that what one person feels to be authentic to them might appear inauthentic to an observer. What is going on when the same-gender performance is felt as authentic by the performer but read as inauthentic by the viewer? One of the most crucial elements is rehearsal.

For an expression to be read as authentic, it must be rehearsed. If we mistakenly think of authentic expressions as having to do with some essential nature, then this can seem surprising. But Butler's theory of performativity offers the insight that gender expressions are performances—series of behaviors that are practiced with enough diligence over time that the resulting expressions both feel and appear authentic.

> The view that gender is performative sought to show that what we take to be an internal essence of gender is manufactured through a sustained set of acts, posited through the gendered stylization of the body. In this way, it showed that what we take to be an 'internal' feature of ourselves is one that we anticipate and produce through certain bodily acts, at an extreme, a hallucinatory effect of naturalized gestures.[5]

The gender produced by these stylized acts—how I dress my body, how I walk across the stage, the way I tilt my head and smile coyly at my customer—is naturalized, appearing as the source of the repeated acts rather than as the product created by their repetition. The rehearsal involved in these gender performances is hidden so it appears that expressions of gender are essential consequences of chromosomes, hormones, or genitalia.

For people who transition across the gender binary, there is a period of rehearsal. And in fact, for cis people, there is a period of rehearsal as well, but typically that rehearsal occurs during childhood and adolescence—a time when it is culturally expected that these first attempts at gendered performances will be awkward and poorly done. It takes time to learn the skills of masculine and feminine performance. In many trans narratives the first encounters with these skills create a moment of affirmation and clarity. Though this experience of authenticity arrives for some trans people in their first moments of drag, cross-dressing, or gender play, these new expressions may not be read as authentic by onlookers until they have had an opportunity to practice them.

This period of gender rehearsal is just as true for gender nonconforming people; however, the process may appear less clear from the outside since they are not moving from one end of our imagined binary to the other. When I use my hyphenated name "Ella-Gabriel," I see the confusion my fluidity causes many of the people around me. When the barista calls out "Gabe" and a person with breasts and long hair comes to pick it up, I see the recalibration of expectation in her eyes.

This illegibility is largely due to **gendered bundling**—the coding of human attributes as feminine and masculine in the binary system. These bundles are easily visible when considering gender stereotypes: Men are meant to be strong, independent, assertive. Women are meant to be nurturing, relational, passive. Men have short hair and wear pants. Women have long hair and wear dresses. These are gross generalizations, and I can immediately think of plenty of cismen and ciswomen who do not fit these characteristics. At the same time, the bundles of gendered characteristics are recognizable and socially reinforced through media portrayals, dress codes, and hiring practices, both in strip clubs and in the rest of society.

Gendered bundling is visible in the way that strip clubs regulate their dancers. Strip clubs (at least the corporate chain clubs that have dominated the market for the past twenty years) curate a narrow range of feminine archetypes, aesthetics, and body types.[6] It pays to have some variety, as different people are attracted to different kinds of dancers, but simultaneously clubs use the regulation of dancers' bodies and aesthetics to create a brand and to appeal to specific market segments. I worked at a gentlemen's club in the downtown of a small Midwestern city. The clientele was majority white and middle class—a mix of businessmen, sports fans coming from the downtown stadiums, and people attending conventions at the convention center next door. The regulations on dancers' bodies, dress, and makeup were all intended to maintain the comfort of this demographic by creating an aspirational luxury aesthetic. Dancers were not allowed to have undercuts, sideshaves, buzzed heads, or unnatural hair colors like pink or blue. Tattoos had to be minimal and "classy" as defined by the owner. High heels had to be at least 6 inches and must be worn at all times, except in Champagne rooms (where they might tear the upholstery of the couches). Dancers must wear evening gowns over their lingerie. Evening gowns were defined as a gown that touched the floor, or at least skimmed your toes in your platform heels. The gowns were otherwise nothing like you would imagine wearing to a wedding, fundraiser, or any other fancy event outside of the club. While the hem might be threatening to trip you, the skirts were typically slitted on either side. Necklines displayed as much cleavage as possible. Backs were left open. Some dresses were merely a series of thin straps on top. In effect, the gowns were a symbolic gesture of sophistication, part of the aspirational aesthetic of leisure activities.

This aspirational aesthetic is also raced, which affects which dancers can work at the club and how they must present themselves. Most of my coworkers were white, a few were Asian, and a few more were Black. It was common knowledge that the managers had informal quotas and wanted the majority of dancers to be white. I heard from several of my Black coworkers that the darker your skin was, the more challenging to make money at that club. I only had one Black coworker who wore her natural hair texture. Most Black dancers wore weaves or wigs, conforming to white beauty ideals.

Some of the remaining independently owned clubs, especially divey working-class clubs, make space for a larger variety of bodies and aesthetics. Henri preferred to work in mom-and-pop clubs for just that reason:

> Corporate clubs don't like me anyway. A lot of them have really specific body standards and tend to be, at least in my experience, very whitewashed. The body modifications present weren't tattoos and piercings, they were, you know, implants and Botox and stuff like that … which is rad, but like I said, there wasn't representation of other body types. There was a mutual lack of interest for management and myself.[7]

For Henri, their performance of femininity as "an alternative girl" with green hair, tattoos, and piercings is critical to their larger performance as a sex worker. They told me that most of their clients are looking for a "manic pixie dream girl" experience. Their image helps to sell that larger performance. In this respect, at least there's a synchronicity between Henri's interior authenticity and the performed authenticity perceived by their clients. Though even working at independent clubs and leaning into an unconventional presentation have their limits. Henri remembered losing customers and income once when they cut their hair particularly short. Though many of their customers and clients know that Henri is queer, they still take care to play up a high femme iteration of themselves, even when they are just promoting themselves on social media between shifts. This requires putting on false eyelashes and a full face of makeup, volumizing their hair, and switching out of the comfy flannel they actually wear between shifts. For Henri to maintain the performed authenticity of their gender, they must provide coherence across contexts: it's important that regulars see the same performance reflected in the club and on Instagram.[8]

Lala also worked at independently owned strip clubs and at a peep show. She already identified as genderqueer when she began working in the sex industry, and found that she didn't need to alter her regular low femme presentation very much. She wore makeup but leaned into an "alternative" look, with tattoos, short hair, and a sideshave. This was well in line with her coworkers as well. Several other dancers were Suicide Girls—pierced and tattooed models for the alternative erotica site that became popular in the early aughts. It wasn't until Lala took a job at a dungeon to support herself through graduate school that she had to severely alter her gender presentation, putting on the drag of high femme:

> It's so ironic, because you think fetish work, especially being a domme, being a bit butcher, being a bit tough would be even less of a problem than in dancing.

Not in my experience working in this place anyway. I had to change a lot of things about my appearance while I was working there in order to make money. I had to grow my hair out. I had a side shave and I grew my hair out. I started getting fake nails with nail art. I changed the way I did my makeup [to be less natural and more glamorous] … I basically had to change my appearance totally to make money at that place. Because I would have clients ask me like, "Oh, are you a lesbian?" or they would see me and say "I didn't want to see you at first because I thought you were too butch." Very explicitly people would tell me I was not performing my gender correctly.[9]

Though Lala expected her low femme presentation and alternative aesthetic to be an asset at the dungeon, in reality both customers and management required a more glamorous high femme presentation—one that could mask any butchness/masculinity/queerness normally readable in her performance of gender. Perhaps the concept of a woman performing power-plays in the dungeon felt too threatening if she also expressed masculinity?

Lala's dungeon regulated their employees' gender performances through a code of conduct similar to the gentlemen's club where I worked. Workers had to be in full makeup at all times and to dress in particular fetish outfits. High heels also had to be worn at all times unless someone was in a character archetype costume that allowed an exception, such as cheerleader outfits, which could be worn with white tennis shoes.

The work of high femme performance required by the club can require so much labor that it is difficult to explore more masculine or androgynous presentations while still thriving in the industry. If you have to shave off all of your body hair for each shift, you can't walk around rocking hairy legs and pits. If you lose money when you cut your hair too short, then you either keep your hair long or invest in some high-quality wigs. If you're expected to have long, painted nails that's an investment you display in your off-hours as well.

Frank theorizes that the value of strip clubs lies in their support of masculinizing processes.[10] Strip club performances provide affirmation for a customer's sexuality and gender. In this way they are more about masculinization than about sex, because genital sex is not actually provided on premises.

Few strippers make the majority of their income from stage dancing alone. A big part of the work is having conversations with customers, building a relationship, and crafting a fantasy together. In this process, customers will sometimes buy lap dances or time in a private room with the dancer. They may also simply pay the dancer to sit with them at a table or at the bar and continue talking. Sometimes these interactions can be incredibly intimate, with customers sharing emotional confessions. My coworkers and I often joked that we were naked therapists.

I frequently had customers who were recent widowers or divorcees. Our time flirting served as a way for them to reconnect with desire and with feeling desired after experiences of profound loss. As a performer, I worked to elicit my desire for them, focusing on some part I could find attractive. From there I could spin a web of authentic warmth and regard. At the same time, a level of inauthenticity that ran underneath the interaction—the knowledge that the customer was paying me for my time and attention, meant that he could express himself far more freely than I imagine he would on a real date. If he shared how lonely and miserable he was without his former wife, he didn't have to be afraid that I would express less attraction to him or walk away. In this way, the customer got to experience desire (supporting their masculinity) and connect emotionally with another person (supporting a common human need) while avoiding the chance of rejection (protecting their masculinity from being undermined).

At other times my femme performance was valued as a signal of the customer's virility and purchasing power, or served as an affirmation of the customer's heterosexuality. I would frequently be hired by a bachelor party to give the bachelor a private lap dance. At my club, lap dances occurred in private curtained booths, separated from the main floor. This meant that as I walked the bachelor down the hall, I had several minutes to suss out his level of enthusiasm. It was not atypical for the bachelor to be neutral at best. Occasionally, when a bachelor appeared particularly uncomfortable, I would offer that we could just hang out in the booth and talk or check our phones. Then when the song was over, I could take him back to his buddies, rave about how wild he was, and no one was wiser. Many bachelors took me up on the offer with evident relief on their faces. Together we took some time to relax, and then fulfilled all of the publicly viewable elements of this masculinizing practice. I would return the bachelor to his table of friends, give a saucy comment about how they needed to watch this "handsy, bad boy," the bachelor would be embarrassed, and his friends would be delighted.

A few bachelors insisted that they wanted the lap dance. I imagine some were uncomfortable with having the performances we were both engaged in laid bare. Or perhaps they disliked me calling their masculine performance (with the connotation of constant heterosexual desire) into question. In either case, I would give a lap dance to an extremely stressed-out bachelor with a clenched jaw and held breath. It was incredibly awkward.

Katherine Frank notes how strip clubs offer a cover for male intimacy. The nude dancer, and the performance of desire for her, serves as a "heterosexual-safety precaution" allowing men to bond while denying any homoeroticism.[11] By making a performance of straightness essential to the social activity, homophobic panic is quelled, and men can feel comfortable directly expressing their love and care for one another. This was clearly the function of the bachelor parties I served.

Men in strip clubs aren't necessarily only performing for friends they came with to the club. Some men come to the club alone, but perform for the other men present by demonstrating their purchasing power. Frank remarks that while she was stripping, men would comment to her about how much, or how little, they observed other men spending in the club. Other customers who she interviewed outside of the club were even more direct about the importance of these performances to them: "You're one-upping. It has nothing to do with sex. It has really very little to do with the women. You're there to impress, to try to impress the other men."[12] Chris also experienced this dynamic when they were stripping:

> The ones [men] I remember were performing a specific kind of prowess by being able to keep people at their tables … They would keep dropping the money periodically just to stay with them … I can't tell how much of it was them being lonely and wanting connection from someone who was way younger than them and usually cute and how much of it was them waiting to be showing off. Like, "I've got them at my table, I've got two or three girls chatting at my table now."[13]

These observations were also in line with what I observed from men in the club where I worked. Raining money down on a stripper on stage was a sure-fire way for a customer to know eyes would be on him. Walking across the floor to take the elevator to a private suite was also a way to demonstrate purchasing power and to imply that they might receive "extras" (such as sex acts restricted in the club) in this private space.

At times the masculine performance of club regulars can simply mimic the power dynamics of a traditional patriarchal family. Henri talked about how in their early days stripping, customers attempted to enact the performance of being a provider through their interactions with them, seeing their payment of dancers as a kind of patronage:

> You know there's the "captain-save-a-ho." The provider, you know, "I can give you something better than this, if you leave with me … You're too pretty to be working at a club … I'm your Daddy now … " All of those archetypes feel like a song and dance, what cis heterosexuality society says that's what masculinity is.[14]

The phrase "a song and dance" hits me in the gut. Because when working in the club, it becomes so clear how much these masculine and feminine performances are songs and dances. Routines dug deep into muscle memory that gave the performer some sense of safety, satisfaction, or pleasure as they repeat the familiar steps, dancing to that catchy tune. It can feel really good to follow a social script, to know what to do in a situation. Gender roles provide that easy affirmation and security through their constant repetition.

Though the feminine performance skills of stripping were obvious, success in the industry also requires the development of some masculine-coded skills as well. To keep myself safe I had to be ready to drop my fun, compliant, flirtatious persona and instead exert cold and direct boundaries. I had to drop my voice, make direct eye contact, and use my heels as a weapon. I might break apart the fantasy and make more explicit the exchange that was occurring and how exactly his behavior was out of line. If he got back in line, by zipping his pants back up and giving me an extra big tip, then I was prepared to revert back to my prior performance. In this way, stripping became a porthole, allowing me to zip between gender norms and (generally) be rewarded for it.

In truth, even as stripping demystified feminine performance for me, it simultaneously denaturalized masculinity because I witnessed its various performances over and over again. While I was learning how to perform the skills of high femininity, I was also seeing over and over the masculinizing performances around me in the club. In fact, my income depended on recognizing these masculine performances—and what role I could play in supporting them. I came to see how fragile masculinity was, how it constantly needed to be affirmed. I saw man after man walking a thin tightrope of correct behavior—the same sort of tightrope I felt myself on as I tried and failed to fit into the femininity around me in middle school. And more often than not, these men seemed entirely unaware of their high wire act. To them it seemed … real. Real as in the only possible choice and, therefore, not a choice at all.

At the same time as I was coming to experience the performativity of gender, I also began to notice which elements of these disparate performances felt most authentic to me. The key was realizing how resentful I felt during my non-work hours when I found myself being expected to perform femininity I didn't truly desire performing. When was I laughing at jokes I did not find funny? Why was I supporting masculine performances in my free-time? Why did it feel so good to wear about 10 percent of the makeup I would have worn at the club but with baggy pants and big, beat up combat boots?

Over the next five years, I made more friends who identified as nonbinary. This was a relatively new concept for me. Though my own particular mix of gendered performances isn't the same as most of these friends, conversations with them led me to finally articulate my own genderqueerness—years after I quit stripping and was able to somewhat separate my livelihood from my performance of gender.

Nonbinary community was also key to Chris's discovery of their own nonbinary identity. One of their kids came out as nonbinary and in supporting them, Chris began to realize that was the term they had been searching for to describe themselves back in their days stripping:

> During that time period I started talking about not being cis but didn't have the language for it. And because I had so much femininity at work when I wasn't at work, I was wearing boxer shorts and men's clothing. Even if I wore a sundress or something like that, I would wear boxers under it. There was sort of like this resisting feminine lingerie and feminine dress that happened during that time period.[15]

Still other elements of feminine identity—like being identified as a mom—felt very comfortable for Chris. This is part of the complication of genderqueer identities, their refusal to fit into either side of the binary. Nonbinary and genderqueer people unbundle the attributes that the binary so rigidly assigns to masculine and feminine, and that unbundling can look chaotic and illegible from the outside.[16]

Henri's unbundling of gendered attributes has been served by compartmentalizing their work year. In the winter, they continue to strip and during the growing season they work as a farmer in rural Vermont. Having six months away from the club each year has allowed them to explore androgynous presentation for the first time. Additionally, the masculine-coding of physical farm labor has given them an opportunity to lean into their own masculinity: "Literally, you're in the dirt and you're shoveling cow shit and you're doing these things that conflict, like actively conflict, with high femme performance as most people understand that. And that kind of offered some relief because I was like, oh I don't have to do this."[17]

At the same time that Henri was finding a sense of liberation in embodying this masculine-coded labor, they were consistently challenged by other farmworkers for the elements of femininity they continued to either choose to present, or which were read upon their body:

> I actually caught a lot of flak when I started farming for being very feminine and putting eyeliner on for the chickens. I got a lot of shit about that, but then later on I kind of realized I can do my eyeliner and that is not going to inhibit my ability to do my job .... Most of the farms here are multi-generational and run by like crunchy old dudes who are like "This is a man's fucking work! You're too little to drive a tractor." And so this is kind of a matter of actually just fucking inserting myself in there being like "actually I can totally do this as well, still bearing in mind where I come from, I can absolutely do this."... I was told more than once that I was too small to use heavy pieces of machinery, but then I would just find people who were willing to train me on that machinery.[18]

In farming, Henri experienced the fragility of masculinity, the need to consistently prove their competence in masculine-coded work. They've had more opportunities to unbundle gendered attributes and to find the combination of expressions that feel true to them. And they've also discovered the ways in which gendered performances are also intensely regulated outside of the strip club.

Like Henri, Lala has also found her performance of gender to be highly regulated in non-sex work spaces. Lala has finished grad school and now works as an adjunct professor, where the femme performances expected of her as an academic are just as narrow and rigid as the dungeon she used to work at:

> When I go to a job interview of any type, even if it's on Zoom, I wear as much makeup as if I was to do sex work. I have to make myself look as femme as I fucking can .... If I didn't do that people would think that I looked like trash or that I wasn't making enough effort.[19]

Like Chris's strip club audition, Lala's academic interviews are also gender auditions. But the demand for femme performance that Lala experiences goes beyond academic job interviews; it's also a part of how she presents herself as a teacher:

> [When teaching] I also wear a dress and I wear makeup because I feel like if I don't students may—not necessarily consciously—form opinions about me, based on the way I'm not meeting their gender expectations. I've had some really bad experiences with teaching evaluations. One time a student was making all kinds of comments about my body. Commenting on the fact that I didn't wear a bra, saying that my tattoos were distracting.[20]

These expectations are another tightrope—a narrow band of acceptable presentations that while slightly different from sex work, are still policed by the employers (club managers, university departments) and the customers (strip club regulars, students). Lala points out that these expectations of presentation are also classed and raced. Lala has been frequently encouraged in both sex work and academic contexts to straighten her naturally curly hair in order to look more sexy or more professional. The white beauty ideal of straight hair signals acceptability in both contexts.

She also adds the hardest part of the femme performance required in academia is in interpersonal performances. While in stripping I found myself required to perform femme in a way that supported my customers' masculine performances, Lala finds that she has to perform a kind of maternal archetype for students. This involves smiling an unnatural amount and going out of her way to be accessible to students, beyond what she sees expected of male instructors. If she fails to meet this expectation, she also sees the results in negative student evaluations.

Something that comes up repeatedly in my conversations with Lala, Henri, and Chris is feeling illegible. Even within queer communities, someone assigned female at birth (AFAB) often needs to present as extremely androgynous or masculine in order to be read as nonbinary or genderqueer. We are each constantly finding our own balance between presenting in a way that feels authentic to our desires and aesthetics and having our genders be visible to some segment of our community. In the past Chris has overcompensated by getting more masculine haircuts:

> I used to have really long curls until last year. And every time I got a haircut I would go a little bit shorter and a little bit shorter, because maybe then they'll get the nonbinary part. And then I went short enough that I'm like "I think this is shorter than I actually like my hair." I kept saying "how can I perform more masculine?" but then there came a point where I'm like it doesn't matter how much I'm not performing femininity. People are gonna see me the way they want to see me and it's not about how short my hair is or how I'm dressing in that moment. It's about their assumptions. And that's been hard. I'm trying to figure out is there a way I can express myself that people will be more likely to validate me and the answer is no. Do whatever the fuck you want anyway … It's making me shift to a more internal locus.[21]

To move through the world as nonbinary, genderqueer, or genderfluid does not mean that one walks down the street entirely liberated from gender. Instead, we find ourselves stuck in the tension between internal authenticity and external perceptions of our authenticity. If gender is a performance, what happens when the people around you cannot recognize what you are performing? And in a place where we are all put into rehearsals for our drafted roles before we have even mastered language, how can we expect any better from our audiences?

Stripping denaturalized femininity and masculinity by immersing me in heightened forms of each. It laid bare the process of gender auditioning, gender rehearsal, and gendered bundling. But as Chris, Henri, and Lala's stories laid bare, these gender-regulating practices are by no means exclusive to the strip club. As I continue to strip away the traits that feel unwelcome and rehearse the characteristics that have been in exile, I take comfort in the recognition that authenticity arrives from a confluence of rehearsal and desire.

✳✳✳

At the strip club, men always want to know your real name. In her research Frank even found that customers would get frustrated when she told them that her stage name was her real name. She found it was common among her coworkers—and it was certainly common among mine—to give a fake "real" name in order to fulfill this fantasy of privileged intimacy. Frank notes that inherent in this desire is the idea that a name is somehow revealing of ourselves.[22]

If that is the case, I can't imagine anyone who has more revealing names than trans, nonbinary, and genderqueer people. We choose names that we grow into or that we feel should have been ours all along. We capture the selves we are, the selves we desire, the people we are practicing embodying every day. Perhaps that is why my new experimental genderqueer name, Ella-Gabriel, feels so uncomfortably vulnerable. It reveals who I think I am and who I am trying to be. The hot high femme and the bookish dyke in flannel. The feminist sex worker welcoming back the masculine parts that have been living in exile for so many years. More than a binary, a whole spectrum within myself.

The truth is, Ella-Gabriel doesn't feel like me quite yet. I haven't rehearsed enough. But what I've learned from stripping is that it takes practice for something to feel natural. It takes rehearsal for it to feel real. It is the desire for this new name that tells me it is right. So, bring your hands together. Pull out your $20s and $50s. And please welcome Ella-Gabriel to the stage.

Notes

1   Judith Butler, *Gender Trouble* (New York: Routledge, 1990), 152.

2   Jessica Berson, *The Naked Result: How Exotic Dance Became Big Business* (New York: Oxford University Press, 2016), 2–3.

3   Chris, Interview by author over Zoom, June 28, 2021.

4   Chris, Interview.

5   Butler, *Gender Trouble*, xv–xvi.

6   Berson, *The Naked Result*, 14–16.

7   Henri, Interview by author over Zoom, July 13, 2021.

8   Henri, Interview.

9   Lala, Interview by author over Zoom, July 6, 2021.

10   Katherine Frank, *G-Strings and Sympathy: Strip Club Regulars and Male Desire* (Durham: Duke University Press, 2002), 20–2.

11   Frank, *G-Strings*, 142.

12   Frank, *G-Strings*, 70.

13   Chris, Interview.

14   Henri, Interview.

15 Chris, Interview.
16 Chris, Interview.
17 Henri, Interview.
18 Henri, Interview.
19 Henri, Interview.
20 Lala, Interview.
21 Chris, Interview.
22 Frank, *G-Strings,* 192.

Bibliography

Berson, Jessica. *The Naked Result: How Exotic Dance Became Big Business.* New York: Oxford University Press, 2016.
Butler, Judith. *Gender Trouble.* New York: Routledge, 1990.
Frank, Katherine. *G-Strings and Sympathy: Strip Club Regulars and Male Desire.* Durham: Duke University Press, 2002.

Chapter 7

THE TAR BABY PRINCIPLE | EXPERIMENT 0.1— A TRICKSTER'S SILENCE

by Ra Malika Imhotep

I. Lil Cotton Flower Is ... The Marvelous Tar Baby

Blackness. A light shines on an empty play space. A glass bowl filled with strips of paper is centered between two bottles of molasses. Offstage I am reading a found poem putting Hortense Spillers into dialogue with Lucille Clifton, Toni Morrison and Ntozake Shange.

Let's face it.

I am a marked woman
But not everybody knows my name

Let's face it.

My country needs me and if I were not here I would have to be invented

Let's face it.

In order to speak a truer word concerning my self, I must strip down through layers of attenuated meanings, made in excess in time over time, assigned by a particular historical order

Let's face it.
there await whatever marvels of my own inventiveness.

Let's face it.

I must strip down.

In the service of a collective function.

Let's face it.
Being alive and being a woman and being colored is a metaphysical dilemma
I haven't yet conquered.

Let's face it

The names by which I am called in the public place

Do not exhaust me

Let's face it.

Everyday something has tried to kill me

And has failed.

> *Then there is music. Black lesbian singer-songwriter X'ene Sky's piano cover of Nina Simone's "Wild as The Wind" plays. I enter stage right barefoot wearing a white cotton nightgown and a black chiffon apron. My yarn braids are pulled back into a high ponytail. I am wearing red lipstick. My movements are a slow and deliberate series of gestures I arrived at in conversation with Bajan dancer and performance-maker Valencia James. I caress my face, grab my neck with both hands, clench the sides of my stomach, spread my legs. This cycle carries me to each corner of the stage before I find center. At some point I am crawling. Rolling around giving my best "afro-modern contemporary" bodywork.*

Before freedom and again 400 years into its afterlife, Brer Fox grabbed up some tar and turpentine and let me make myself through his hands.

> *I walk into the play space. Centerstage with my back to the audience, hands undoing the apron. It falls in front of me.*

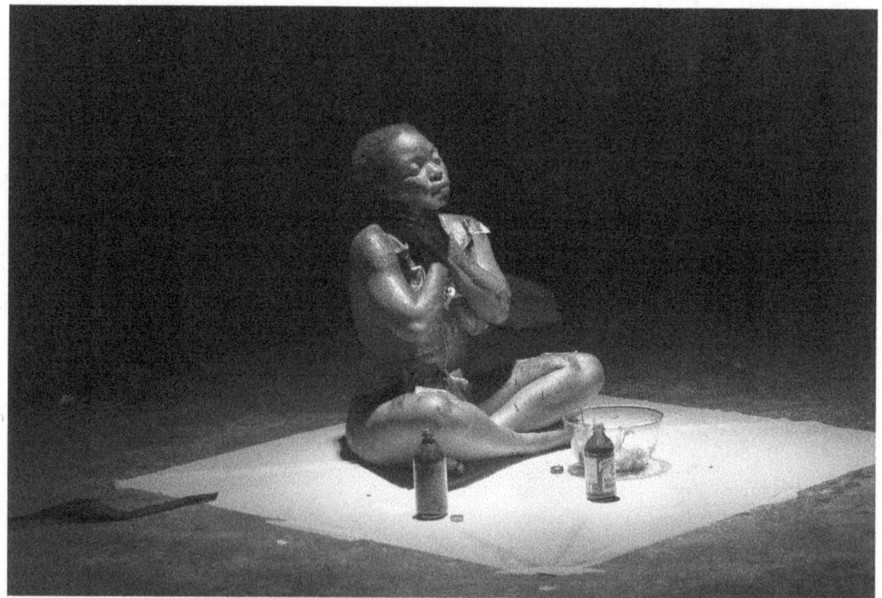

Image 9 Ra Malika Imhotep, credit Jeff Millies.

Grinning and feeling all accomplished he surrendered to this muse, mistaking my tenor for that his own greed. You see, the morning i came to him Brer Fox was out to get the best of that ol' Brer Rabbi—the quick moving trickster always pullin' the wool over Brer Fox, Brer Bear and even Ol'Massa.

Payin' them no mind, i made use of Brer Fox's ol' hands and fix'd myself up real nice and round in all the right places: two pearls through which to see, a wood button for a nose, a thick red slash of lip—all set into the soft Blackness of my face.

My hands slow waft up to my sides then bend at the elbows casting an eerie "hands up don't shoot" silhouette against the white screen before me. They fall down to find the buttons on the front of my gown. It falls as I bend forward.
(The crowd doesn't know whether to cheer or remain silent in witness.)

i whisper'd into that ol' Fox's ear to dress me up nice and alluring, and he fetch a few spools of yarn to weave atop my head and set me down right at the lip of the river where as i can watch the water glitter. little did he know, this here water is my Ma Dear. She the only one i answer too.

While i settle into my prettiness, Brer Fox look on and commence to singing to himself about the rabbit he finna catch on my account and what a nice dinner that meat'll make once it meet his eatin' plate.

And so's i just sit there, lookin' out at the water, havin' deep conversations his ears ain't pitched to catch. Thanking Ma Dear for letting me take form this evening. Not paying much mind to the Fox but thanking him for his hands all the same.

I turn to face the audience. Rhinestoned pasties catching the light. My body a smooth length of even brown. My face carries no distinct emotion but a focused gaze out. I drop to my knees and let my weight fall stage-left as I start to remove the strips of paper from the glass bowl. I arrange them on the ground in front of the bowl before reaching for the bottles of molasses. One is a deep-ebony-almost-black, the other lightened with copper mica pigments.

Then trot up that ol' Brer Rabbit—moving so fast he almost missed this lil' ol' black thing sitting at the river's edge.

At the sight of that Rabbit, Brer Fox jump under the bush cross the road and hide.

Then Brer Rabbit pause, double back and give me a deep glance over—lookin' real close with some secret heat behind his eyes. First Brer Rabbit get to talm'bout how i'm is a "sassy ol' Jay bird"

I smile as I raise the lighter bottle mixing the pigment with each flip of my wrist. After a little struggle with the cap I pick up both bottles and empty them into the glass bowl. Making the two sticky streams dance around each other as the pool at the bottom of the bowl.

and I'm almost flattered 'cept for that flame in his eye tell me to keep to myself.

Brer Rabbit commence to getting awfully familiar. He say "hey there, brown sugar how 'bout you let me have a lick at yo sweetness!" and my Tar Baby self just sits there, ain't sayin' nothin'—Brer Fox still tucked away under the bush, softly humming his eatin' song as he watch.

When satisfied, I put down the bottles and place my hands into the bowl. Mixing the molasses, then raising my hands and watching with delight as gravity pulls the sticky mess down to coat my fingertips.

Brer Rabbit say "okay now! *Earth Mama* why don't you bend over and carry my load" Tar Baby ain't sayin' nothin' and Brer Fox, he lay low.

I begin to coat my arms. My eyes following the molasses with sustained attention. I coat my right leg then reach for a strip of paper that reads "BROWN SUGAR." I coat my thigh in the molasses mixture then stick on the paper. REPEAT ON LEFT LEG.

Brer Rabbit keep searching for a name I'm primed to respond to, he seem to speak from a list that start off calm but then grow indignant: alright then *peaches*? He grumbles … how 'bout it *sapphire*?, oh you must think you *god's holy fool*?—

I dip my hands back in the bowl and smile as I lift them to my face. I coat my cheeks in the molasses mixture then slide both hands around my neck recalling the cycle of gestures from the beginning of the performance. I affix a strip of paper that reads "SAPPHIRE" to the center of my chest.

"'How you come on, den?" Brer Rabbit, ask … gettin' big mad.

Tar Baby stay still, en Brer Fox, he lay low.

Brer Rabbit fix his mouth to say, "black as I is, my nose up so high I caint even smell my own breath."

Then "EARTH MAMA" across my belly and right shin. "JEZEBEL" along the side of my left knee cap. "PEACHES" on my chest atop of "SAPPHIRE." "MISS EBONY FIRST" on my belly. "EARTH MAMA" moves to my right shoulder.

Say he got something to fix me. And I'm just there, ain't sayin' nothin' as the sun heat me up into softness.

Brer Rabbit puff up his chest and says: "I'mma learn you how to talk to a respectable man like me if it's the last act of this here show." And I don't know who he think he talkin' to but being the Tar Baby I am, I keep my mouth shut. Sitting pretty. Getting soft in all the right places.

Brer Rabbit yelling now. He say, "*Cain't you hear me calling you, miss honey*? Or is you as dumb as you is black? If you don't fix yo' face and greet me imma bus' you wiiiiiide open."

& Ain't much of nothing for me to do in the face of no madrabbitnigga so I just stay still. Wondering if Brer Fox still watching, i can't hear him humming no more …

Hands dip back into the bowl of molasses then raise to cover my face. My eyes are closed. Now covered in the molasses mixture. I caress my face, grab hold of my neck, my belly, then slide my hands down my open legs.

Brer Rabbit keep on yelling …
Tar Baby, keep on sayin' nothin' …
Then that niggarabbit draw back his fist and it land right upside my head where the sun been kissin' and he get stuck. He try to grab at my neck and that hand get stuck too. He kick his legs up right at the *di space between* my legs. He yanking and pulling and twisting just getting' more tied up in my sticky mess of a body.

Hands dip back into the bowl. I bring my arms before my face and caress them. My left hand sliding down my right forearm as my finger curls softly towards my face. REPEAT. Right hand over left arm.

In the struggle I commence to melt 'round myself and it look like we dancing in a pool of molasses.
& I aint never say nothin'
"If you don't let me loose" he shout "I'mma kick the natal stuffing outta you" I don't say nothin' but I think deep about where I was befo all dis. In the dark wet warmth of Ma Dear's belly. The natal stuff I used to swim in. that which this here rabbit is tryna beat out of me.
& I ain't say nothin'

I brace my shoulders and fold my legs underneath me. My forearms fall towards my knees. I assume a meditative posture and take a series of visibly deep breaths as molasses drips from my face.

Then here come that ol' fox talm' bout "Howdy Brer Rabbit … you look sorta stuck up this mawnin."
Brer Fox laugh and laugh and laugh. Laugh Like he done forgot how I moved through his hands this morning. What a pretty thing I made myself before he trotted me out for some Rabbit meat.

With my eyes closed i turn to the side and lay down with my knees raised.

Right as the turpentine start to drip out the round of button hole of my eyes, Ma Dear, the river, rear up real big flooding the marsh. She grab me from off the log and start to mixing her sweet waters all around that rabbit and I.
Soon I am loosed from him. Loosed from the slug of flesh that held him and I together.

Soon I give up my self in a dark warmth, the color of tar.

And Ma Dear say, "Baby, I tried to told bout messing with these skinfolks. They don't know how to hold something soft and black as you. Next time be sure to fix yourself with teeth to smile and a tongue sharp enough to cut."

I caress myself as I gather all the strips of paper from my sticky brown body and pull them into a ball that I hold prayerfully at my chest. Laying there I take another series of visibly deep breaths. FADE TO BLACK.

II. The Theory

Let's face it. I am a marked woman, but not everybody knows my name. "Peaches" and "Brown Sugar," "Sapphire" and "Earth Mother," "Aunty," "Granny," God's "Holy Fool," a "Miss Ebony First," or "Black Woman at the Podium": I describe a locus of confounded identities, a meeting ground of investments and privations in the national treasury of rhetorical wealth. My country needs me, and if I were not here, I would have to be.[1]

Centered before you on stage I carry a chorus of [ungendered] black femme genius.
These names marked into my flesh are inescapable.
So I dance with them. nothing left behind.
I steal my stories back and offer up a truer word.

When Black feminist philosopher and literary critic Hortense Spillers says "my country needs me, and if I were not here I would have to be invented" in her 1987 essay "Mama's Baby, Papa's Maybe: An American Grammar Book," I see Brer Fox grabbing hold of some turpentine and tar to make him up an object that will serve to feed him. In the time of slavery and into its afterlife, representations of Black femininity have been sources of celebration and contention. Scholars of antebellum history and political economy have illuminated the ways Black women's reproductive capacity functioned as the principal site of their value, fundamentally shaping their experience of slavery and their expressions of sociality and resistance.[2] In this context, the Black feminine body was made to represent both the desires and disgusts of imperialist white supremacist capitalist patriarchy.

Burlesque is a word of multiple significations. With regard to genre, it is "a literary, dramatic or musical work intended to cause laughter by caricaturing the manner or spirit of serious works, or by ludicrous treatment of their subjects."[3] In contemporary parlance and practice it is most associated with staged striptease performance. Robert C. Allen begins his historiography of American Burlesque with Briton Lydia Thompson's 1868 debut in New York. Thompson's blonde beauty, charismatic sexuality, and crass disregard for propriety made her comedic performances of European masculinities a praised spectacle that provoked "hysterical antiburlesque discourse" which consequently inspired larger crowds.[4] One white theater critic of the era described the monstrosity of burlesque as that which defies the natural and the conventional by forcing "the conventional and the natural together just at the points where they are most remote."[5] Allen extends this to characterize burlesque as "one of several 19th century entertainment forms that is grounded in the aesthetics of transgression, inversion, and the grotesque."[6] In her transgression of convention, the burlesque performer, he continues, represents a construction of the "low other."

Defined by Peter Stallybrass and Allon White, the low other is that which is "despised and denied at the level of political organization and social being whilst it is instrumentally constitutive of the shared imaginary repertoires of the dominant culture."[7] Here "the low other" resounds as a synonym for Spiller's configuration of the "pornotrope" wherein the material history of the United States (and by extension the modern world) the "Black woman" is constructed as the irresistible yet destructive low other against which proper "morality," "sexuality," "femininity," and "womanhood" are defined. In a sense, the "Black woman" is the archetypal burlesque but as indicted by the histories of segregation that I return to later in my discussion of the "Chitlin Circuit," the dark-skinned female body was often barred from the most celebrated burlesque establishments. But as performance historian Jayna Brown points out, the gestural vocabularies of Black femininity (shimmy dances, snake hips, and other "primitive" movements) as first appropriated through the form of female minstrelsy would go on to shape the performance repertoire of American burlesque.[8]

American lexographer and cultural critic, H.L. Menken coined the term "ecdysiast" (ec-deze-e-ast) to taunt mid-century white burlesque performers who were struggling to defend their craft and careers from Depression-era moral panics. In 1940 burlesque performer Georgia Sothern wrote to H.L. Mencken and several other American lexographers pleading for a new word that might interrupt the stigma's associated with "strip-tease" performance: "It happens that I am a practitioner of the fine art of strip-teasing. Strip-teasing is a formal and rhythmic disrobing of the body in public. In recent years there has been a great deal of uninformed criticism levelled against my profession."[9]

Taken from the Greek ekdysis, meaning "a stripping or casting off," it had been used scientifically since the mid-nineteenth century in reference to animals like snakes and birds that shed and molt, respectively. This antiquated term strikes me as relevant to contemporary neo-burlesque for several reasons. The term's contested history and political utility seem to anticipate contemporary discourse on the classist and often racialized distinctions made between neo-burlesque, stripping, and other variants of sex work. I am also drawn to *ecdysiast* for its other-than-human referent to the act of stripping off layers of one's own skin. While Mencken may have initially meant it as a pejorative association, it calls to mind the fleshy ante-human erotics I always heard in Spiller's declaration that *i/we must strip down*.[10] My work on the neo-burlesque stage performs an embodied citation of this Spillerian declaration. Thus, I mark myself a *Spillerian Ecdysiast* self-consciously utilizing choreographies of the erotic and public economies of desire to court my own marvels. This embodied citation of Black feminist theory brings the scriptive textures of the text to the body, my body.

The moves I make through the conceptualization and performance of theoretically charged Black feminist burlesque acts consider the Black folkloric figure of the Tar Baby a useful heuristic for understanding the "irresistible, destructive sensuality" Spiller's attributes to Black feminine flesh in the context of US chattel slavery. Tar is black and sticky—its material both performs and signifies its Blackness, and in its Blackness it demands engagement. In the folktale, it is the voiceless glamour of the Tar Baby that entraps Brer Rabbit. The tar of her body draws him in and holds him as prey.

Most readings of the Tar Baby folktale center Brer Rabbit as the archetypal trickster figure. In Black literary and cultural discourse, identification with Brer Rabbit has been understood as a central component of the trickster tale's importance to the Black folk tradition and by extension the Black world.[11] Read for their depictions of masculinist cunning, these trickster tales give Black folk's space to envision themselves as "smarter than massa." The briar patch has been hailed as the field/the ancestral lands/the ghetto/the hood—and all the other "unlivable" geographies in which Black folks make and sustain life. While these readings are warranted, I'm "stuck on" the gendered Blackness of the Tar Baby and what seeing (and refusing to discard) this figure as more than just a means to an end might open up for critical inquiry and for the lived experience of Black Femininity. In what follows I explore examples from a queer Black feminist performance history to offer what I am calling a "Black trickster genealogy for American Burlesque." Starting with the mid-century erotic fire dances of Lawanda Page, and ultimately reaching back even further to Ida Forsyne's early-twentieth-century European tour as "Topsy," through the contemporary spacetime of my own Black feminist performance interventions on the neo-burlesque stage, this cyclical, anachronistic genealogy refuses to discard the central roles that Black feminine figures have played in establishing the sexual cultures dramatized in contemporary American burlesque.

In what some might consider a counterintuitive application of the Tar Baby folktales' meaning, L.H. Stalling asserts that a revisionist Tar Baby, like that fictionalized by Toni Morrison in her novel of the same name, works as "an active being, less constructed by other individuals or beings but still caught in between roles and representations and one's own self," to exemplify the queer aesthetics and rhetorical strategies that enliven the work of Black feminine figures in performance. Specifically, Stallings reads the Tar Baby trope in the "chitlinfyin(g) drag" (a mode of low-class Black vernacular camp) employed by twentieth-century Black female comediennes, namely, LaWanda Page.[12]

Page's entertainment career began as a dancer and burlesque performer in the 1930s billed as "The Bronze Goddess of Fire" traveling a circuit of performance venues and social establishments that catered to Black audiences in the eras of *de jure* and *de facto* racial segregation in the United States. This informal conglomerate of Black entertainment venues was colloquially referred to as the

"Chitlin Circuit." While the Chitlin Circuit was not an explicitly queer space, its function, as described by Stallings, "did address the needs of Black people consistently ascribed to the realms of [non-normative sexualities]."[13] While white burlesque performers were navigating censure in the mainstream theater scenes of New York and Los Angeles, Black exotic dancers, and burlesque performers, who were often already marginalized within those venues, were able to sustain their careers within the anti-normative Black spaces of the Chitlin Circuit. Touring the Chitlin Circuit, "The Bronze Goddess of Fire" met the comedian Redd Foxx and years later Redd Foxx would cast Lawanda Page as the unforgettable "antiwomen," Aunt Esther on his sitcom Sanford & Son.[14] For Stallings, Page's appearance as both the exotic "othered woman" lighting cigarettes with her fingertips and the slick-mouthed elder aunt refusing to perform femininity in ways that the male trickster/comedian demands symbolically connect Page's performance work to the figure of the Tar Baby.[15]

In scripted comedic battles with Red Foxx, Lawanda Page's character is always made a punch line through the denial of her femininity and desirability. When positioned as the Tar Baby (Aunt Ester) to Redd Foxx's Brer Rabbit (Fred Sanford), Page appears to lose the game of dozens, but her cultural significance as a voice of queered excessive Black femininities points us toward other modes of survival.[16] In my own scholarly work, I refer to these shapeshifting aesthetic and performance strategies employed by Black women and gender nonconforming Black femmes in response to the threats of patriarchal violence and other masculinist interruptions as the condition of *being-in-blackfeminineflesh*. Thus, I engage the Tar Baby through critical analysis, creative writing, and performance as an emblem of the sticky trickster technologies that enable anti-normative Black survivals. By bringing the Tar Baby into the performance lexicon of American burlesque, I work to expose the racial fault lines of contemporary erotic entertainment.

The Marvelous Tar Baby act troubles the distinction between silence and agency by utilizing an *interior* voice to interrupt discursive silence. The Tar Baby, a folkloric character who canonically "says nothing," remains silent in the world of the story while audiences privy to my/Lil Cotton Flower's performance get to hear their withheld perspective. Staging the Tar Baby's internal dialogue does not interrupt the external drama and violence of their hailing in the scene of the folktale. They continue to "say nothin" to the host of character's that surround and instrumentalize them; even as their internal dialogue reimagines the terms of these relationships ("Brer Fox grabbed some tar and turpentine and *let me make myself* [emphasis added] through his hands")[17].

Rewriting the Tar Baby's silence as an external choice that does not foreclose the potential of internal reflection and depth is a performative invocation of what Kevin Quashie has termed the "interior self-measure" of Black expressive quiet.[18] The performance genre of neo-burlesque is particularly suited for this kind of public presentation of Black feminine interiority. As explicated by Mecca Jamilah Sullivan, Black queer performers within the neo-burlesque industry often stage "a black queer feminist intersectional critique of and through the erotic" that brings us into dialogue with a tradition of Black feminist performance that branches out from Ntozake Shange's 1973 invention of the "choreopoem."[19] Using what Sullivan diacritically terms "body/language," the choreopoem and its queer progeny proffer an "expressivity defined by embodiment" in which voicing and silence coexist in tandem and in tension.[20]

Sullivan's invitation to consider the sensual storytelling that shapes Black feminist burlesque as a form of "queer choreopoetic performance" helps me make sense of the contradiction I feel in connecting the Tar Baby's declarative silence to my act of embodied voicing. The quiet erotic expressions of my Black femme body merge with the poetic interiority of the Tar Baby to invoke what Spiller's terms "the nuantial"—a space of nuance that the Black life-world at-large, and the Black woman's sexual-world in particular, have been disallowed.[21] Shange's innovation of the choreopoem—a form where multiplicities of distinctly Black feminine body and voice are interdependent and staged publicly—intervenes against this structural refusal to see the nuance of Black feminine subjectivity. Within this tradition of Black feminist performative and literary embodied utterance heard, witnessed, and/or felt, I am brought to the way of Afrekete, trickster-goddess of the erotic. Refusing easy comprehension, layers of vernacular orality and embodied silence within The Marvelous Tar Baby tale as voiced and embodied by me, as Lil Cotton Flower, portray a history of Black femininity as publicly hailed (into the scene of racialized and gendered violence) and internally understood (as a figure that experiences yet transcends that violence through its own erotic self-fashioning and connection to the natural world).

III. Confessions of a Spillerian Ecdysiast

My first ever burlesque act, entitled "Topsy's Cotton Belt," was danced in tribute to Ida Forsyne, Black Patti, and the long legacy of Black women vaudeville performers and chorus girls that laughed, twisted, shouted, and smiled as they laid the foundation for modern burlesque. I was inspired to experiment with burlesque as a medium for Black feminist storytelling by a line in Jayna Brown's book *Babylon Girls: Black Women Performers and the Shaping of Modernity*. In the chapter "Letting the Flesh Fly: Topsy, Time, Torture, and Transfiguration," Brown writes:

> Female minstrelsy has its own history, shaped by notions of the black female body's abilities, availability, and utility. In the mid-nineteenth century, "female minstrelsy" was an official stage circuit term. It evolved into and was renamed "burlesque" in the 1880s but carried forward the practices of racial mimicry from earlier stage conventions. Early burlesque was female-dominated popular stage work that was often satirical and always about dance, presaging the later chorus line dancers.[22]

And suddenly I was overwhelmed by the thought of lithe white-bodied ingenues in their glittery tasseled pasties feasting on Topsy's remains. As elucidated by Brown, the untamable young Black slave girl Topsy, from Harriet Beecher-Stowe's *Uncle*

Tom's Cabin, embodies the "childlike simplicity" projected on to Black folks in the late eighteenth and nineteenth centuries. In staged adaptations of *Uncle Tom's Cabin*, Topsy was a character designed to be played by a white woman in Blackface. As such, Topsy existed as a "therapeutic opportunity [for white female performers] to access realms of freedom [proper] womanhood was otherwise constructed against."[23] As Topsy, and in other female minstrel derivatives, including burlesque, white women got to "act out" and disregard the stoic purity they had been culturally ascribed to. In these performances of freedom they invoked their power over and access to the Black female body.[24] But when Black female performers like Ida Forsyne played Topsy, Brown argues, the character's movements register a spiritual reclamation of the Black body. Free from the respectability politics of the New Negro and seemingly immune to the violence of chattel slavery, Topsy embodied "the disruptive creativity of the black female child," whose acts of transcendence reflect that of Black performers from the nineteenth century to present times.[25] Brown's provocative argument is supported by Forsyne's own articulations of her body in performance. Though she did not have access to the kinds of literacy utilized by contemporary Black feminist performance artists to articulate their own relationships to their work, Forsyne was written *about* throughout the early twentieth century and left behind at least one trace of her own perspective in an interview conducted by Marshall and Jean Stearns between 1960 and 1966 for their critical account of the evolution of "American vernacular dance."[26]

While Forsyne never performed as the character Topsy in staged renditions of *Uncle Tom's Cabin*, due to the ubiquity of *Uncle Tom's Cabin* and the archetypal caricatures it gave life to, Forsyne was billed as "Topsy, The Famous Negro Dancer" when she toured London in 1906 with *The Tennessee Students*.[27] Naturally "little, black and cute," Forsyne couldn't *not* appear as "Topsy" on stage. The bodily comportment she was born into rendered her an unnatural sight, "the little lady who 'was not born but just grew.'"[28] Topsy is an imagined object; Forsyne was a Black female dancer, the conflation of the two anticipates what has been discussed in recent works in Black performance studies as object performance.[29] Black feminist object performance makes use of this fungibility between living Black female performer and unreal racialized gendered performance trope. As Topsy, Forsyne performed her own burlesque, emerging from a potato sack center-stage backed by a line of white ballet dancers who were paid extra to perform in blackface. Described by Brown, Forsyne as Topsy would reveal herself "limb by limb, then danced wildly until a shot rang out and she fell to the floor."[30] Forsyne herself articulates this fall as rolling "over and over and up." But when the Stearns wrote of the act in the book project for which Forsyne was interviewed, they described her movement as "over and over and dead." In this discrepancy, Brown sees the interplay between the tropes of inescapable suffering and inhuman resilience that overwrite Black performance in the popular imagination.[31]

Understanding Forsyne's "Topsy Sack Dance" (1906) as a burlesque act is a needed intervention in the historization of both Black dance and burlesque performance in the United States. In its originary sense, minstrelsy was always a burlesque. On the minstrel stage the subject was Black life but because white supremacy was the popular sensibility of the time, the performances were presumed to be representative and, even more heinously, accurate. Wriggling herself out of a potato sack, limb by limb, dancing wildly across the stage until a shot rang out and then falling to the ground rolling over and over and *up*, Forsyne referenced "the historical memory of living as a commodity, as well as the black child's [and black woman's] familiar proximity to violence, cruelty, and death."[32] She made a burlesque of the quotidian suffering she had momentarily escaped as a Black child born in Chicago in the wake of Reconstruction. And she also performed a dramatic reveal inside a physical theater narrative that resonates with the performance structures of much contemporary burlesque.

I made the decision to consciously stage these histories in my burlesque because their erasure bolsters oppressive patterns of consumption that make the space of the stage unsafe for the low other. When first performing "Topsy's Cotton Belt" in San Francisco, I knew I needed to end that act by spinning over and over and falling "up." I repeated the phrase "over and over and up" in my head as Nina Simone's rendition of "Save Me" built to its rhythmic conclusion. I spun my body as Nina scatted out "save save save" and fell to the ground with the song's last note. A friend in the audience said I looked possessed as I caressed my out-of-breath body before hurriedly rising to clear the stage for the next performer. Based on audience applause, I won that first showcase. As I walked through the crowd a white male from the audience tapped me on the shoulder and told me that my act was "well-played"; another commented on my smile. They had gotten something I didn't intend to give. Something felt incomplete.

In retrospect, I understand "The Marvelous Tar Baby" as a sequel to "Topsy's Cotton Belt," maybe even an attempt to correct for the things my first act missed. It didn't start that way. It started with me sitting in my room feeling unsafe in the world (maybe another Black girl had been murdered, I can't be sure). I wanted to write a folktale and didn't know where to start so I read the one most familiar to me: Joel Chandler Harris's 1880 rendition of the marvelous Tar Baby. I couldn't get over how violent it was. I didn't remember it that way. But the violence registered with me, and I decided to write from the Tar Baby's perspective—which I felt was my perspective.

I turn to Spillerian Ecdysis, as a way to claim my inheritance as Topsy/Forsyne progeny and as a provocation towards the present longed for in Lorraine O'Grady's 1994 essay "Olympia's Maid: Reclaiming Black Female Subjectivity." O'Grady writes:

> When, I ask, do we start to see images of the black female body by black women made as acts of autoexpression, the discrete stage that must immediately precede or occur simultaneously with acts of auto-critique? When, in other words, does the present begin? ... now seems a paradigm for the willingness to look, to get past embarrassment and retrieve the mutilated body, as Spillers warns we must if we are to gain the clear-sightedness needed to overthrow hierarchical binaries: "Neither the shameface of the embarrassed, nor the not-looking-back of the self-assured is of much interest to us," Spillers writes, "and will not help at all if rigor is our dream."[33]

I'm struck by the rhetorical ease with which O'Grady "tags" Spillers's into her own ruminations. It models a practice of citation that is enabled by the conversational lilt that undergirds most of Spillers's prose. She is talking to us and with us. Handing us language to help choreograph the ways we think about and feel into ourselves. Perhaps most famously this occurs in the opening of 1987's "Mama's Baby, Papa's Maybe," the direct address which I have already demonstrated has a way of sticking to the reader, summoning up an internal amen corner before she, Spillers's, tears up everything we thought we knew about slavery and its marks on us. But it happens instructively in other moments throughout her writing (I would even say it happens in every essay if you read with an ear trained on a certain kind of Southern slick-talkin' genius).

I am wondering now if it is all an attempt at sublimation. Me following the charge from an ovaric piece of critical writing, asserting my sex on to the figure of a folktale learning something new about my own ability to survive through the repetition of this act. As I coat myself in molasses, I imagine I am bathing. Baptizing myself in the fragrant sticky Blackness. Becoming at once edible and medicinal (traits that are always, already read on to my Black femme body). I am also haunted by the history latent in Blackstrap molasses, a by-product of the global sugar economy as heavy with Black sweat and suffering as the cotton plant. I think about Karen Finley covering herself in chocolate as a feminist statement about consumption. I think about Yoko Ono sitting still allowing the audience to approach her with scissors and do as they will. These are the referents my performance conjured in the minds of peers and mentors. Through the lens of feminist performance art, I am offering a contemplation of racialized femininity, consumption, and vulnerability. To my own mind, I am also engaging in a call and response dialogue with the folkloric traditions I was born into.

But to be honest, I am still afraid that those who see me, my work, or photos of my flesh will dismiss it all as frivolous nudity or worse, self-exploitation. I wonder if they will grant me the benefit of my own depths or even dare to face the histories surfaced onto my skin. I wonder if they will even take the time to hear me, or if they rather I just didn't say nothin …

But true to my trickster lineage, I remember: my silence will not protect me.[34] These are all my stories, my power. My Tar Baby sensibilities are both bait *and* switch. They attract, they disgust, they stain, they cleanse. In this genealogy of dark and messy provocation, I am but one figure in a long line of inescapable shadows. Without me, there is no light.

Fade to Black

Notes

1   Hortense J. Spillers, "Mama's Baby, Papa's Maybe: An American Grammar Book," *Diacritics* 17, no. 2 (1987): 65. https://doi.org/10.2307/464747.

2	Lindon Barrett, *Blackness and Value: Seeing Double* (Cambridge: Cambridge University Press, 1998); Saidiya V. Hartman, *Scenes of Subjection: Terror, Slavery, and Self-Making in Nineteenth-Century America* (New York: Oxford University Press, 1997); Kimberly Juanita Brown, *The Repeating Body: Slavery's Visual Resonance in the Contemporary* (Durham: Duke University Press Books, 2015); Adrienne D. Davis, *"Don't Let Nobody Bother Yo' Principle": The Sexual Economy of American Slavery*, *Black Sexual Economies* (Champaign, IL: University of Illinois Press, 2019).

3	"Burlesque," *Merriam-Webster's Online Dictionary*, https://www.merriam-webster.com/dictionary/burlesque.

4	Robert C. Allen, *Horrible Prettiness: Burlesque and American Culture* (Chapel Hill, NC: University of North Carolina Press, 1991), 16.

5	Allen, *Horrible Prettiness*, 25.

6	Allen, *Horrible Prettiness*, 26.

7	Peter Stallybrass and Allon White, *The Politics and Poetics of Transgression* (Ithaca, NY: Cornell University Press, 1986), 5.

8	Jayna Brown, *Babylon Girls: Black Women Performers and the Shaping of the Modern* (Durham: Duke University Press Books, 2008).

9	H. L. Mencken, *The American Language Supplement 1 :The American Language: An Inquiry Into the Development of English in the United States*, 4th ed. (New York: Alfred A. Knopf, 1945); Andrea Friedman, "'The Habitats of Sex-Crazed Perverts': Campaigns against Burlesque in Depression-Era New York City," *Journal of the History of Sexuality* 7, no. 2 (1996): 203–38.

10	Thinking here about recent trends in Black Studies that critique western humanism through critical engagements with Blackness and animality. Spillers and Sylvia Wynter are forebears of this theoretical tendency. Spillers taught us how Black flesh had never been permitted to be a properly regarded body in the Western sense. Wynter taught us the political constructions of Western Man1 and Man2 were imperial aberrations of human beings. Spillers, "Mama's Baby." Sylvia Wynter, "Unsettling the Coloniality of Being/Power/Truth/Freedom: Towards the Human, After Man, Its Overrepresentation—An Argument," *CR: The New Centennial Review* 3, no. 3 (2003): 257–337, https://doi.org/10.1353/ncr.2004.0015. Zakiyyah Iman Jackson, *Becoming Human: Matter and Meaning in an Antiblack World* (New York: New York University Press, 2020). Alexander G. Weheliye, *Habeas Viscus: Racializing Assemblages, Biopolitics, and Black Feminist Theories of the Human*, Illustrated ed. (Durham: Duke University Press Books, 2014).

11	Lawrence W. Levine, *Black Culture and Black Consciousness: Afro-American Folk Thought from Slavery to Freedom*, New ed. (Oxford: Oxford University Press, 1978).

12	L. H. Stallings, *Mutha Is Half a Word: Intersections of Folklore, Vernacular, Myth, and Queerness in Black Female Culture*, 1 ed. (Columbus: Ohio State University Press, 2007), 124.

13	Stallings, *Mutha Is Half a Word*, 127.

14	Stallings, *Mutha Is Half a Word*, 129.

15	Stallings, *Mutha Is Half a Word*, 129.

16	"dozens" denotes the Black vernacular tradition of social banter. The game of dozen is played on school yards, street corners, and living rooms and one could convincingly argue that within the Black queer community, this practice has been rearticulated as "reading" and "throwing shade."

17	Ra Malika Imhotep, "Lil Cotton Tells a Tale," in *gossypiin* (Pasadena: Red Hen Press, 2022).

18   Kevin Quashie, *The Sovereignty of Quiet: Beyond Resistance in Black Culture* (New Brunswick: Rutgers University Press, 2012), 45.
19   Ntozake Shange, *For Colored Girls Who Have Considered Suicide/when the Rainbow Is Enuf* (San Francisco: Shameless Hussy, 1973); Mecca Jamiliah Sullivan, *The Poetics of Difference: Queer Feminist Forms in the African Diaspora* (Champaign: University of Illinois Press, 2021), 101.
20   Sullivan, *The Poetics of Differences*, 94–5.
21   Hortense Spillers, *Black, White, and In Color: Essays on American Literature and Culture* (Chicago: University of Chicago Press, 2003), 15.
22   Jayna Brown, *Babylon Girls: Black Women Performers and the Shaping of Modernity* (Durham: Duke University Press, 2008), 57.
23   Brown, *Babylon Girls*, 71.
24   Brown, *Babylon Girls*, 72; Spillers, "Mama's Baby," 77.
25   Brown, *Babylon Girls*, 58.
26   Marshall Stearns and Jean Stearns, *Jazz Dance: The Story of American Vernacular Dance* (New York City: Hachette Books, 1994).
27   Stearns and Stearns, *Jazz Dance*, 252.
28   Stearns and Stearns, *Jazz Dance*, 252.
29   See Uri McMillan, *Embodied Avatars: Genealogies of Black Feminist Art and Performance* (New York: New York University Press, 2015); Amber Jamilla Musser, *Sensual Excess: Queer Femininity and Brown Jouissance* (New York: New York University Press, 2018).
30   Brown, *Babylon Girls*, 62.
31   Brown, *Babylon Girls*, 62.
32   Brown, *Babylon Girls*, 62.
33   Lorraine O'Grady, "Olympia's Maid: Reclaiming Black Female Subjectivity," 1992, 6, lorraineogrady.com.
34   Audre Lorde, "The Transformation of Silence into Language and Action," *Sinister Wisdom* 6 (1978).

Bibliography

Allen, Robert C. *Horrible Prettiness: Burlesque and American Culture*. Chapel Hill: The University of North Carolina Press, 2000.
Brown, Jayna. *Babylon Girls: Black Women Performers and the Shaping of the Modern*. Durham: Duke University Press, 2008.
Friedman, Andrea. "'The Habitats of Sex-Crazed Perverts': Campaigns against Burlesque in Depression-Era New York City." *Journal of the History of Sexuality* 7, no. 2 (1996): 203–38.
Horton-Stallings, LaMonda. *Mutha' Is Half a Word: Intersections of Folklore, Vernacular, Myth, and Queerness in Black Female Culture*. Columbus: The Ohio State University Press, 2016.
Jackson, Zakiyyah Iman. *Becoming Human Matter and Meaning in an Antiblack World*. New York: New York University Press, 2020.
Levine, Lawrence W. *Black Culture and Black Consciousness: Afro-American Folk Thought From Slavery to Freedom*. Oxford: Oxford University Press, 1978.

Lorde, Audre. "The Transformation of Silence into Action." *Sinister Wisdom* 6, no. 6 (1978): 11–15.

McMillan, Uri. *Embodied Avatars: Genealogies of Black Feminist Art and Performance.* New York: New York University Press, 2015.

Mencken, H. L. *The American Language Supplement 1: The American Language: An Inquiry Into the Development of English in the United State.* New York: Albert A. Knopf, 1945.

Merriam-Webster's online Dictionary. "Burlesque." https://www.merriam-webster.com/dictionary/burlesque.

Musser, Amber Jamilla. *Sensual Excess: Queer Femininity and Brown Jouissance.* New York: New York University Press, 2018.

O'Grady, Lorraine. "Olympia's Maid: Reclaiming Black Female Subjectivity." *Lorraine O'Grady*, 1992. https://lorraineogrady.com/.

Quashie, Kevin. *The Sovereignty of Quiet: Beyond Resistance in Black Culture.* New Brunswick: Rutgers University Press, 2012.

Satterfield, Susan. "Livy and the *Pax Deum*." *Classical Philology* 111, no. 2 (April 2016): 165–76.

Spillers, Hortense J. "Mama's Baby, Papa's Maybe: An American Grammar Book." *Diacritics* 17, no. 2 (1987): 64–81.

Spillers, Hortense J. *Black, White, and in Color: Essays on American Literature and Culture.* Chicago: University of Chicago Press, 2003.

Stallybrass, Peter and Allon White. *The Politics and Poetics of Transgression.* Ithaca: Cornell University Press, 1986.

Stearns, Marshall Winslow and Jean Stearns. *Jazz Dance: The Story of American Vernacular Dance.* New York: Da Capo Press, 1994.

Sullivan, Mecca Jamilah. *The Poetics of Difference: Queer Feminist Forms in the African Diaspora.* Champagne: University of Illinois Press, 2021.

Weheliye, Alexander G. *Habeas Viscus: Racializing Assemblages, Biopolitics, and Black Feminist Theories of the Human.* Durham: Duke University Press, 2014.

Wynter, Sylvia. "Unsettling the Coloniality of Being/Power/Truth/Freedom: Towards the Human, After Man, Its Overrepresentation—An Argument." *CR: The New Centennial Review* 3, no. 3 (2003): 257–337. https://doi.org/10.1353/ncr.2004.0015.

Intermission I

"THE ELSC FILES"

by Julie Cook

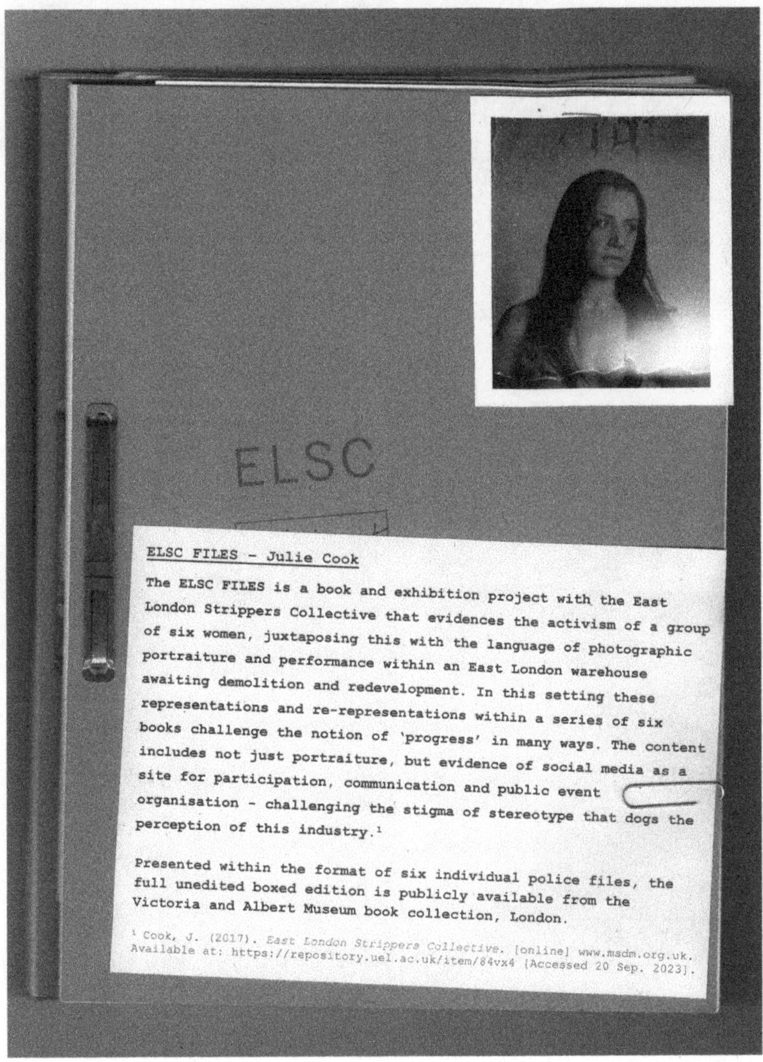

ELSC FILES - Julie Cook

The ELSC FILES is a book and exhibition project with the East London Strippers Collective that evidences the activism of a group of six women, juxtaposing this with the language of photographic portraiture and performance within an East London warehouse awaiting demolition and redevelopment. In this setting these representations and re-representations within a series of six books challenge the notion of 'progress' in many ways. The content includes not just portraiture, but evidence of social media as a site for participation, communication and public event organisation - challenging the stigma of stereotype that dogs the perception of this industry.[1]

Presented within the format of six individual police files, the full unedited boxed edition is publicly available from the Victoria and Albert Museum book collection, London.

[1] Cook, J. (2017). *East London Strippers Collective*. [online] www.msdm.org.uk. Available at: https://repository.uel.ac.uk/item/84vx4 [Accessed 20 Sep. 2023].

Image 10 File 2, Edie Lamort. ELSC FILES, 2018 (Boxed Artists' Book Series of 6 by Julie Cook).

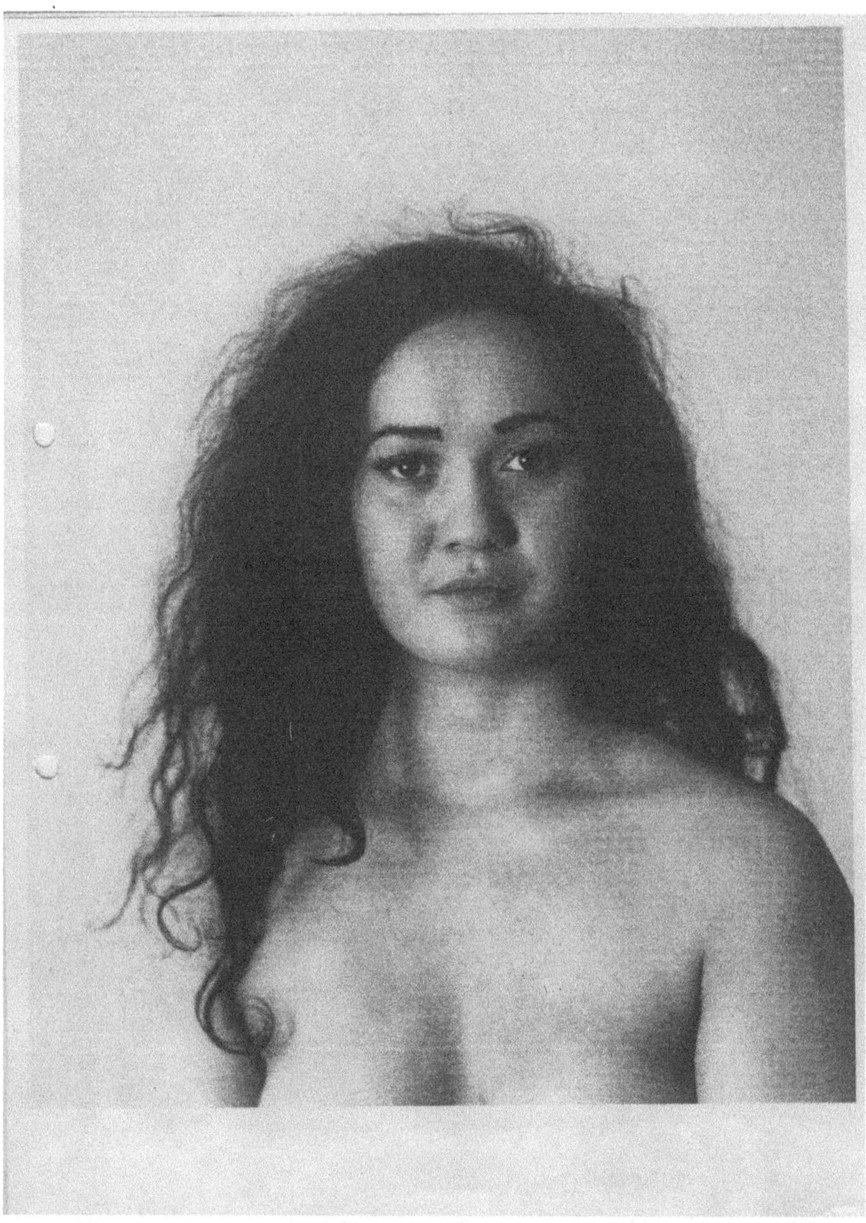

Image 11 File 4, Kitty Velour. ELSC FILES, 2018 (Boxed Artists' Book Series of 6 by Julie Cook).

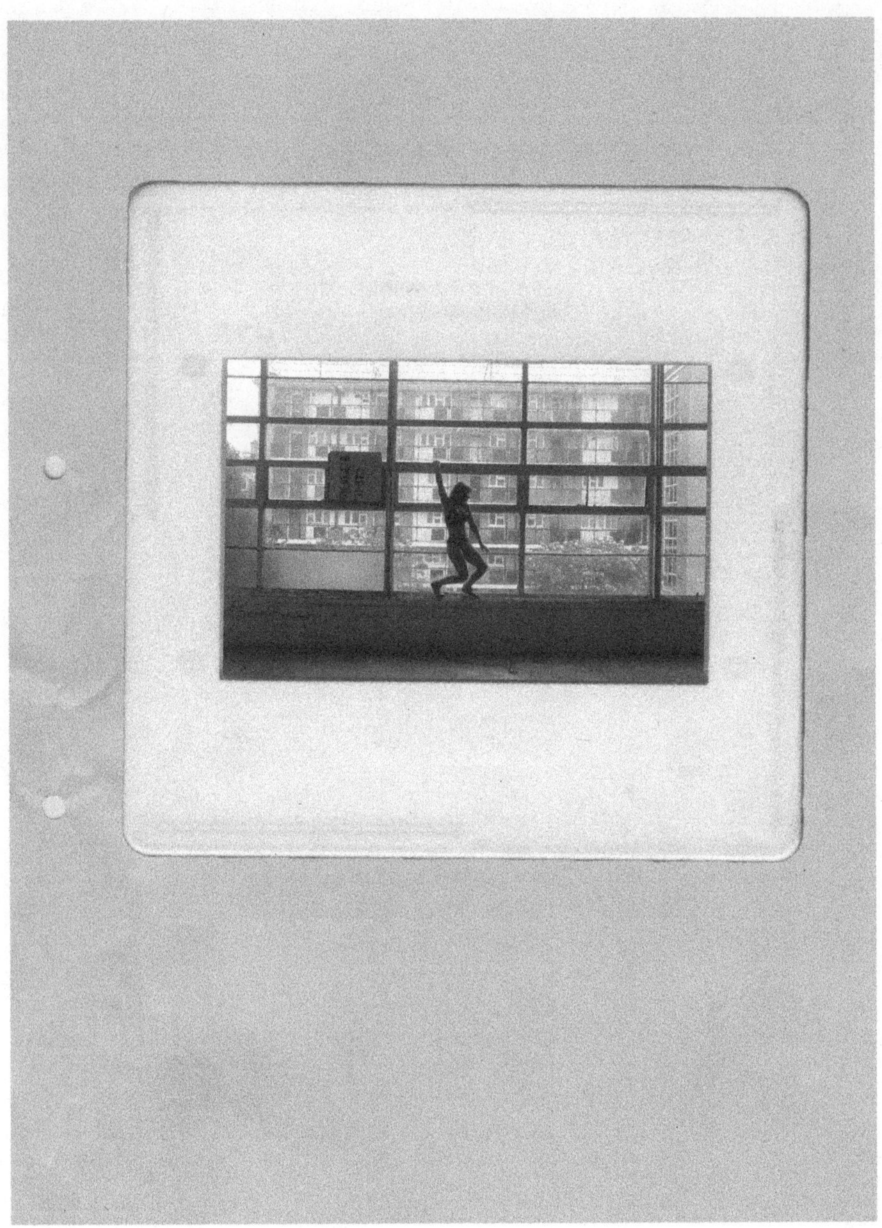

Image 12 File 5, Foxy. ELSC FILES, 2018 (Boxed Artists' Book Series of 6 by Julie Cook).

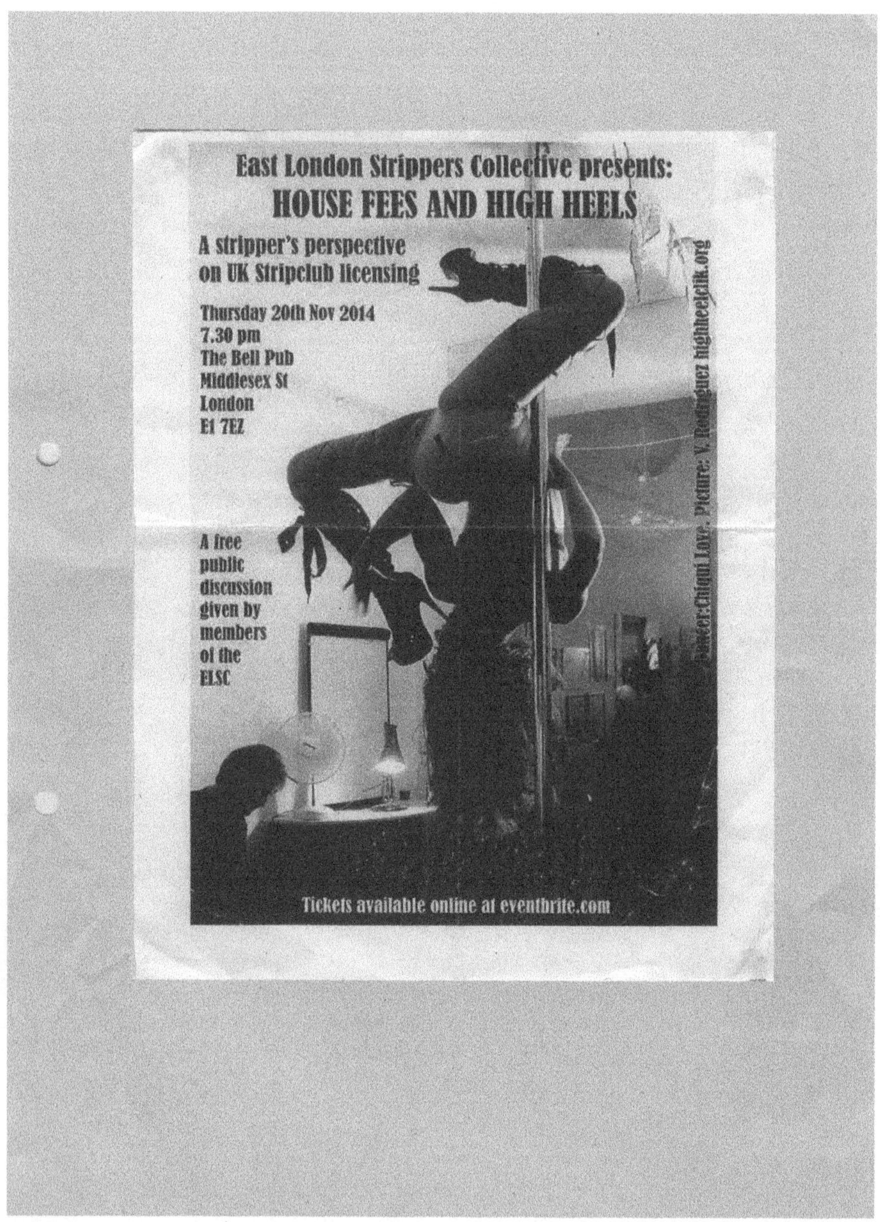

Image 13 File 6, Vera Rodriguez. ELSC FILES, 2018 (Boxed Artists' Book Series of 6 by Julie Cook).

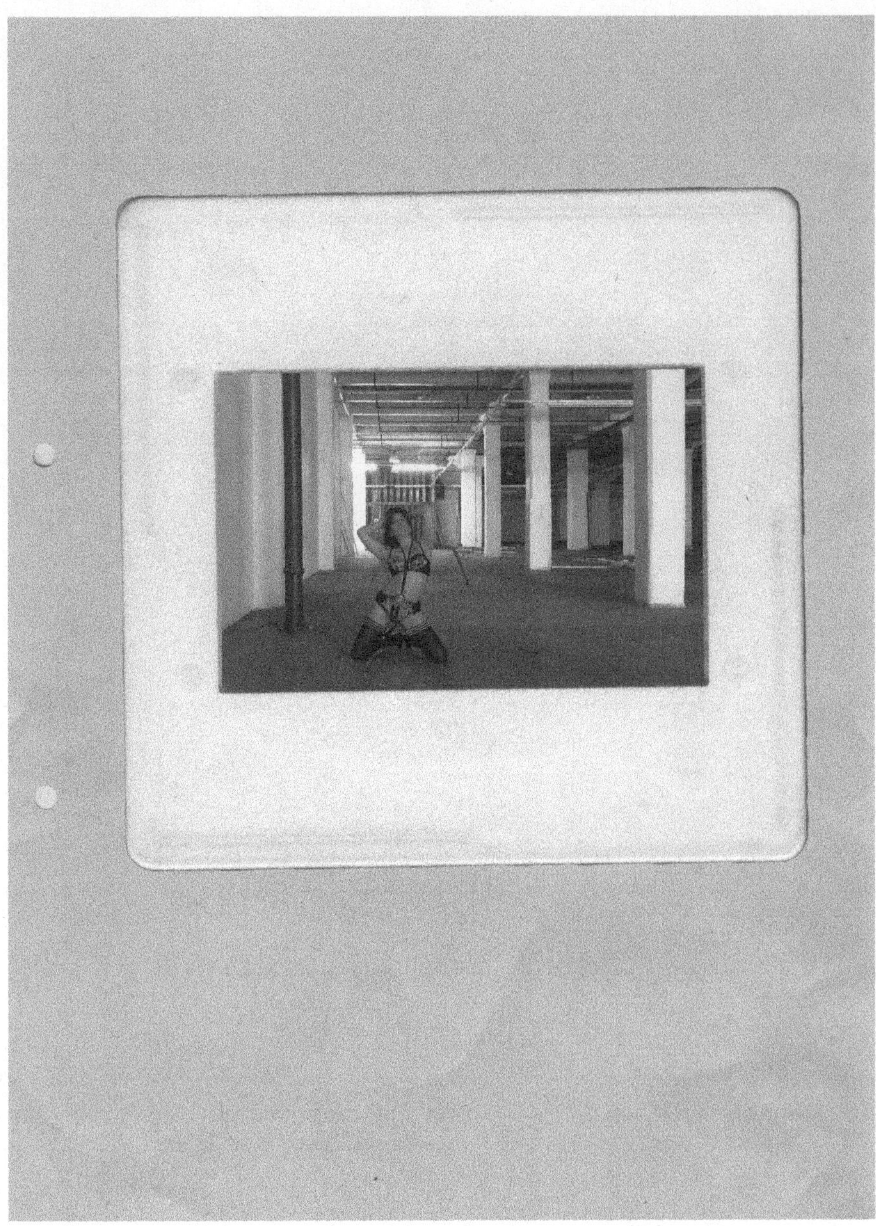

Image 14 File 5, Chiqui Love. ELSC FILES, 2018 (Boxed Artists' Book Series of 6 by Julie Cook).

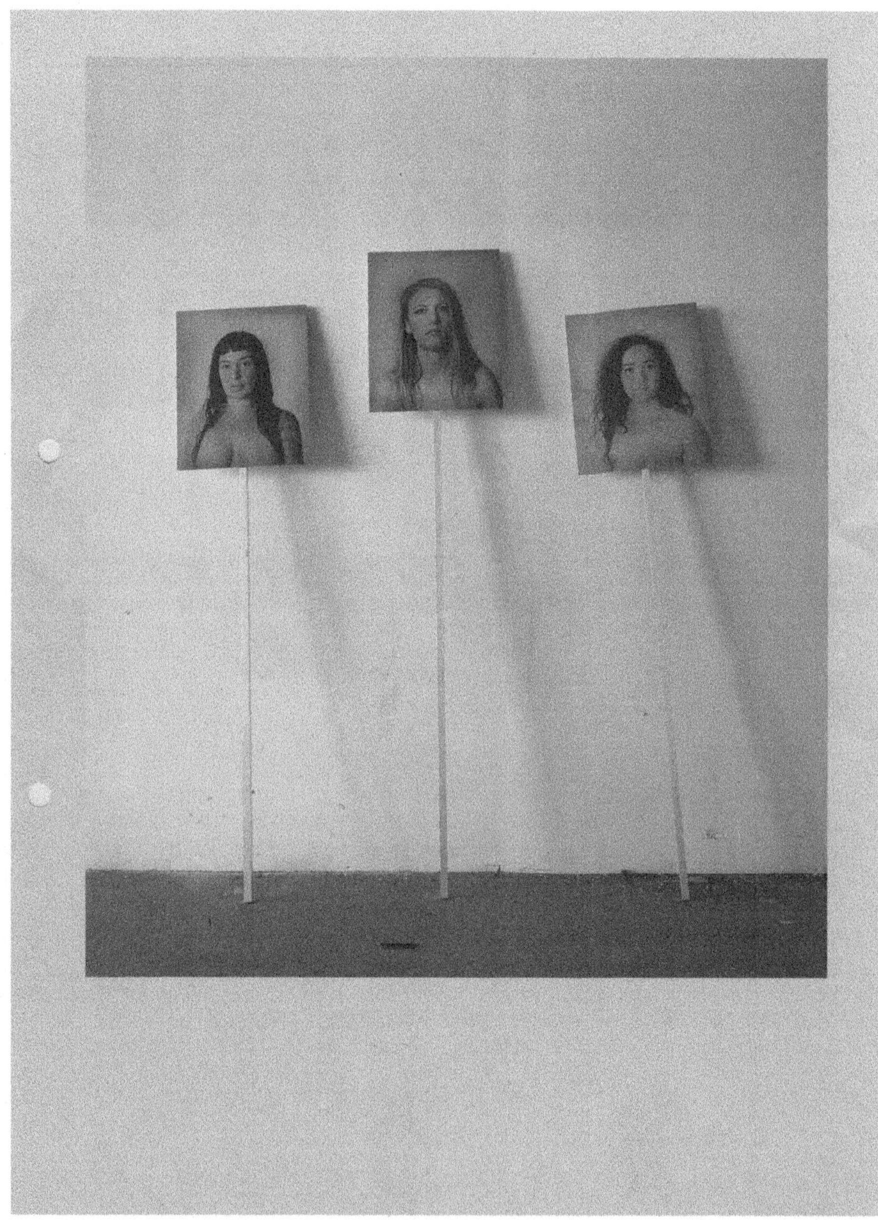

Image 15 File 1, Stacey Clare. ELSC FILES, 2018 (Boxed Artists' Book Series of 6 by Julie Cook).

Act II

MONOLOGUES

Chapter 8

TITILLATION: RADICAL VISIBILITY OR WHEN I FOUND OUT I HAD CANCER, I WATCHED *DIRTY DANCING* OVER AND OVER AGAIN

by Emily Underwood-Lee

My one-woman show *Titillation* (2010) tells the story of my journey to womanhood and my understanding of femininity.[1] I perform the ways in which being diagnosed with breast cancer shook these conceptions and the attendant changes this caused in my body through treatment, menopause, and radical surgery. I employ my desire for Patrick Swayze, particularly in his portrayal of Johnny Castle in the film *Dirty Dancing* (1987), and Swayze's very public cancer story. The performance culminates in a striptease where I remove my clothes, and also my prosthetic breasts that I wear during the performance. I have toured *Titillation* in England and Wales and the work has been shown at theater venues, in universities, and in specialist conferences for both performance studies scholars and healthcare professionals. In this brief chapter, I examine the prosthesis and the heroic cancer narrative as two forms of inadequate fetish, which I propose are a substitute for the putative un-wholeness of the cancer-marked body. I place my analysis alongside extracts of the opening and closing scenes of *Titillation* and images of the performance.

Titillation Verse 2

3. I wanted to be a ballerina and I twirled and twirled.

TURN FINGER

5. I watched her leave for an evening at the theater. She wore a bright electric blue dress and a blue clip in her hair that sparkled brighter than the sapphires pinned to her floor-length black coat.

HAND DOWN LEFT SIDE OF BODY

7. I learnt that if you are young and beautiful and you offer tired, thirsty travelers ripe, juicy grapes, they will do whatever you want, so long as you are dressed in green.

HIPS FROM SIDE TO SIDE

8. I watched a woman wearing too much lace spinning around and around.

CIRCLE HIPS

12. I understood the power of the scent of skin warmed by the sun and flowers after a long sleep.

SLOWLY RAISE ARMS OVER HEAD

14. I learned that I would initiate the action

SIGH INTO MICROPHONE, DROP HANDS

But he would then take control and those large hands would make your waist feel tiny.

LIFT HANDS TO FRONT AND THEN ONTO WAIST

15. Beige iridescent lipstick.

POUT, LICK LIPS, PAUSE

17. I had my tiny waist and my fantastic tits and I seduced a rock star.

HANDS UP TO POINTY BREASTS

19. I thought I could conquer the world.

This is how I learnt how to be a woman.

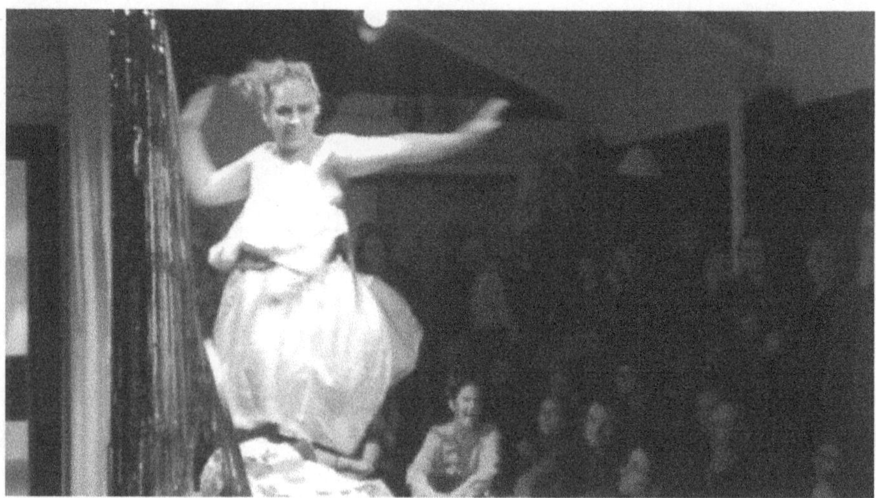

Image 16 *Titillation* performed at Everyman Theatre, Liverpool, 2010, credit Underwood-Lee.

I created *Titillation* in 2010. The piece was made in the context of my academic research into objectification on stage and was specifically intended to explore the objectification of bodies that are visually marked as female and femme presenting, but which challenge normalized constructions of femininity. At the time of making *Titillation*, my own body, as a white, relatively young woman, whose gender matches that I was assigned at birth, initially signals as conventionally feminine, and yet, since undergoing treatment for breast cancer, I have had my breasts, ovaries, and fallopian tubes removed, and have large scars across my chest and stomach.[2] The literal lack of these female reproductive organs marks me as "not quite" woman, something less or un-whole and beyond hegemonic conceptions of what signifies us as female.

Slavoj Žižek describes the fetish as "the embodiment of the Lie which enables us to sustain the unbearable truth."[3] In Zizek's argument, lack, which I am here employing to explore the lack of the breast, necessitates a fetish. However, the need for the fetish always, on some level, reminds us of the lack for which it is standing in; thus, the cancer-marked body demands a fetish and, in doing so, always evokes the lack and the threat that it represents. The fetish, in the form of the prosthesis or heroic cancer "survivor" story, is never able to completely obfuscate this threat. The cancer-marked body always asserts its otherness and is hence revealed to be lacking again, unable to measure up to a putative ideal. When layering the fetish over the marks of cancer, the construction of the fetish is revealed through its failure. In *Titillation*, I play with the failure of the prosthesis and the heroic narrative to stand in for or sustain the cancer-marked body. I employ burlesque conventions in the hope that my cancer-marked body moves from un-whole threat to object of desire. I sought to find a way to present my doubly marked body, as both desirable and desiring.

Samantha Crompvoets argues for a reassessment of the mastectomized body as un-whole, stating that this un-wholeness is created through a series of medical narratives and interventions which reduce women who have undergone breast cancer treatment to a series of parts. She further suggests that the use of breast prosthesis is an inadequate substitute for the missing breast: "the process of being made to feel un-whole is not simply the result of losing a breast ... The premise that a woman's ability to regain this complete sense of self and wholeness by adhering a piece of silicone or foam to one's mastectomy site is evidently flawed."[4] As Crompvoets discusses, a prosthesis is often the medical establishment's offered solution to the "problem" of mastectomy, but a prosthesis simply masks the site of mastectomy, functioning as fetish. In my performance, I removed my prosthesis and attempted to reclaim my marked body as a site of femininity. I refused to see my surgically altered self as less than, as un-whole, or as lacking. The performance is somewhat confrontational as I directly address the audience, get up close to them, and play with burlesque tropes to mark my body as an object of desire. In these acts I am attempting to make radically visible both the marks of cancer on my body and the prosthesis as inadequate substitute for the breast. Audre Lorde speaks of the hostility shown to her when making visible her surgically altered body in a breast clinic simply by not wearing a prosthesis:

A woman who has one breast and refuses to hide that fact behind a pathetic puff of lambswool which has no relationship nor likeness to her own breasts, a woman who is attempting to come to terms with her changed landscape and changed timetable of life and with her own body and pain and beauty and strength, that woman is seen as a threat to the "morale" of a breast surgeon's office![5]

In *Titillation*, I remove my breast prosthesis and perform a dance with them, jiggling them, holding them at arm's length, and making the pasties I have attached to them twirl and shimmy. This is my attempt to reveal the prosthesis in all their threatening inadequacy. I ask the audience to look at the prosthesis, really look at them, and to sustain that gaze. The fetish is decorated with glitter and tassels, able to twirl with the best of them, even performing difficult figure of eight motions (made all the easier by the fact that I am holding the prosthesis in my hands and employing the delicate motor skills of my fingers, rather than the unruly motion of the natural breast on the torso, in the ultimate burlesque trick).

Just as my prostheses are revealed as insufficient fetish in *Titillation*, I also attempt to undermine any notion of cancer survival as a heroic struggle or life-enhancing awakening. Mary K. DeShazer, in her work on breast-cancer narratives, suggests that by reclaiming the marks of our cancer, and turning them from signs of lack to signs of experience, we can confront culturally constructed notions of femininity.[6] While I value DeShazer's configuration of people who bear the marks of cancer as presenting an alternative version of femininity, I want to complicate this still further. I want to challenge the conception of my scars and absent breasts, a signal of my being less than woman, and I also want to refute notions that I have become *more than* through cancer treatment and counter heroic narratives, which Arthur Frank describes as "Quest Narratives" after Joseph Campbell.[7] Frank articulates the quest narrative as a journey of discovery, where the ill person needs to travel through illness in order to return changed and with great knowledge that can be shared with others who are yet to undertake this journey: "the communicative body seeks to share the boon that it has gained upon its own return. Others need this boon for the journeys that they will necessarily undertake."[8] Here we see the fetish enacted again, this time the knowledge gained through the arduous "journey" of cancer obfuscates the threat that the less than whole body of the person who has been through cancer treatment represents.

This heroic story is well rehearsed in representations of cancer. Many a cancer campaign has profiled cancer "survivors" who have gone on to climb mountains, run marathons, or have gained unique insights into the value of life and now live "every minute to the full." In *Titillation*, I attempted to subvert this heroic journey by allowing myself to linger in the details and to present an uncertain ending, remaining on stage after the climactic moment at which my striptease has ended and finishing the show with a speech about the uncertainty of the future following a cancer diagnosis. This speech is delivered simply while standing at the microphone, hospital gown, bra, and prosthesis removed, my cancer-marked body displayed as, what I hope can be, a site of radical visibility and resistance.

Titillation Verse 8

> *THE DANCE, I REMOVE THE SHOULDERS OF MY GOWN, MY RED SILK BRA, MY BREASTS, I TWIRL, RIDICULOUS AND FANTASTIC, REPULSIVE AND TEMPTING, TASSELS FLY, JELLY BREASTS WRINKLE, SCARS ARE REVEALED, GLITTER, GLITTER, GLITTER. I'M GOING TO SHOW, WHO IS GOING TO LOOK?*
>
> 31. I got the first of my scars and lost my hair.
> 32. I lost my left breast.
> 33. The right one went as well.
> 34. My ovaries are next on the list.
>
> This is how I forgot how to be a woman.
>
> *CONTINUE DANCING*
>
> Patrick never got better. I don't know if I will but, right now, I'm still here.

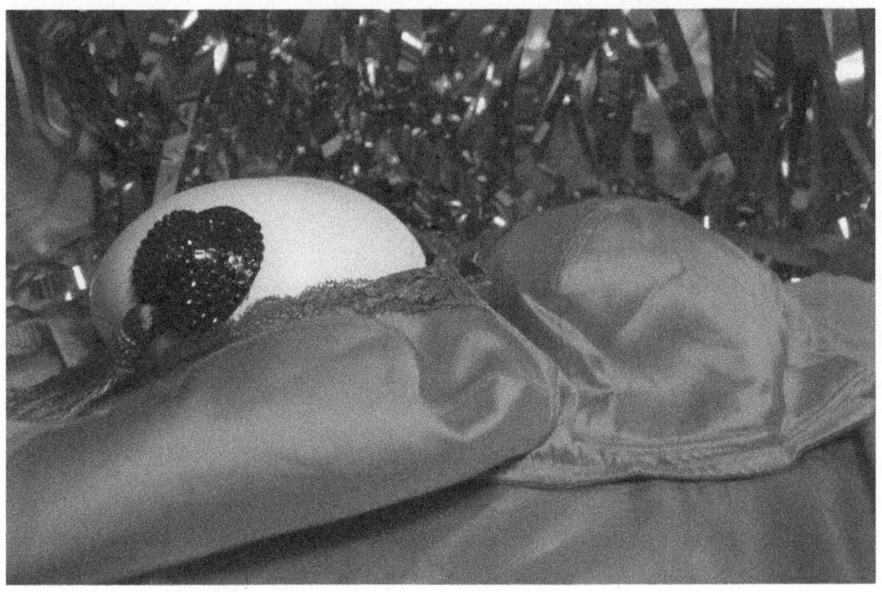

Image 17 *Titillation* promotional image, credit Underwood-Lee.

Notes

1   *Titillation* featured choreography by Kylie Ann Smith. I received financial support from the Arts Council of Wales to make the performance and have had financial support from the AHRC Connected Communities scheme as part of the Connected Communities Festival. There is also a second version of the show, *Titillation Grade 3*, which reworks the script to include film contributions by Sean Tuan John.

2   I was thirty-four at the time of making *Titillation* and toured the show throughout my mid-thirties.

3   Slavoj Žižek, *Enjoy Your Symptom!: Jacques Lacan in Hollywood and Out* (London: Taylor and Francis, 2013), x.

4   Samantha Crompvoets, "Prosthetic Fantasies: Loss, Recovery, and the Marketing of Wholeness after Breast Cancer," *Social Semiotics* 22, no. 1 (2012): 118.

5   Audre Lorde, *The Cancer Journals* (San Francisco: Spinsters Inc, 1980), 59–60.

6   Mary K. DeShazer, *Mammographies: The Cultural Discourses of Breast Cancer Narratives* (Ann Arbor: University of Michigan Press, 2013), 123.

7   Arthur Frank, *The Wounded Storyteller*, 2nd ed. (London: University of Chicago Press, 2013).

8   Frank, *The Wounded Storyteller*, 127.

Bibliography

Ardonlino, Emile, director. *Dirty Dancing*. Vestron Pictures, 1987, 1 hr., 40 min.

Crompvoets, Samantha. "Prosthetic Fantasies: Loss, Recovery, and the Marketing of Wholeness after Breast Cancer." *Social Semiotics* 22, no. 1 (2012): 107–20.

DeShazer, Mary K. *Mammographies: The Cultural Discourses of Breast Cancer Narratives*. Ann Arbor: University of Michigan Press, 2013.

Frank, Arthur. *The Wounded Storyteller*, 2nd ed. London: University of Chicago Press, 2013.

Lorde, Audre. *The Cancer Journals*. San Francisco: Spinsters Inc., 1980.

Underwood-Lee, Emily. *Titillation*, various venues, 2010–16.

Žižek, Slajov. *Enjoy Your Symptom!: Jacques Lacan in Hollywood and Out*. London: Taylor and Francis, 2013.

Chapter 9

THE BECOMING OF MISS AURORABOOBREALIS:
FROM FOURTEEN-YEAR-OLD CLUB KID TO
CO-FOUNDER OF BROWN GIRLS BURLESQUE

by DawN Crandell

I was a fourteen-year-old punk rock kid living in rural upstate New York when I started dancing at a club in Albany. QE2, once a 1950s-style hamburger joint, was turned into a nightclub in the '80s by Charlene Shortsleeve. It was the center of the Albany underground scene, and the whole Capital Distinct of New York State.

My Mom was cool with it. She figured if I was old enough to get the hour-long ride both ways and stay out all night dancing, then I was old enough to deal with the consequences of having to function in school while exhausted the next day. Mom must have known, known I needed this. QE2 became my communal experience, musical education, and a deep release, all wrapped into one ecstatic weekly experience.

I will never forget my first time.

I walked through the entrance to the front bar that was once the counter of the hamburger joint. The dingy linoleum floor held stories as new ones were about to be made. I was quickly ushered to the back of the club for the eighteen-and-over party. The dance floor was crammed with black-clad kids stomping and spinning their way to ecstasy. We wore ripped up fishnets, combat boots—Doc Martens for those who could afford them, Army surplus store versions for the rest of us—tight miniskirts, and bustiers. DJ James (later DJ Saint James) was spinning everything from KMFDM to Siouxsie and the Banshees to Fishbone, The Cure, Public Enemy, Operation Ivy, Ministry.

We danced. And danced.

Then the urge to be seen overcame me. I locked eyes with my best friend, Mary, and without uttering a word, we bolted across the room with a single-minded intention. *The cage.* The cage stood off the main dance floor, elevated above the crowd. One person could dance in there comfortably, but Mary and I managed to Tetris our bodies in by getting as physically close as possible. Any closer and we would have been dry humping.

We let loose in that cage. I fed off the rush of having all eyes on me, my young flesh intentionally exposed as sexually explicit songs like "The Only Time" by Nine

Inch Nails and "I Sit on Acid" by Lords of Acid boomed through the speakers. On more than one occasion, we would fit four of us in there, stacked and sandwiched together, a pulsating mass of teenage hormones and flesh. The cage was the pinnacle of the QE2 experience for us.

I became one of the QE2 regulars, an unofficial crew of outcasts and weirdos. A few years later, one of our crew was dating a guy who was a roadie for the S&M industrial band Sleep Chamber. They usually performed with the Barbitchuettes, a group of young women who danced at the band's shows in revealing clothing. When Sleep Chamber got booked at the Limelight in New York City, they weren't able to bring the Barbitchuettes with them from Boston.

The QE2 crew stepped in.
It was my first time going to New York City,
I lied to Mom this time.

We crammed two car loads of excited teenagers into borrowed vehicles and sped down state with wild abandon. When we finally reached the West Side Highway, we hollered the lyrics to the Beastie Boys' "No Sleep till Brooklyn" out the windows.

By the time we got to Chelsea and found parking, we were so late, we started running through the streets. I could feel the energy pulsing through the city, and my body. We ran up to the front door of the Limelight out of breath and slightly frantic.

"Please," we pleaded with the bouncer, "We are supposed to be dancing with the band!" We could hear the drums banging and the crowd howling inside. He gave us a hard time about our IDs, but we were persistent. He finally agreed to let us in.

We rushed into the club. I whipped off my coat and bolted straight for the stage. I was wearing high-cut lingerie from the 1980s and little else. We all posed at the back of the stage looking like sexy cutout paper dolls when, in reality, we were scantily clad teenage girls who had snuck out of their parents' home in upstate New York for this moment.

We took turns descending to the main stage in groups of two. We had been told to dance around the band—all men in their twenties and thirties—and touch them and each other. The band watched us as if we were nothing more than sexy bodies, devoid of personhood. I was used to the subversive counterculture of QE2, and this felt different to me. I felt like I was on display.

But I also felt an inexplicable burst of energy and joy. I looked out at the sea of over 500 people rocking out to Sleep Chamber, and felt a rush of excitement. I got into my character, and became part of this incredible collective experience.

Something changed in me that night. I was starting to find myself. And I knew it was complicated, but there was a type of agency to be found in putting my own sexuality and body on display.

✳✳✳

By nineteen I had started stripping.

One of the QE2 crew, Raven, worked at a local strip club. She had pale skin, dyed black hair, and a Gothic look. She made no effort to hide her job, and this normalized stripping for me. I figured stripping was better than waiting tables. Men treated women the same, but with stripping, I wouldn't have to carry heavy trays. Plus it gave me the opportunity to dance as work.

Stripping quickly became a cornerstone of my identity. I used my stripping as a kind of Litmus test. When I met a new person, I would introduce myself: "Hello I'm DawN, and I'm a stripper." If they were shocked or judgy, I knew we couldn't be friends.

I started playing with the staging of gender and sexuality with satire at Sarah Lawrence, a progressive college just thirty minutes north of New York City. My junior year they instituted "Sleaze Week" which encouraged us students to explore our explicitly sexy side in a supportive environment. I would go to Coming Out Dances in my stripper outfits.

Sophomore year I created a piece for Cross-Dress Cabaret that I now consider my first burlesque piece. It was set in a strip club. I came out in a suit, looking like a boss. A few of my friends were scattered on the stage playing various strip club characters. As I moved through the space, I interacted with the patrons, giving them energy and lap dances. I intentionally ignored my one friend, Tommy, who I had asked to play a stereotypical strip club asshole.

Here, I had the power to choose who I interacted with, and how. To me, this piece was a satirical look at strip clubs' characters and strip clubs in general, a celebration and a critique.

While I was bringing stripping to Sarah Lawrence, I started learning about burlesque from my stripper friends. My worlds were colliding in exciting ways. I was working in my house club in upstate New York chatting backstage with Xeavier, a white, petite woman who had strength in body and spirit. She had long, black hair down to her ass, and moved like liquid around a stripper pole.

"There's this Miss Exotic World competition," Xeavier told me, "where you can be really creative and artistic." This was back when Exotic World was at the ranch with Dixie Evans sashaying around imitating Marilyn Monroe. I became intrigued.

I was working in Yonkers when another stripper friend told me about the Blue Angel in New York City. "You're not going to make as much money," she told me, "but you can do cooler shit and be artsy. And a woman owns it." I went to one of the Blue Angel shows, and to this day can still remember this stunning glow-in-the-dark paint act I saw.

And then in 2004 I saw my first burlesque show—BadAss Burlesque at the Knitting Factory. I fell in love instantly. The piece that hooked me was by Darlinda Just Darlinda. She came out in this old school yellow negligee as this Zombie-like housewife, and she started shaving herself, and then she started bleeding. It was poignant and amazing, a commentary on womanhood and beauty all rolled into one messy, sexy act.

I realized that this thing called "burlesque" could be a container for the type of performance art meets stripping that I had already been doing. And that burlesque didn't have to be just sexy or just pretty. It could be whatever I wanted it to be. The burlesque stage was like a blank canvas. And, to me, it celebrated all the fun parts of stripping without all the annoying bits like hustling and dealing with the customers.

I became a fan. I started going to burlesque shows semi-regularly. When I graduated from Goddard with my MFA in Interdisciplinary Arts in 2007, I invited folks to the Slipper Room to see a burlesque show. I showed up, excited for the show, my brain all afresh with twentieth-century Black Radical Artists and the concept of institution building that I had been studying.

After one of the acts, I leaned over to my friend Maya. "I've had this idea for a few years to start this all woman-of-color burlesque troupe," I told her. From 2004 to 2007, I had seen one brown body on a burlesque stage in New York City. One brown body. In three fucking years. In New York City. At the time, I wondered: there's got to be other people of color who are doing this. Why am I not seeing them? Are they not getting booked? What's going on?

Maya, being the Taurus she is, responded without hesitation: "Let's do it."
And that's how Brown Girls Burlesque was born.

✳✳✳

We had our first meeting in Maya's living room the next month. A bunch of beautiful women of color all from different artistic backgrounds showed up. We sat on cozy couches in her basement apartment in Fort Greene Brooklyn. The vibe was laid back, but the energy started to buzz as we told the group our idea for Brown Girls Burlesque.

"We're not going to wait for the white folks to put us in their shows," I said to the group. "Let's create our own shit." I saw several women nod their heads.

Smokey Fantastic raised her hand to speak. She told us a story, a somewhat cautionary tale. She was the only one of us who had done burlesque before. She had been booked for a gig, and after the show, the producer told her that what she did wasn't burlesque. They refused to book her again. A few months later, she saw her image on a new flyer that that same producer was using to promote a show. It was so messed up they used her image without her permission, after claiming she was not doing burlesque.

"This is why I want to start Brown Girls Burlesque," I said after Smokey finished telling her story. "We don't need to be told that what we are doing is not legitimate. Let's just do it ourselves." So that's what we did. We did it ourselves. Made a space for bodies like ours to shine on stage and to feel welcome in the audience.

Brown Girls Burlesque (BGB) started meeting regularly at Maya's to talk about ideas for acts and shows. Since we came from a variety of creative backgrounds, we all had something unique to contribute. Some of us were dancers and choreographers, actors and singers, poets and writers. I brought my graduate-school research of Black radical artists—Katherine Dunham, Paul Robeson, and Amira Baraka—and the concept of institution building.

Many of the original BGB members came from Sarah Lawrence. We had a strong student-of-color community there, so that was a big influence in creating an all women-of-color troupe. We wanted to build more than individual performances—we wanted to create a coalition.

We did research. We got our hands on a book about neo-burlesque, and there was a half-page mention of Harlem Shake, the iconic all-Black burlesque troupe from Oakland California. We looked them up, and it turned out their founder, Simone de la Getto, was similarly dismayed by seeing so few women of color in burlesque, and was inspired to create opportunities for herself to dance with other Black bodies. They were trailblazers and beacons of light for us.

After doing our research and meeting and workshoping ideas and acts, it was finally time to stage our first show, the *Jimi Experience*, an all Jimi Hendrix show. It exceeded all of our expectations.

✳✳✳

On October 12, 2007, I arrived at the Pussycat Lounge in New York City. The door on the left led to a traditional strip-club on the first floor. I dragged my suitcase through the door on the right that led down a long narrow hallway. At the end of the hallway, I lugged my suitcase up the creaking stairs to the second floor. The venue had a rock 'n' roll vibe. Standing-room only. Small stage set a couple of feet off the ground. Within a few minutes, the space started to fill. There was electricity in the air and the audience was alive, ready for the festivities.

The show started. I watched the other acts from the side of the stage. When I scanned my eyes across the crowd, I saw all these beautiful Black and brown bodies loving what we were giving them. I noticed two friends of mine making out with wild abandon, and it made me smile.

Then it was my turn. The host sauntered to the middle of the stage and got the audience hyped for my act. "Please welcome to the stage, Miss AuroraBoobRealis!" The crowd went wild with screams that I could feel all the way in the core of my body and spirit. The first notes of Jimi's "Manic Depression" wailed loudly through the speakers. The type of loud where I felt it in my body in the best way. I was wearing a tight, velvet strapless onesie in a vibrant purplish fuschia—one of my stripper costumes—and a matching thong. At the time, I wore my hair in a purple dreaded mohawk.

I was embodying both the manic and the depression, a wild undulating frenzy of purple. I was feeling myself. And the audience was feeling me. There were screams of joy. The already-amped audience grew louder and louder in their appreciation. I shimmied and shook my curves, a twenty-first-century Black shake dancer, giving my all for the stage. I was unapologetically celebrating my sexuality, my aliveness.

To curate a whole show comprised of women of color in 2007 in New York City was a political act. Every time I step on stage, it is a political act. It meant so much to own the complexity of our experiences and our imaginations, and to do so unapologetically.

That first show was incredible not just for us, but for the audience. We had all invited our networks, but we were frankly surprised by the turnout. After we had met our 200-person capacity, we started turning people away at the door. When we saw that flood of people, we knew then that this was going to be bigger than just our friends and family. We were fulfilling a need, and we knew people were hungry to feel and experience what we were giving.

There was this palpable, collective energy that got created, and it was infectious. From the get go, our audiences have been filled with wild, amazing brown and Black and queer bodies with tons of style. They were just waiting for people who looked like them and spoke in similar ways and had common cultural references to bring it to them. We inspired each other, really. And we brought our Black and brown excellence to an art form that we loved, but that was flawed in many ways.

Representation in burlesque has changed today, but there's still progress to be made. My story is one story among many. It is not the first, and I am happy to say that it certainly won't be the last. The stage is ours to take as we step boldly into the spotlight.

Chapter 10

"WHEN IN DOUBT, BODY ROLL": STORIES OF STRIPPER ACCIDENTS

by Zahra Stardust

Circa 2012, Larrakia country, Darwin. It's 40 degrees Celsius and foundation is dripping down my face. Mascara is stinging my eyes. I can no longer remember the source of the bruises but can feel the swelling as I bend down to rifle through my essentials. I can smell the fake tan in my armpits and peel off a couple of flakes from behind my knees.

Everything is strung together with either zippers or Velcro. The boots held together with gaffer tape. White dust covers my palms and inner thighs. Hairspray glitter coats my torso. I scrape off leftover candlewax from my chest with a baby wipe.

I am on the showgirl contract at the Honey Pot Club. It's my seventh of the ten shows we are contracted to do each week, and this is my last of a three-week stint. It sounds glamorous, but for me, life as a stripper mostly consists of laundry and parking fines. Here we do three fifteen-minute shows at three different venues within the space of an hour and a half, so I arrive literally saturated in sweat.

Some of the bruises have obvious origins. From crawling around concrete floors, from laybacks on the pole, from my bra clip digging into the middle vertebrae. But then there are the general mystery bruises. I do handstands into people's laps to distract them from the fact that I have got heat rash, I'm highly flammable, and I haven't washed my g-string since last weekend.

I am well practiced at dancing with minimal infrastructure. Sometimes at the lunchtime shows in Sydney, the bar managers suddenly turn on our music without notice, and we emerge from the toilets in broad daylight, competing with the horse racing or football. We basically get up on the pool table in the middle of someone's game and start taking off our clothes.

In the daytime, most of the strippers live together in the Honey Pot house, where we spend most of our time lying about in underwear and no make-up complaining about how dead the club is and watching all five seasons of some television show I have never heard of but which is suddenly captivating. I can barely get off the moldy couch to reach the two-minute noodles.

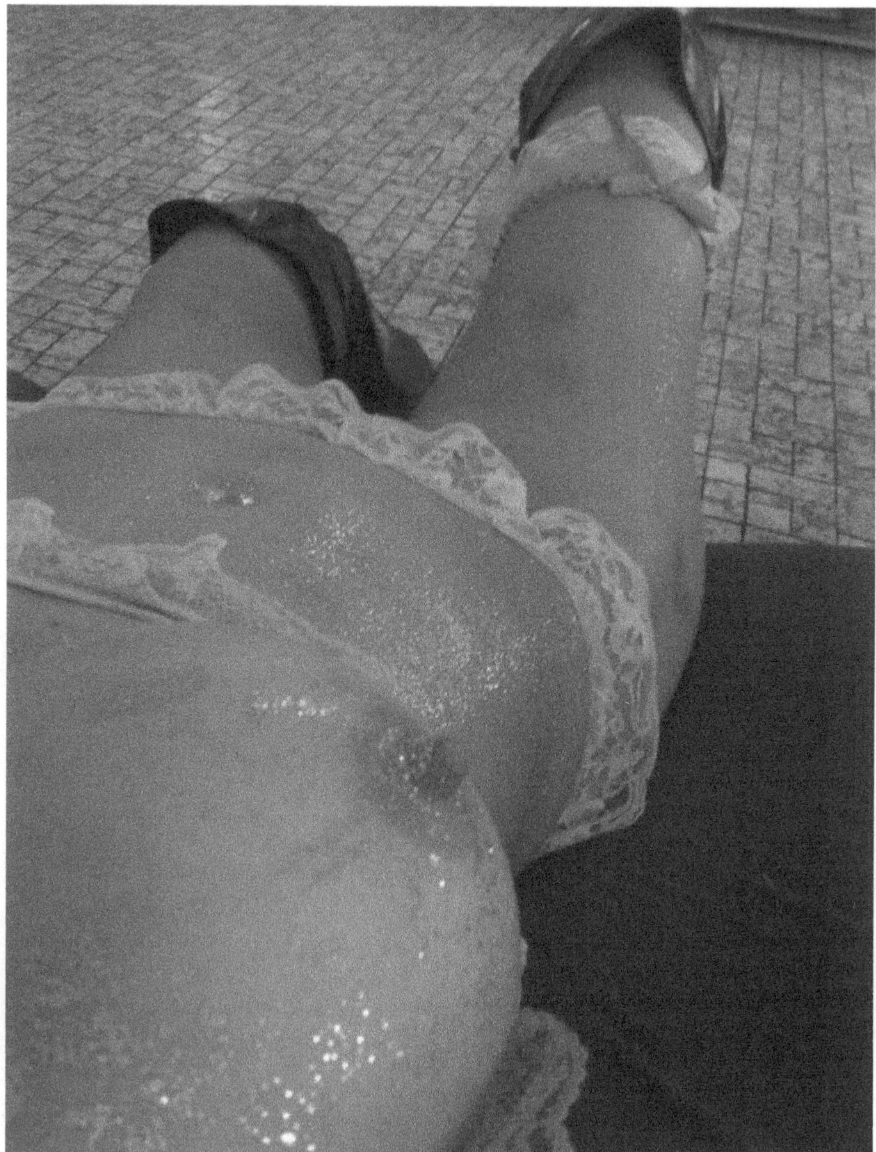

Image 18 Bruises, credit Belinda Mason.

Four nights a week, we do shifts in the Honey Pot Club. It's freezing cold. The air conditioning only has two settings: On or Off. Apart from the security, bar staff, and management, all the dancers are in very little clothing. But there's only so long we can huddle in the bathrooms for warmth before they want us back on the floor for the 2 a.m. lesbian double.

Tonight, I am doing a private show for a buck's party. My main concern is to try and prevent the customers from spilling beer on my rug, putting their dirty hands on my clean toys, or surreptitiously filming my show. I've chosen a vibrator that is modest in size because there's minimal time for warm up. But some days, if I am feeling like a bit of a size queen, I choose something a little more impressive (for professional development).

I am lying on my back and have reached the last track in the mix. I reach into my bag of tricks and begin to lube up my dildos. Until I notice there is something not quite right.

It is worth pointing out at this point that I am well experienced at stripper accidents. On my first ever night of work, I broke a customer's nose. It sounds dramatic, but this kind of risk ought to be relatively foreseeable when you are doing a fan kick on a tiny podium and the customers lean in too closely.

Then, there was the occasion when I fell over in the first ten seconds of my feature show because I opted for seven-inch heels instead of six, and the ankle boots just did not have the same support as the knee-highs. The time when I burnt my hands from lighting hair mousse on fire or ended up with welts on my labia from using the wrong kind of candle wax that melted at too high a temperature. Or the time when I lost a sea sponge inside myself and nobody could find it, and two days later a doctor retrieved it with a speculum and forceps.

One particularly memorable stripper fail was at Calendar Girls in Christchurch, Aotearoa. I had forgotten my shower gel for the bath show. Instead, I used ordinary detergent from the club kitchen. I had done the big entrance, a song of chair work, a song of floor work, a song of pole tricks, and was nude and ready for the slow, sexy finale. *Rhianna* came on and I got out my soapy bath. I stood there perfectly poised: one knee bent, chin up, back arched, sponge above my head. And then I poured acid-like, oven-cleaning quality detergent directly into my eyes.

I could not see anything for the remainder of the four-minute song. My eyes were on fire so I could not get up from the floor. Minxing about the floor for a song was not really the problem. The worst part was that at the end of the show, we were meant to do a lap around the audience to collect our tips. But instead, I spent a good twenty minutes backstage pouring water into my eyes with shot glasses and emerged bloodshot and frazzled.

My most spectacular stripper mishap was at the Imperial Hotel, a queer pub in Newtown, Sydney, the time I thought it was a sensible idea to cut off fetish tape with a Stanley knife because it matched my outfit. It was a tradie theme, and so I had a series of tools I found in the "Ladies" section of the hardware store to match my pink high-vis "safety" vest. Needless to say, I cut right through to my muscle and ended up in the hospital with fourteen stitches. This was a good lesson in why color coordination and thematic consistency should not take precedence over occupational health and safety.

But back in Darwin, I am lying on a tarp in someone's backyard, surrounded by about twenty men and somebody's mother. I am making eyes at the audience and lubing up my toys, thinking—this is all going well, I am going to take my $350, buy my groceries and perhaps pay off some credit card debt.

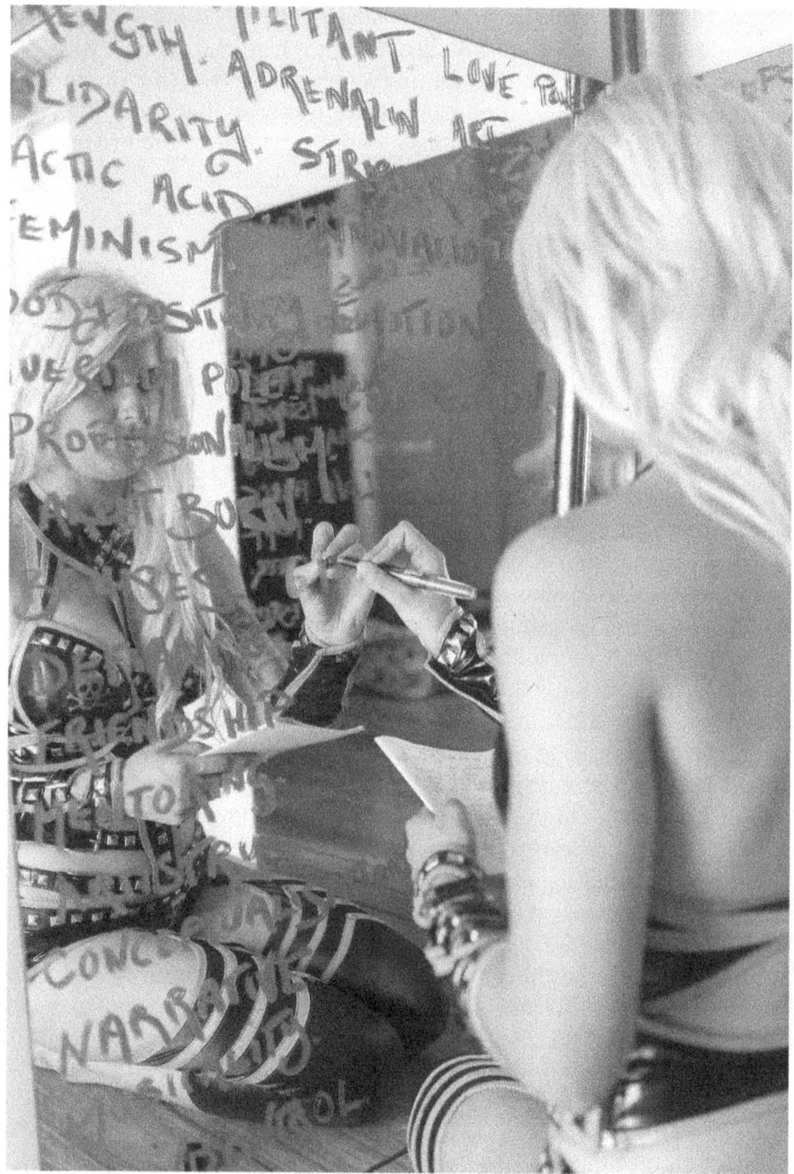

Image 19 Mirror writing, credit Belinda Mason.

I realize that it is not lube the second it hits my labia. I know it is not lube, the second I feel it sting. I look down into my polka dot bag of show toys. It is not lube. It is hand sanitizer. I have just put a generous dollop of hand sanitizer on my vibrator and inserted it into my body.

The crowd leans in eagerly as I grimace for a second. But never fear—I am a professional! I remember what I always told my pole dancing students in the event of some kind of stage disaster. For those moments when you have a complete mind blank or forget the entirety of the choreography: "If in doubt, just body roll."

I take a deep breath and lie there smiling, pointing my toes, and letting this dry, antiseptic, alcoholic irritant seep into my internal membranes. I flick my hair, smile seductively and, like a true professional, I just body roll in time to the music.

There's an old industry adage, one that seeks to refute the idea that stripping is inherently risky or dangerous. The biggest risk, the saying goes, is that you might end up with glitter in your eyes. That risk is real—glitter will scratch the fuck out of your eyeballs.

But it's not just glitter—you can tear your labia on the pole, get a flying dildo to the face, or slip on silicone lube. Stripping is serious business. If I've learnt one thing from the last fifteen years as a professional undresser, it's to strap in your labia for a wild ride ahead.

Chapter 11

PERFORMING INTIMATE EXPERIENCES AS A QUEER BLACK BODY

by Toussaint Jeanlouis

I walked into the recently renovated Diamond Horseshoe, originally operated by Billy Rose as a nightclub that was later turned into a theater, at the Paramount Hotel in New York City buzzing with energy of its historical past. I had been cast to perform as a butler in *Queen of the Night* (2014–16), an immersive theater show that combined circus, dance, food, perfume: a sensorial spectacle curated by an all-star creative team. One goal of *Queen of the Night* was to arouse people's senses. A delectable full meal was served as guests feasted from ornate bird cages overflowing with lobster, chicken, and garlic butter chive biscuits that melt in your mouth. A scent designer created olfactory experiences specific to our characters and bodies. As I walked by a patron, they could smell the bergamot from my warm skin lingering in the air.

I wore a costume designed by Thom Browne: halter top tuxedo shirt with pleats, and tux shorts that finished at the knee. During the run of the show, a codpiece was added to the outfit. My makeup: mascara, gold eyeshadow, and fingernails painted black. I was given soft-toe, hard-heel shoes with no arch support that made my feet hurt and over time caused long-term pain in my back. But here I was, available to give spectators an experience they would never forget.

We had six weeks of rehearsals to develop our approach to the one-on-one intimate experiences that were the cornerstone of *Queen of the Night*. I developed a character named Barcnel, a combination of Colonias and Bartholomew. My intention was for Barcnel to be shrouded in mystery but also confident in his sensuality. I imagined him to be a healer for others—a shaman for the heart.

A one-on-one I created was set to be performed in a tight room space underneath a stairwell behind a closed door. I had to crouch and crawl to get in. There, I sat with the guest and asked them: "What does love feel like in your body? What would you want to say to someone you love?" I would give them a notepad to write down whatever came to mind. If the person they were thinking about was present, they could give their thoughts to them, or they could hold on to it for later. Sometimes they would choose somebody they met that night to give their note. The experience was theirs.

Part of the show's development included working with a dominatrix to learn how to give reciprocal energy, and how to guide spectators through their immersive theater experience. I created a one-on-one that was placed in a hallway where audience members were able to walk past the participant and myself, witnessing the experience. The lighting was warm and magnetic, and intoxicating smells swirled in the air. On the wall was a sconce made of a huge gold hand with a light behind it. I would bring the person to the palm-lit hand, extend my hand directing them to look at the light, and then ask them to close their eyes. I whispered in their ear, "You're the Mouse, and I'm the Lion." And then I would gently come up behind them and squeeze their calf really, really tight. And then slowly release it. Then I may go to their thigh, squeeze it, and slowly release. Next, their arm. I may go to their ribs to press on their diaphragm a bit. The decision to restrict and release parts of the body came from questions I asked myself: What does it feel like to be held tightly? What does it feel like to be let go? What does the line between love and hate feel like? What does fear and joy feel like? What does it feel like to be alive?

I would wrap my arms around them tight, slowly release, then whisper in their ear: "Now *you* are the Lion, and *I* am the Mouse." Then, I would direct them to face me. I opened my arms to give them the option to hug me back, to flip the roles. Sometimes they would. Sometimes they didn't know what to do. I let them decide. Once someone held me so tight and as they began to cry, they exhaled and said: "I haven't been held in so long. Thank you for letting me know that's what I needed." Sometimes a person would give a long, intense hug, and they would start rubbing me in an uncomfortable way, letting me know they were aroused. I would have to tolerate that unwanted physical attention for a beat, and then tell them "thank you," and confidently walk away.

As I understood it, we were not allowed to say "No." We had to redirect so participants may continue their experience of sensual awakening. Every night I had to navigate who I approached for a one-on-one. Barcnel was stoic and underneath that shy, so fist-bumps or loud exclamations like "Yo!," were not an option. Making eye contact was the primary tool I used to connect. Yet making direct eye contact can be frightening, intimidating, and threatening for most people. It can be for me.

Men often felt like a challenge partly because of my own insecurity of intimacy with men. The intimacy I was seeking was not founded in sexuality, but a "knowing connection," a vulnerability we don't always allow ourselves, especially in a fast-paced city like New York. And so, I was always navigating the boundary of heteronormativity to get men comfortable with me in an intimate way. And with women, the power dynamics were slightly different. It was about offering them a space to feel equally in control, and encourage them to stand in their power. I may have smiled and quickly stopped, asking myself "What am I inviting with this smile?" I wanted *them* to feel safe. *I* wanted to feel safe. I might see them again in passing, grin and nod, but not speak. It was the allure of the unknown.

Being a 6 feet 3 inches-tall Black cis male, I long ago had to learn how to be malleable in every moment for my safety. Every night, going back into that show with new audiences and new experiences required me to constantly reinvent myself. If I was anxious about interacting with people, to ground and focus myself I would ask: "What is the common thread in all of us?" I created my own script, and had these checkpoints, but inevitably the unforeseen came up. It was psychologically and emotionally tolling. I still had to remain relatable and open at all times, available to do my job.

Some nights I might do something a little different to find inner joy, inspired by the moment. Instead of dancing two feet apart, I might take somebody's hand and respectfully dance with them as the stoic Barcnel would. In those moments, I received unwanted encounters: patrons groping me or kissing me without permission. "Don't say no, redirect" feverishly ran through my mind. We were expected to tolerate the drunken rich patron's behavior no matter what. The rehearsals had no drunk patrons. We weren't given any tools on how to navigate that. Many of us had triggers, trauma from sexual abuse or what has happened to us in our lives. The show forced us to navigate our triggers with what was happening to us in real time. This didn't foster a safe environment despite how fun it appeared.

I would have liked an action plan so that it didn't feel so unsafe. Or feel like I was going to be reprimanded for trying to make myself safe. At some point during the run, I injured my shoulder. I was one of four butlers who carried another performer through the space perched on an elaborate platform.

Can I please switch sides? I asked. I was told no.

It hurts, I begged. I was told no, you can't switch sides.

I can't do it on this side, I said, asking for the blocking to be changed temporarily so I could use my other shoulder. I was told no.

The irony was I was told no, but during the show, I was expected to always say yes.

✳✳✳

One night we were coming to the end of the show. The finale included feeding attendees a delicious, chocolate mousse cake. I always hoped for leftovers. It was very decadent and sensual. I was sitting on the edge of a table feeding people. I made eye contact with a man I had seen earlier in the night and never took on a one-on-one. He was certainly drunk now, but I connected with him. I thought I was safe on a table in the open, *and* this was the closing ritual. As I always did, I delicately scooped a perfect bite of the desert and he allowed me to feed him. He let the mousse coat his mouth, and then ran his tongue around his lips peering back into my eyes.

"More," he demanded. 'Last one,' I said, and fed him some more. A woman to my right was staring at the exchange. She said, "Look at what he's doing!" At first, I didn't know what she was talking about. And then I looked down, and I saw the man was groping my crotch, in front of all these people. My cod piece was padded with a magnet, so I hadn't felt it. But I knew I would not be allowed to push him away. Instead, I moved his hand and said, "Thank you. Have a great night." After being assaulted in front of people, I had to sit there and continue to feed rich entitled people cake.

In reality—which is hard to say because the trauma triggered many emotions—nobody was protecting us in the dark. Nobody was there to hear someone say something really sexual or objectifying, or to see someone pressing up against my body. And, ultimately, I figured I put myself in this position. I created my character and my one-on-one experiences. I was being encouraged, post-devising, to perform in a way that my work wasn't created for. I did not feel my body was my own, and that was a large part of the recurring trauma I was experiencing each night. Not having bodily autonomy is something that many performers experience. It's as though because we are paid, we are giving up control of our bodies and our minds.

And, in this case, I also gave up my intellectual property. The contract stated if I took this character anywhere else, legal counsel would come after me. I did not own my own artistic production, pieces of my personal story. So who am I as an artist? How do I exist if someone else owns my artistic production? What happens when someone else owns everything? What do I become?

Not only was I facing the loss of bodily autonomy, but I was encountering micro aggressions from the dressing room to the stage. One night I was escorting the Queen through the crowd as attendees ate an elaborate meal paired with fine wine. I looked stoically ahead, focusing on giving energy to the Queen and protecting her. As I walked by this one table, an older white woman with gray hair and large glasses leaned over and said out loud for all to hear: "Are you her slave?" I had to think quickly as there was no script for this and no one had ever asked me this during the show.

"Aw Darling, that ended in 1865," I muttered. There's no appropriate sexy response when someone asks if you are a slave. I wanted her to understand that what she just said was in no way appropriate. But I was expected to stay in character. I could give a little sass, but I had to make that sass sexy, when really that's the last thing I wanted to do at that moment. The whole experience of performing at *Queen of the Night* forced me to navigate my own traumas and behaviors. Of wanting to be seen, wanting to be heard, and feeling connected. And being in this Black body, I was struggling. The audiences were predominantly white and rich. And I was expected to connect with people who, outside of this space, would likely not even speak to me.

❋❋❋

One night during the show run, everybody was in their most elaborate regalia, looking fabulous and having the time of our lives. We were downstairs in the theater, giving attendees a sensorial experience to remember. After the show was over, we poured into the streets—buzzed and alive with energy—and were inundated with a huge protest in Times Square. Eric Garner had been murdered by the police, choked to death, in July 2014. The protestors were smearing what looked like blood on the ground.

Moving from that privileged space of the theater to the reality of Black bodies in open spaces in America was really intense and uncomfortable. I had the freedom to perform as an artist. I was doing what I loved. But I couldn't help wonder: did these people really care what I and people like me were going through? After treating privileged people to sensorial debauchery, I had to go back to the real world and face a completely different reality. I had to walk the streets and protect myself. Protect myself on a different level than I did every night while doing the show.

The vulnerability of my body in free spaces became amplified with Eric Garner, and again in the years that followed with the deaths of Black men, women, and children by the hands of those who were enlisted to serve and protect. When I look back on the show, I think about the ways I was not seen, heard, or respected. I was looking for validation, people to acknowledge the harm that they had devised and/or allowed. I realize my body will always be on the block. I could be wearing the fanciest suit, but because of someone else's perceptions, I will still be on the block. So how do I share who I am with others?

I know that there's a strength in being vulnerable. It scares a lot of people to be vulnerable, to be open and honest rather than shut down or shy away. This is complicated with layers of masculinity for we are not allowed to be vulnerable. Toxic masculinity guarantees that. But my inner core is soft. I am a big, soft, Black man. In our culture, that is incomprehensible. I'm expected to be stoic, strong, hard. There's a presumption I should be able to protect myself, that I shouldn't have these issues happening to me. So I stayed silent.

Chapter 12

"READING NANA: THÉÂTRE DES VARIÉTÉS"

by Sharon Kivland

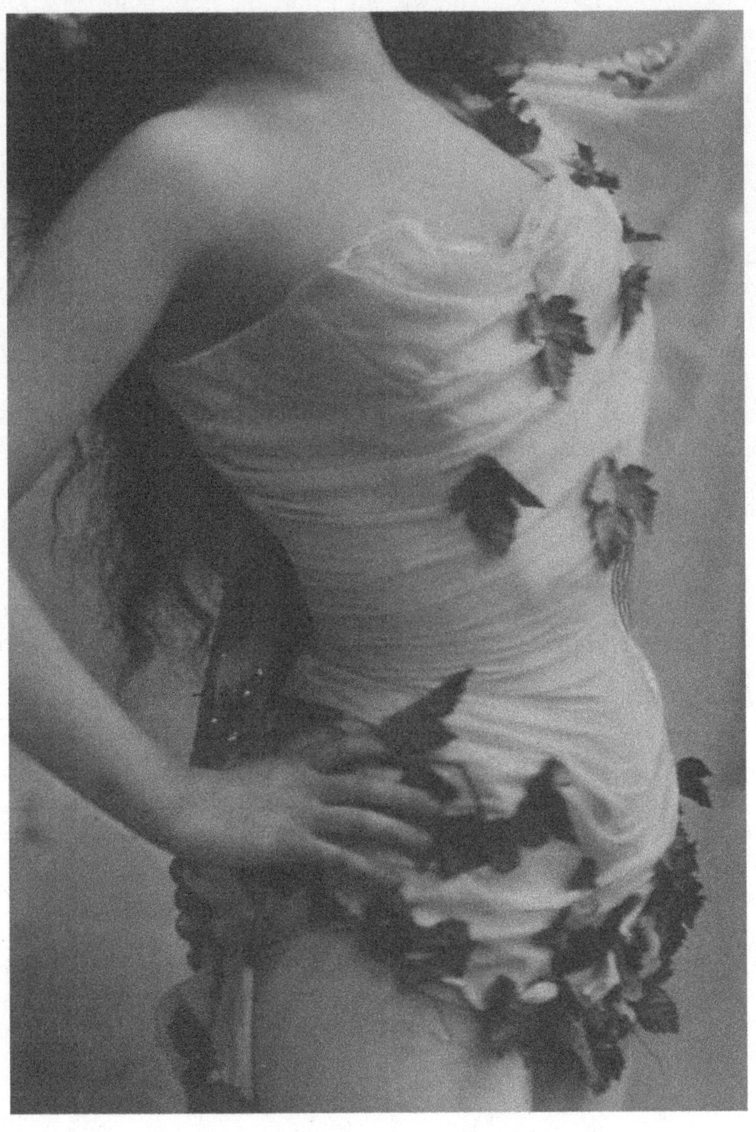

Image 20 Invitation card for the exhibition, Sharon Kivland, *Ma Nana (encore), autre filles, et quelques petites explosions*, Galerie des petits carreaux, Paris, 2013.

I have been reading *Nana* by Émile Zola for a number of years. Zola's novel, his "true story of the *demi-monde*," was published in installments, first appearing in October 1879 in *Le Voltaire*. The definitive version in book form was published on February 15 by Charpentier. I read and I re-read the book, in both French and English. I digested the book, condensing it, organizing it into themes, appearances; yes, I assimilated it.

I read (one might say perform) my assimilations, and I have danced one, according to Jean-Luc Godard's film version, inviting others to join me. Some parts of my reading have been published in installments in *Crux Desperationes*, edited by Riccardo Boglione. They have been assembled as a whole novel that is largely incomplete, just as Nana or *Nana* slips from the grasp, in *Reading Nana: An Experimental Novel.*[1] A supplement of emptiness and silence has been added, also read to an audience and read at Miss Read in Berlin in 2017. A later supplement was a little *conversazione* in *Crux Desperationes*, 2021, later also published in *Soananyway* in 2022.

Nana's value lies in that she can be exchanged. Her value lies in that another has had her. Her body has useful qualities, and these qualities are also of value. Nana or *Nana* is of value because she has been used; her potential for use is realized and finely calibrated. The cleavage between her use and exchange is less clearly demarcated. She eludes possession, no matter how many times she is had, no matter how many times it is read. There is no portrait of her, though Manet painted one which or who is like her. A horse was named for her, described in more detail than she. I have taken it upon myself to depict her, to speak for her and as her: a woman who is a book, a book that is a woman. In this iteration, Nana/*Nana* is a script, awaiting her/its readers.

[*In the auditorium of the theatre, in the virtually empty stalls, in the half-light of the dimly glowing chandelier*]
And what about Nana, the new star? It has been Nana here and Nana there. She is something invented. She has a delightful voice. She's tone-deaf. She is an excellent actress. She is a great lump of a girl. She doesn't know what to do with her hands and feet.
[*Downstairs, in the big marble-paved vestibule, in the crude gas-light*]
Nana has something else, dammit, and something that takes the place of everything else. It has been scented out and it smells damnably strong in her. She has only to appear and the whole audience will be hanging out their tongues. She'll go far. A skin! Oh, what a skin she's got. The manager knew what the little tarts were worth.
[*On the pavement outside, the row of gas-jets blazing*]
She's a slut. The public will soon send her packing.

[*Around the box office, a din of voices. Nana's name is sounding with all the lilting vivacity of its two syllables. The men standing in front of the playbill spell it out aloud*]
Where has Nana come from? Why didn't you tell me you knew Nana? Nana, hey, Nana!

[The auditorium. The first act. The orchestra strikes up the lively notes of a waltz with a cheeky rhythm full of roguish laughter. People call out: Silence! The audience is frozen into immobility. The curtain goes up. Venus appears. Very tall and well-built for her eighteen years, in her goddess's white tunic and with her long hair hanging loosely over her shoulders, Nana comes down towards the footlights with quiet self-assurance. Greeting the audience with a laugh, she launches into her big song: "When Venus roams at eventide … "]

We've ever heard a more tuneless voice, or one less skillfully controlled. She sings like a trombone. She doesn't even know how to comport herself on stage. She thrusts her arms out in front. She sways her body in a vulgar and ungraceful manner. We are disarmed. We laugh. We no longer think of hissing. We are fascinated by her shapely figure. Oh, oh! Jolly good, bravo! We break into rapturous applause. Our gaiety increases. We cannot deny she is an amusing creature, a lovely girl. Her laughter makes a delightful little dimple appear in her chin. She's not in the least embarrassed. She is on good terms with us. She seems to be admitting with a wink that she has no talent at all, but that doesn't matter, because she has something else. Her shrill voice tickles so deftly it sends a shiver through us. She smiles her smile, which lights up her little red mouth and shines in her great bright blue eyes. She tilts up her nose with pleasure and her pink nostrils quiver, while a bright flush colors her cheeks. She still sways backwards and forwards, but we no longer consider this ugly. We point our opera glasses at her. Her voice fails her, so she thrusts out one hip which is roundly outlined under the flimsy tunic, bends backwards, so her breasts are shown to good advantage and stretches out her arms. We applaud from all sides. She goes upstage and reveals to us the nape of her neck, a neck on which her reddish hair looks like an animal's fleece. We become positively frantic. As the curtain comes down, we are on our feet, making for the doors. We stamp and jostle, we think it is idiotic, we all think this.

[The passage outside the stalls, the foot of the stairs]
I know the girl. I am certain I have seen her before. At the Casino, I think, and she got herself picked up there, she was so drunk. I don't know where it was, but like you, I've certainly met her before. It's disgusting that the public should give a reception like that to the first slut that comes along. Soon there won't be any decent women left on the stage. Oh, she's got some flesh on her, and no mistake. Something to get your teeth into. Beastly, beastly! Stunning, stunning! Very good. Better still if she were to cultivate her voice.

[The second act, set in a cheap dance hall, the Boule Noire, *at carnival time]*
It strikes us as rich entertainment. We seize upon allusions; we suggest indecent meanings. Our exclamations give obscene twists to inoffensive phrases. It has been a long time since we wallowed in such irreverent nonsense. It makes a change for us. Nana is so white and plump, she looks so natural for this part that calls for big hips and a loud mouth, she has immediately captured us. That hefty wench who slaps her thighs and clucks like a hen, she gives off an odor of life, a potent female charm, that intoxicates us. We allow her to get away with everything. She can hold

herself awkwardly, sing every note out of tune, it doesn't matter: she only has to turn around and laugh for us to shout our applause. When she gives her special thrust of the hip, we light up and we glow with passion. It is a triumph when she leads the dance. We applaud. We cheer.

[*The corridor of the first-tier boxes*]
This Nana, surely she's the girl we saw one evening on the corner of the Rue de Provence? By Jove, I knew I'd seen her before. You know, my dear, I think Nana's very good.

[*Act three. A grotto on Mount Etna, hollowed out of a silver mine and glowing like gold coins*]
A shiver runs through us. Nana is naked, flaunting her nakedness with a cool audacity, sure of the sovereign power of her flesh. She is wearing nothing but a veil of gauze; and her round shoulders, her Amazon breasts, the rosy points of which stand up stiff and straight as spears, her broad hips which sway to and fro voluptuously, her thighs—the thighs of a buxom blonde—we can divine her whole body, indeed clearly discern it, in all its foamlike whiteness, beneath the filmy fabric. This is Venus rising from the waves, with no veil save her tresses. And when Nana raises her arms, in the glare of the footlights we can see the golden hairs in her armpits. We do not applaud. We do not laugh any more. Our faces are tense and serious, our nostrils narrowed, our mouths prickly and parched. A wind seems to have passed over us, a soft wind laden with hidden menace. All of a sudden, in the good-natured child a woman stands revealed, a disturbing woman with all the impulsive madness of her sex, opening the gate of the unknown world of desire. Nana is still smiling, but with the deadly smile of a man-eater. God is all we can say to each other. We are gripped completely. A murmur arises from us, swelling like a growing sigh. Some of us clap our hands. Every pair of our opera glasses is fixed on Venus. Little by little Nana has taken possession of us. Every one of us is under her spell. A wave of lust is flowing from her as from a bitch on heat, and it has spread further and further until it has filled us all. Now her slightest movements fan the flames of our desire, and with the twitch of her little finger she can stir our flesh. Our backs arch and quiver as if unseen violin-bows have been drawn across our muscles; and on the nape of our necks the down stirs in the hot stray breath from some woman's lips. We are half-lifted from our seats by passion. We are pale. We are apoplectic. Our ears are blood-red and twitching. Our mouths are agape and our faces mottled with red. Our eyes are cat-like, phosphorescent, speckled with gold. We are suffocating, our very hair growing heavy on our perspiring heads. In the three hours we have been here, our breath has filled the atmosphere with a hot human scent. We seem to be swaying, seized by a fit of giddiness in our fatigue and excitement, and possessed by those drowsy midnight urges which fumble between the sheets. Nana, in front of us, who are crowded together and overwhelmed by the nervous exhaustion which comes toward the end of a performance, remains victorious by virtue of her marble flesh, and that sex of hers which is powerful enough to destroy us all and remain unaffected in

return. We are on our feet and making for the exit, while in the midst of giving thunderous applause and frenzied shouts of Nana, Nana!

[*The corridors, tumbled heaps of clothing, then the exit of the theatre*]
We jostle the attendants. We line the foyer. We light cigars and walk off, humming: "When Venus roams at eventide …" We fill the foyer. We are a herd of men with parched lips and ardent eyes, still burning from the enjoyment of Nana.

Note

1   Sharon Kivland, *Reading Nana: An Experimental Novel* (London: MA BIBLIOTHÈQUE, 2017).

Bibliography

Kivland, Sharon. *Reading Nana: An Experimental Novel.* London: MA BIBLIOTHÈQUE, 2017. Serialized in *Crux Desperationis*, edited by Riccardo Boglione, between 2011 and 2020, Montevideo, Uruguay.
Kivland, Sharon. "Conversazione." *Sonanyway* 2, no. 10 (September 2021): n.p. https://www.soanywaymagazine.org/issue-ten.
Zola, Émile. *Nana.* Paris: G. Charpentier, 1881.

Chapter 13

"STRIPPING OFF SHAME AND REVEALING HOT JOY"

by Anna Brooke

It was a hot summer night with humidity that threatened to loosen the adhesive that was keeping me legal. The backstage was a cramped, sweaty jumble of bodies in various states of undress. Our costumes, props, bags, and makeup cases were all over the place as we got ready for the second act. Condensation from our drinks pooled under the glasses, creating small, wet circles on the ledges that held them.

I was up next for my gogo set. I checked myself in the mirror, wig freshly pinned and glitter reapplied. I wore a netted dress stretched over my glistening body, my g-string prominent and ready for all the dollar bills that would get tucked in at all angles, my heels tall and sharp. I was ready to dance. I adjusted the flower in my hair as I walked out onto the dark stage. On the other side of the tall, red velvet curtain stood and sat a crowd thrilled by the first set and hungry for the second. I could hear them laughing, yelling, and steeping in the heat like us, except they had air conditioning on that side. The excitement was palpable, and I loved it. I poked my head out of the side to let the DJ know I was ready and positioned myself behind the curtains. I rolled my shoulders back, shook my hands out, and took a big breath.

"Ladies and gentlemen, for your go-go pleasure, please give a warm welcome to Legs Malone!"

The music started. I extended one arm out, suggestively stroking the curtain. A few whistles and cheers rose up. I withdrew my hand and poked one leg through the curtain. The whistles and hollers got louder. I turned around, parted the curtains, and slowly pressed my g-stringed rear out. The crowd went wild. I was in heaven.

The first time I ever got on stage, I killed it. It was the Montessori Christmas pageant and I was about three or four years old. I have no memory of this moment, but my mom tells the story so well that I can put myself back in this tinsel-tinged moment in time. I was in the front row and apparently sang every word of the songs with gusto, full gesticulations, and joyous enthusiasm. My mom tells of how parents came up to her afterward and commented on my stellar performance. Clearly, I had arrived.

As fate would have it, it was the very act of performance that liberated me from a quiet, self-imposed prison of being a "good girl" and all the harm that entailed. It opened my eyes to the blindness I had long mistaken for clear sight. Love blew me wide open, and burlesque was my liberation. But what was I being liberated from?

Bodies carry a lot of meaning, and certain bodies have been assigned more privilege, access, and currency than others. Think about the line outside a hot nightclub—only certain people are going to gain admission based on their appearance. I was conditioned to behave in certain ways so as to gain access to privileged spaces. Waking up from the harmful constraints of what I had been taught to value (thinness, beauty, good behavior, whiteness) and opening my eyes into their inherent prejudices and judgments have been a rude and hard process. If it weren't for the embodied joy, naked mirth, and wild, glittery fun of burlesque, I would still be clinging to the limitations of the life I left so long ago.

I grew up in a very small, wealthy community outside of New York City. During the summertime, we all went to the local pool, a members-only recreational panopticon where everyone could see and watch each other. It was commonplace to have running commentary on whoever was walking in or out of the pool's gates. The constant surveillance seemed to be part and parcel of the whole experience. This seemed normal to do when, in truth, it was exceptionally toxic.

I was ten years old when I realized that my body was different. It was a hot summer's day in the late 1980s. Some friends and I were stretched out on the green plastic lounge chairs that ringed the pool, drinking soda and shooting the breeze as kids do. I was wearing my favorite aquamarine swimsuit that was dotted with flamingos and palm trees, doing my best to get a tan.

"Look at those gams!" Elaine exclaimed as she looked down at my outstretched body. Elaine was my childhood best friend's eccentric stepmom whose booming voice was well known around the pool. She would swan around with her floppy hat, breezy cover-up, and nosy intentions, herself a newer arrival whose loud tones of voice and dress were a topic of hushed conversation around the pool.

I knew a compliment when I heard one—there was no judgmental tone to her voice—but I had never heard someone comment so suddenly and so loudly about my body. I remember being confused by the word "gams" as I stared up at her. All I could see were my legs, long, white, gangly, and covered in moles and freckles which I despised. I was constantly taunted for being so pale, which made me obsessively lay out in the sun, praying to get darker. Instead of a tan, all I got were countless sunburns, a few cases of sun poisoning, and, later, several precancerous moles that had to be sliced off and scooped out of my body.

Later that afternoon, I went to my room, closed the door, and looked at myself in the full-length mirror. Elaine's words echoed in my head and I began to see my growing body in a new way. I was not developed or old enough to have the body I wanted to have. I was desperate to grow up so I could wear the dresses I saw hanging in my mom's closet, the high heels I saw tucked away, and the bras I could never imagine filling. Suddenly, there was hope.

Sitting at the pool, summer after summer, I became obsessed with inhabiting and performing beauty. I was still subscribing to *Sassy*, but whenever the new issues of *Cosmopolitan* or *Vogue* hit the stands, I would eagerly snap them up. I pored through their pages, soaking in each model's pose, angle, hip to waist ratio, or whatever was being celebrated and sold on every page. These women were perfect, embodying some ideal of beauty that seemed both valuable and rare. I overheard my mother mention that these magazines were way too mature for me, but she never took them away or told me directly that I was too young to be reading them. I rarely read the articles because I didn't care about them. All I wanted were the airbrushed images of unattainable beauty whose ranks I dreamt of one day joining.

By this time, I was a late-blooming, tall, gangly middle-school kid with braces, a flat chest, and terrible dandruff. I was constantly made fun of which made me want to disappear. I prayed that one day I would be there on those same magazine pages alongside these women whose beauty I worshiped, because then I would be safe from withering judgment. I repeatedly watched ugly duckling stories, where the awkward child grows up into a beautiful woman. I prayed with all my might that I would be released from my excruciating adolescence into the ease and luxury of beauty and the access it afforded.

My day came, but it was not what I expected. When I was in my twenties, I worked as an intern for a major fashion media company in Paris. I assisted production on huge shoots with famous supermodels, and got a rare behind-the-scenes view on the beauty I had devoted myself to. At one big shoot, I came side to side with a very famous supermodel and saw that her thighs were the size of my upper arms. In that moment, any attachment I had to having a thinner-than-healthy body evaporated. I realized that biology had dealt us two very different hands (and bones), and there was nothing I could do about it. I had been obsessed with looking like women who biologically make up less than 0.001 percent of the population. It became clear to me that any thought of ever looking like them was a pipe dream.

Although I mostly dropped that dysmorphic attachment, it remained. Want to look acceptable? Dress a certain way. Want to feel accepted? Behave a certain way. Want to fit in seamlessly to the social molds provided by systems and ancestors past? Act a certain way. Anything that lay outside of those parameters was looked down upon, judged, and torn apart by the arbiters of taste and power. This had been so deeply seared into my nervous system that I felt beholden to it and powerless to change it.

Years later in college, while wearing revealing clothes when bar hopping with my best friend, we were accosted by an older woman who drunkenly yelled at us that our skirts were too short and we were being too loud. That may well have been the case, but who's to say she wasn't simply reacting to her own pent-up desire to slap on some red lipstick, a mini-skirt, and hit the town? It was easier to come at two young women who were giving themselves ample permission to whoop it up than to give herself the same permission, societal standards be damned.

I rarely saw women who were happy or even joyful with their own bodies. I imagine there may well have been moments of real, embodied joy for them—I just never saw any. To be naturally, authentically joyful on one's own was unusual and thus highly suspect. It meant potentially questionable mental health, fervent religious belief (which was suspect as hell), or a secret pill habit among other reasons. Perhaps the women I saw were too beaten down by rigid societal expectations to be buoyant. I rarely saw any woman I knew enjoy their food, dance with wild abandon, or be generous with themselves in any meaningful way.

There seemed to be a disconnect between embodied joy and how women moved about their lives. Once women became mothers, they disappeared as sensual creatures. If their beauty faded, it was game over. Men, on the other hand, somehow managed to retain their attractiveness despite paunches and bald spots. It was a widely accepted binary I could never and still do not understand.

Instead of enjoyment and its sensual innocence, the core pursuit of all the women I knew and loved was beauty. It was the ultimate asset that every woman felt they needed to strive for. Praise and attention were heaped upon those lucky to be born with certain bone structures, or someone who had just lost a lot of weight, or who had just bought the newest fashion. I watched and learned all the signals, soaking them up like a sponge. Instead of enjoying life and our bodies in their kinetic, soft, messy, joyous glory, we were instead taught to worship the narrow parameters of beauty.

I went on to study art history in school because it was the only thing that ever made sense to me. I was constantly seduced by the beauty I saw hanging on the walls, in galleries and museums. I wanted to touch the cool marble curves of sculpted bodies, caress the generous globs of paint worked into a froth on canvas. I wanted to burst into dance, or tears, when confronted with beauty. I could keep my composure if needed, but what I really wanted to do was *feel* my delight, my joy, and my pleasure. Instead of experimenting with making art myself, I studied it, wrote about it, and helped people make their art by becoming a support for artists, not realizing that I was the one who wanted to be on display.

I like to think of my introduction to burlesque as a form of divine intervention, a sacred correction to a warped mindset. I had found out about this stripteasing artform during a very turbulent time in my life, and I got hooked fast. I was living in London, and the biggest British burlesque star at the time was Immodesty Blaize, a gorgeous, curvy Ava Gardner lookalike who was a delight to watch. She was putting on a show, *The Immodesty Tease Show*, conveniently abbreviated to T.I.T.S. It featured an incredible roster of burlesque talent, including Dirty Martini and Julie Atlas Muz from New York City. Having just finished graduate school where I had learned the priceless value and privilege of watching artists do their work live, I knew that this show was a gift I wanted to give myself. I also had just found out that the days in my dream city of London were numbered. My visa application had been denied for the second time, and the appeal was not looking good. I was heartbroken, but the future was calling. So, two tickets were purchased, and off I went with a fellow budding burlesque friend to see T.I.T.S.

The show began with a bang and was a rip-roaring delight. Drag king Murray Hill came out and introduced himself as the host of the show. He started cracking jokes that made my New York heart sing with nostalgia and delight. He introduced each star one at a time with hilarious quips and a rhythmic delivery that evoked Don Rickles. The burlesque dancers used every one of their god-given faculties and body parts to thrill, titillate, and make us roar with laughter. I was flying high when Murray announced Dirty Martini.

When Dirty stepped on stage, my jaw dropped. I had studied art history for years and had never once seen a body in person that looked like hers. The luscious Venus-like women I had studied in Renaissance art had nothing on Dirty's curves. She commanded everyone's attention, her exceptional stage presence beaming out and her eye-popping figure strutting, bumping, and grinding while elegantly clad in rhinestones and swirling fabric. Her beauty and what she did with those dangerous curves made me feel as if time itself had stopped.

As I watched her, every single one of my self-hating, fat-shaming, body dysmorphic thoughts came up and turned to mist on the wind. My old limitations quietly imploded. I suddenly saw more than just Dirty at that moment. I saw a soul in motion in perfect alignment with sacred purpose, a heart radiant with expression, and a body lit up with joy.

More than a mere performer, she became before my eyes a sacred channel of sensuality that spun joyous tassels in the face of all the systemic, practiced limitations that lay outside of this one, brilliant moment. Nothing could have prepared me for this sudden education, a flash realization that everything I had been taught was false, that women are glorious, sensual, sexual creatures whose bodies and art deserve to be celebrated and supported.

You could say her act literally blew my mind.

As if I had not already had enough, Julie Atlas Muz then came onto the stage and knocked me clear off my heels. "You don't own me," the music crooned as she unwound herself victoriously, riotously, furiously from a rope coiled around her from head to toe. I had never seen a woman so in charge of her own body, owning every second of her act, and delivering a punch line or big reveal that had the audience howling, cheering, and hollering. Her command of the music, manipulation of her props, incredibly well-educated body, and total ownership of the piece were monumental for me to witness.

As I sat on the tube on the way home, my head hazy with drink and spectacle, I realized that something inside of me had changed. I had not wanted to return to my home city of New York before that night and had been bracing myself for my inevitable re-entry. Thanks to T.I.T.S., I realized I was going home to one of the most vibrant burlesque scenes on planet Earth. Suddenly, I had something to look forward to, and that something I later realized was joy. It did not matter that I was not perfect, or that I wanted to take my clothes off in front of rooms full of strangers. All I could hear was the pounding of my heart and an urgency that seemed to be seeping out of my bones.

Up until that point, my whole life had been an attempt at becoming something I was not. Sure, I had talent and passion, but training and working to be an administrative assistant do not prepare one well for the stage. I knew from an earlier, somewhat disastrous dance audition that if I was not showing up in my fullest capacity, I would not be included. So I immersed myself. On my way to and from work, I listened to music and imagined what moves I would do to different flourishes. I played with choreography to nail certain moves dead into the rhythm of the songs. I came up with ridiculous, hilarious themes that would make me chuckle to myself on the subway. I practiced, got gigs, practiced some more, and got better gigs. And I built a beautiful, colorful career of which I am immensely proud.

Becoming a burlesque performer challenged my conditioning through the sheer forces of joy, sensual delight, and beauty. In the act of stripping, I peeled off the restrictions that had been cultivated in my body and mind, and from the generations that preceded me. I carry long lines of privilege in my bones, but it is a heavy cloak that carries deprivation in its very warp and weft. The stage is the first place I ever felt a deep part of me open up and be received in my wild uniqueness and imperfection. All of the subtle cues I had been studying over my life in order to be a good girl, to be socially acceptable and enjoyable in high-adjacent society suddenly became a palette of possibilities for me to inhabit onstage. Instead of strategically deploying my trained arsenal of behaviors to keep myself safe and hidden from humiliation, I embraced exposure and turned it into a job. I can take up all the space I want with whatever message or performance I am carrying in my body and heart. No one is waiting in the wings to crush my momentum. Sharing, reveling, and dancing my heart out are what makes me tick.

I still carry that old blindness with generations of conditioning to unwind. I may never work the whole way through it. As a recovering perfectionist, that is a hard thing to walk with, but the path itself is paved with reminders to keep focusing on the joy. Being judged is not the same as having my life threatened. Being shamed is not the same as being physically harmed.

By using the weary tropes of thinness, access, and beauty as key pieces of our worth and identity, we are holding ourselves back from our own evolutions that we so richly deserve. When we afford any attention to these rigid, body-as-worth concepts, we do nothing to relieve the pressures that suppress our wild, sacred gifts of self-expression. Challenging these crusty old concepts is the first step, and it all begins with our own relationship to ourselves and giving ourselves permission to be messy, sensual, imperfect, and marvelously human.

Burlesque taught me how to strip away the deeper beliefs that I was unworthy, not enough, and somehow bad or wrong simply because I was expressing myself however I wanted to. The roars and cheers of the audience were the acknowledgment I had been craving, and as I got used to hearing them and trusting that they were real, something in me forever relaxed.

I have deep, eternal gratitude for my stripper siblings who support, love, and cheer me on even if I feel like a walking hot mess. The fierce, protective love I feel in those dressing rooms activates my willingness to take chances, be weird, and uphold the same for others.

As someone who grew up a good white girl, it took sex, rock n'roll, performance art, and a choice to celebrate my body to make me realize how wildly limited I had been. It took me getting literally naked on stage in front of rooms full of strangers and dancing my heart out to realize that the constructs I had so dutifully obeyed were rooted in control and harmful conditioning that allowed my ignorance to go unchecked and even rewarded. Celebrating our bodies and their truth without hindrance or limitation is the essence of liberation.

Chapter 14

"REQUIEM FOR A STRIPPER'S SUITCASE"

by Stacey Clare

Of all the questions I have been asked during my fifteen years working as a stripper, "what's the worst thing that happened to you?" trumps the lot.

It feels like a coiled spring, loaded with stigma, immediately revealing the attitudes of the person asking it. The question is asked with an expectation that as a sex worker, I must have multiple instances of awful events to draw from. It's often asked without awareness or sensitivity that it may be triggering for me to recall, without warning, the details of things I'd rather forget, and may have stored away in some deep recess of my memory for good reason. People asking this almost always have some horror fantasy of their own in mind, involving abusive customers (maybe even assault), projecting onto me each time this question comes up.

My answer has been crafted over many years of dialogue and experience. While interactions with customers over the years have proven to be a mixed bag, the most upsetting thing that ever happened to me didn't involve a customer at all. And, more to the point, while the memory still smarts today, I am grateful for the event that inspired me to choose the path I'm on now.

The story begins in Shoreditch, East London. In 2010 I moved to London from Scotland, where I began stripping in 2006. Four years of dancing in Glasgow and Edinburgh clubs had served me well, but London was a different ball game. An already-over-saturated market meant clubs were overcrowded with workers and competition between dancers was tight; a change in licensing laws in 2009 meant there were less venues to choose from. The global economic crash had a further knock on effect, leaving more people in dire straits and less money to go around. This had the unfortunate effect of giving more power to bosses and owners of clubs who had no problem treating us as a disposable workforce. And with the business model already tipped in their favor, it meant we had very little power in the workplace.

I'd not been living in London for very long before I heard about a venue called The White Horse. It turned out to be a family-run business, and the head of operations was female. Three generations of women from the same family lived upstairs above the pub, giving the place a proud, matriarchal vibe, despite the predominantly male audience. The customers seemed to be an even mix of local tradesmen and city bankers (for whom Shoreditch had become a sort of playground for the super-rich). Pints were poured in vast quantities as wide screen TVs silently played sports or news headlines; a pool table in the back and several framed pencil drawings of legendary East End boxers all appealed to the male clientele. Yet, underneath the recognizably masculine characteristics of the venue, a subtle femininity was purring away quietly all the time.

The first time I walked in, I kind of fell in love with the place. A pole dancer was in the middle of her act, which was spellbinding to watch. Huge mirrors all around the stage reflected her image back from multiple angles. She was petite, lithe, tanned skin with a short-cropped pixie hairdo and wearing white PVC thigh-high boots, exquisite in her artistry and doing pole tricks that took my breath away. Her physique was astounding as she performed with such precision and prowess that I was instantly inspired to want to work anywhere that hired dancers like her. I filled out an application form at the bar, answering questions that focused more on my hair color, tattoos, and breast size than whether I had any experience of dancing. I handed it back over the bar, and the lady I spoke to, who turned out to be the proprietor, Sue Bristow, told me she wasn't hiring at the moment, but she'd let me know.

I was glad to get a call back not long afterwards and happily went in to audition. After performing my turn on the stage, I followed Sue into her office. She didn't mince her words when she sat down and said, matter of factly in her thick, Barbara-Windsor-Cockney accent: "I'm not sure, you're very thin aren't you? You've got nice tits though." She sort of sang the words "nice tits though" in a high-pitched inflection that I'll never forget as long as I live. She was herself a much bigger lady and I wasn't sure how to respond. I figured I could be as frank in return, so I said, "Well, I haven't got an eating disorder if that's what you mean. I've got my lunch in my bag." I reached down and pulled out a Tupperware box of sandwiches from my bag as evidence, which was all quite bizarre, but seemed to do the trick. She offered me a trial shift in the upstairs club.

The White Horse at that time was actually two venues in one. Downstairs was the White Horse pub, with pound-in-a-glass strip shows: pints, tits, loud cheers and lads, lads, lads. Upstairs was more understated with dark leather seating, Chesterfield armchairs, low lighting with candles and pink washes, that felt more like a private gentlemen's club. The mood was altogether more genteel; it even had a different name—Blush. I passed my trial shift and settled in to working at Blush quite quickly. Conditions were generally good; money flowed reliably and I began to find friends and community there. It was run fairly, and many dancers I got to know had worked there for a long time, because it was the best club to work in when it came to a safe, relaxed, and respectful environment. House fees (the amount of money strippers are expected to pay to work in a venue) were always affordable, and the number of dancers per shift was limited to avoid overcrowding (which was a better environment for customers, as it meant less dancers hustling and competing for tips).

But it wasn't long before I came up against Sue's despotic managerial style. Despite the relatively safe and respectful working environment, we were all still vulnerable to Sue's unpredictable moods. She was old school in many ways and there was no question that she ruled the roost. But this meant she could sack anyone whenever she felt like it, and she used this threat as a management tool. I saw her sack someone for being ten minutes late, despite the dancer being a brilliant performer and a firm favorite with many regular customers. I knew of another dancer who was sacked because of a haircut. There was no real appreciation that performers dance to the beat of our own drum, and that ultimately we were self-employed—so why should being ten minutes late, or getting an unusual hairstyle, be grounds for dismissal? The problem all along was the lack of regulations and no recognition of our rights in the workplace. As precarious workers, we could be fired any minute.

For whatever reason, Sue didn't like me. I liked working there but the threat of losing my job hung over my head like a sword of Damocles the whole time, and as result I suffered from stress. After a couple of years, in 2013 I experienced ongoing health problems that meant I had to take time off work. When I told Sue I was going to have to take a break, she astounded me by being uncharacteristically sympathetic—it turned out she also suffered with chronic health problems and so understood completely. Weird.

On top of ill-health, I was also going through a lot of personal upheaval. Precarious work wasn't the only source of stress, as unstable housing was taking its toll as well. I was moving from one overcrowded, neglected, and altogether unpleasant rented house share in Homerton to an over-priced, poorly appointed, noisy flat on Broadway Market. With all the disruption I'd forgotten about a suitcase I'd left at work. In that suitcase was my entire collection of stripper costumes, from my very first dress to my latest bargain finds. To say this suitcase was valuable to me would be an understatement—it didn't just contain clothes, shoes, and accessories, it also held all my memories, bad and good, from seven years of dancing. It wasn't clear from my health problems whether I would be able to dance again, so it felt like a very precious cache to me.

The items in the suitcase closest to my heart included a number of long gowns. Stripper gowns are like a parody of a ball gown. Some strip clubs used to have a rule about wearing long dresses before midnight, to imply a semblance of modesty (as though fulfilling an almost comedic male fantasy that at midnight we suddenly transform into lust-fueled lingerie-clad nymphos and start dry-humping the fixtures). But as with any other outfit worn by strippers, less is more, and stripper gowns reveal as much flesh as conceivable, with as much cut-away from the design as the fabric will allow.

The first gown I ever bought was a classic example: a black skirt, split at the front to just above the knee, and then simply a black boob tube and some tiny black straps wrapped round my torso, all connected down the front and stitched onto the skirt. I paid £80 for that dress, which came with a thong, all handmade by a lady who made a career from designing, making, and selling stripper dresses, bringing them into clubs, and setting up a stall in the changing rooms. It felt like a lot of money at the time, and it turned out to be a real investment as it lasted for years. I had to reinforce the split above the knee several times, since that was where it took the most strain from walking around in it. But it was a real friend.

Another barely-there silver gown was designed with a halter neck top half connected to a skirt with a metal ring, which was split all the way up each leg and held together with more metal rings. This dress looked best when it was worn without any underwear, and I made plenty of money from taking it off. Another favorite dress was a leopard print backless gown that, instead of a skirt, had long fringe which didn't cover anything, showing off my legs and arse while still complying with the "long-dress" rule.

So many of the outfits were second-hand, since there was always a strong culture of passing outfits on. This sharing and giving-away culture is a huge part of what creates sisterhood among dancers. In fact, I can barely remember a changing room that didn't have one or two clothes hangers displaying an outfit for sale, indicated by a handwritten note (£20 ono, Clara) and sometimes an accompanying phone number. So much of my stuff was bought from other dancers, or gifted, or salvaged.

There was a hot little number I bought from Bambi, aka Felicity Logan, who went on to be an international pole-dance star. She'd been dancing in Australia and travelled to Adelaide for the Clipsal 500, a major annual supercar-racing event. Strippers came from all around to entertain the tens of thousands of punters that descended on the town, and many clubs required dancers to wear special grid-girl outfits, with black and white chequered designs. Bambi was selling her grid-girl costume, black yellow and chequered hot pants, and a long-sleeved crop-top with a zip down the front. I wore it with a black WonderBra and left the zip half undone, which made my cleavage look amazing. It was a cool investment of £10 or £20, and I must have earned thousands back from it.

There was a red set of lingerie that I used to wear with a huge thick red feather boa, made from real ostrich feathers, that was another second-hand bargain bought from Silvia, a Brazilian queen who had been working at the White Horse for years. I remember being given a couple of tiny sequined string bikinis, one navy blue, one turquoise blue, that became firm favorites for a while. There were some amazing Coco De Mer lingerie sets that I'd bagged at an annual clearance market. They would close the shop for a day and charge £5 entry, and we'd rummage through mountains of stuff that they wanted to get rid of, weird sizes or mismatching sets that if you knew how to use a needle and thread you could easily modify and make work. I got a suspender belt that was made of clear plastic, and a gorgeous black bra with gold metal rings and matching pants that were XXL, which I altered by hand to fit me.

There was a neon pink, fishnet body stocking that I rescued from a bin, after another dancer, Erin, had rejected it. I took it home, washed it, stitched up the holes at the toes (that was presumably the reason she binned it), and made such a ridiculous amount of money from it, that I almost couldn't believe I'd ever bothered paying for other outfits. It was ripped at the crotch and since it was fishnet it left nothing to the imagination; I was basically naked apart from the tiny neon-pink thong I wore with it, yet customers paid to see me peel it off my body despite already being able to see right through it. Strange.

There were two pairs of black, thigh-high PVC boots, which weren't cheap but were cheaply made, that I destroyed by pole dancing in them. They had seven-inch heels, which added to my 6'1" height, meant I towered over every customer, intimidating them while I collected their pound coins in my pint jug before getting on stage. It turns out finding boots to pole dance in is a problem because bending at the knees strains the zipper, which eventually gives way. When the first pair I wore broke within a couple of shifts, I complained to the internet fetish footwear company that sold me them, who just sent me out another pair. When they broke just as quickly, I was forever trying to make the boots last longer, having to glue or stitch bits of them together or cut them open to keep the zip going.

There was a purple tube dress that was my absolute favorite number, a simple mini dress with skinny shoulder straps, slashed into thin slices up both sides of my body, which again looked best when it was born without any underwear. I used to wear that with the black boots and dance to "Whole Lotta Love" by Led Zeppelin, or "Archangel" by Burial. There was another long black gown, made of gauze and covered in jewels, that worked best with my hair pinned up as I danced to "Need Your Love So Bad" by Peter Green's Fleetwood Mac. There was a killer black corset that cinched my waist so perfectly, which I found in a second-hand designer outlet, my favorite shop in London. It was in the basement underneath a hairdressers in Angel, and the ceiling was so low I had to stoop down in some places to get in there. The lady that ran it was from Romany heritage, and always had time for a bit of a chat and gossip—I told her all about the strip club customers, and she told me all about the rich ladies who brought her their designer throwaways. I always found something incredible and I clearly remember when I found that corset—she only wanted £40 for it, but brand new it would have cost hundreds.

Another extremely lucrative outfit was a matching bra and knickers set with a black and white zigzag-striped pattern that I had found in Ann Summers, and a pair of shoes with the exact same black and white zigzag pattern from Irregular Choice. They went with a black lace suspender belt and whale-net stockings with lace tops from Ann Summers. I wore the hell out of them when I used to work up North in Newcastle, wondering if black and white stripes would subliminally attract Newcastle Utd football supporters.

There were countless other things: push-up bras, pairs of stockings, suspender belts, and bikinis … the tools of my trade. I'd put them all in the suitcase, with some outfits separated neatly into clear plastic sandwich bags (a tip picked up by observing other dancers), which helped locate some of the harder to find items, especially if they were black. I think back fondly to all the times I've frantically rummaged through a selection of black outfit pieces for a particular black thong, or black stocking, often in the dark in a cramped changing room, eventually having to empty the contents onto a (usually) filthy floor while a tyrannical manager or DJ is calling my name. When I worked in The White Horse, the changing room was actually big enough for everyone and I formed a habit of just emptying the contents of my work bag into the middle of the changing room floor, to the bemusement of the other girls, as I hurried to get ready and then just leaving it there for my costume changes.

Doing shifts in Blush, I would maybe change once or twice throughout the night, but if you were doing a shift downstairs in the pub, you had to bring five outfits, because you'd be doing five stage shows throughout your shift. There was always an expectation that you'd make an effort and Sue wanted us to look glamorous. When I initially started working there, Sue wouldn't let me dance downstairs—I apparently wasn't glamorous enough. I resented this since the shifts downstairs were shorter, and you could make about the same amount of money from doing five shows in a four-hour shift as you did upstairs from hustling and talking to customers for six to eight hours, which was exhausting. I tried explaining this to her once, but it was clear she didn't know what I was going on about—having never been a dancer, she couldn't relate.

During my time off, there was a bit of an overhaul of the business. She spent some money renovating the pub downstairs, and got rid of the pool table from the back room and turned it into a private area with low podiums and poles for us to offer private dances downstairs as well as the stage shows. From a management point of view, it made good sense to consolidate the two spaces into one, and it was less of a headache for her. The upstairs space was lying empty for months, and a few months before I fell ill, I approached her to ask if I could try running a life drawing class with strippers performing pole tricks and modelling for the class. Again, she surprised me by agreeing to the idea, and this was how a number of us began building a little community that later grew into the East London Strippers Collective.

The life drawing class was a success and it took off quickly. Within a few months we were able to fill the room upstairs and Sue was happy to see it flourish, although it wasn't always plain sailing and she was still just as aggressive in her management style.

It was on one of these evenings, whilst running a life drawing class, that my-worst-experience-on-the-job took place. Unbeknownst to me, Sue had got a bee in her bonnet and gone on a rampage to get the downstairs changing room tidied up. She'd told dancers they had a week to collect their things from the changing room and anything left would be thrown out. I hadn't been getting Sue's messages because I'd been taken off her rota while I was ill. As I arrived for the class, I'd noticed Sue and another member of staff were chucking out bin bags, but it wasn't until one of the dancers on shift came upstairs with a grave look on her face and whispered to me, so as not to disturb the life drawing class, that she thought Sue had just thrown out my suitcase. She knew it was mine because she'd seen the red feathers when it was opened—apparently everything that was going to be chucked out was put in the middle of the changing room floor as a last chance before it got thrown out. A number of dancers recognised it as my suitcase, but didn't think to message me until it was too late.

I ran down stairs to the changing room with a feeling of horror in the pit of my stomach, asking everyone where my suitcase was. It was missing from the corner of the room where I'd left it. Several faces looked at me with sympathy, while one of the bar staff told me the rubbish had just been put out at the front on the street. I bolted out the back door and ran round to the front pavement on High street, only to see a rubbish truck driving off into the night. The grief and despair I felt were so overwhelming; I almost vomited on the street. The rest of the evening passed by in a blur, as I went into shock, mortified at the sense of loss compounded by how close I'd been to saving my precious belongings, had I just known even minutes earlier what was happening.

I remember trying to confront Sue that night, but she just blocked anything I had to say. It was like she could see from my face how upset I was, but simply turned away. After I'd calmed down, I tried appealing to her, to see if there was any part of her that cared. I steeled myself to walk into the office and attempt to communicate to her how much losing my entire career's worth of possessions had caused me distress. I promised myself I would remain calm and composed, and it worked— it didn't blow up into a screaming match at all. But what I did discover during that conversation shocked but didn't surprise me. That day Sue revealed to me the sheer contempt she felt toward dancers. "They're *disgusting*" she said in her sing-song Barbara Windsor voice, "the stuff I've found in them changing rooms is *rotten*." No doubt, neglected stripper changing rooms can end up foul places; I had seen it for myself plenty in the past. But I just sat still while she mouthed off, without a shred of awareness or compassion that she had just discarded someone else's treasured possessions.

I had the feeling in that moment that she didn't see me as a person, just a target for all her years of pent up rage. It seemed incredulous that someone would continue doing a job that she hated for so long, managing a group of people that she clearly despised. I left the office with some clarity. Whilst I never got an apology, I had enough insight to realize that she didn't have the capacity to give one. And I found enough strength and compassion to realize that she, at some level, was also suffering. I was able to carry on with the life drawing classes and eventually go back to dancing at The White Horse once more.

It was a year or so after this that I eventually learned more about the history of The White Horse, and heard a story that explained everything. Sue had been brought up in the flat above The White Horse by her mum and dad, Pauline and John Bristow, who had run the pub since 1982. John had managed the pub during an era that was harsh for women in the workplace, and treated the dancers that worked there accordingly. Sue learned how to be a despotic manager from his example. John eventually walked out on the business and the family when he ran off to Spain with one of the dancers—a blonde with nice tits. Pauline hit the bottle, Sue's brother did a bunk, and so she was left to pick up the pieces and take on the family firm. She did well out of it until The White Horse finally shut up shop in 2016, thanks to the relentless gentrification of Shoreditch pricing her out of the area. She went and opened a beauty salon a few streets away in Hackney soon afterwards. I smiled at this when I heard it—a beauty salon, of course. I could still hear her words, "You're in the glamour industry, girls!" ringing in my ears. It was probably what she wanted all along.

As for my suitcase, I still feel the sting of loss and the rage of injustice. Its value can't be calculated simply by counting the money spent on its contents. If I were a carpenter and my boss threw out all my tools, I'd have been well within my rights to take Sue to the small claims court for loss of earnings. But in an industry that doesn't recognize or respect my rights as a worker, that's easier said than done. Had I not been struggling so much, had I been less precarious I might have kept the suitcase closer to me, if only I hadn't left it there. If only this, if only that …

The upshot of it all was that it pushed me into action. When I saw, once and for all, that Sue didn't give a shit about my stuff and wasn't going to take an ounce of responsibility, I thought to myself, "Right, we're on our own then." It was time to stop hoping and waiting for bosses and managers to improve conditions for us. The following year in 2014, a group of dancers, all known to each other from working in Hackney, formed the East London Strippers Collective. Four years later in 2018, a national trade union branch was formed for strippers and sex workers called United Sex Workers, and in 2020 an East London dancer (both a member of the union and ELSC) won a landmark legal case, setting a legal precedent and winning workers' rights for strippers in the UK.

The sex workers' rights movement is growing slowly but surely, and there are countless other stories of appalling workplace abuses. Mine is not the worst, but it still feels incredibly personal to me. I was recently shown a social media post of a fire started by a strip club manager, burning old shoes and clothes left in the changing rooms—an act of dominance and violence directed at women if ever there was one. It's not just the loss of the objects, but the insult of my identity being literally thrown out like a piece of trash. All that was part of me in that suitcase, my carefully crafted stage persona, my ability to perform, earn, express, and exist—dumped in landfill. I hope that by writing it down I may finally put it to rest. I dedicate this story to the memories carried in that suitcase, to the untold joy it brought, to the meaning of every stitch, buckle, clasp, underwire, sequin, rhinestone, zip, feather, ruffle, and plastic high-heel. I still miss you.

Goodbye.

Intermission II

THE WHOOPEE CLUB

by Lara Clifton and Tamara Tyrer, with photos by Sarah Ainslie

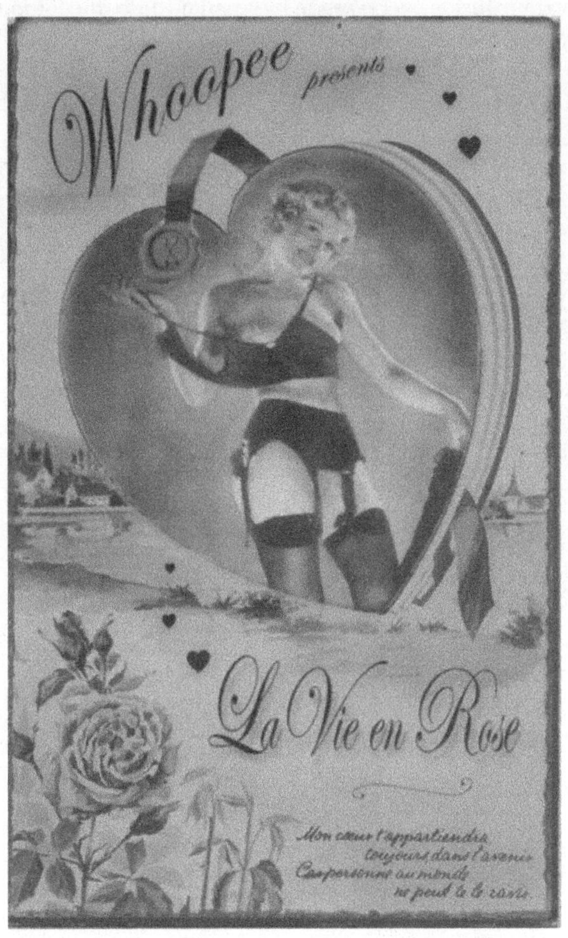

Image 21 "La Vie en Rose," The Atlantic Bar, London (2004) Show Flyer. Designed by Zoe Lloyd.

Tamara Tyrer and Lara Clifton, the creators of The Whoopee Club, re-visit the archive of photos taken by photographer Sarah Ainslie and share their memories. Between 2003 and 2009, *The Whoopee Club* created immersive and fantastical site-specific experiences, juxtaposing nightclub, live art, and dance with vaudeville, burlesque, and cabaret. Whoopee stood at the forefront of a new exploration of gender, gaining huge press attention concerning what it meant for women and men to perform burlesque on stage in the 2000s. Whoopee's performances were all-inclusive and non-binary, exploring femininity, masculinity, drag, gender, and everything in-between.

> **Clifton**: This is classic Walter. He looked like such an English gentleman. Every act was unique and had a theme, but there was always striptease. Walter came on stage looking exactly like Steed from *The Avengers*. He had the best strip trousers ever—made by Atsuko Kudo, the famous designer who happened to be his wife—that ripped off sublimely, revealing beautiful ladies underwear.
>
> He put tassels on his balls, he had tassels on his pants, which he twirled around. He used stress balls as tits. He would throw them around, and part of the job of stage manager was to find the stress-ball tits.
>
> This is at The Cobden Club and you can see in the photo there's a guitar—we performed with a live band, The Flash Monkey.
>
> **Tyrer**: The Cobden Club was perfect, wasn't it? It had that beautiful stage with a red curtain. It hadn't been redone or modernized at all. It was quite a magical place really.
>
> **Clifton**: Tamara found The Cobden Club as an extra in a film. It was a venue neither of us had heard of and it was like it was waiting for us.

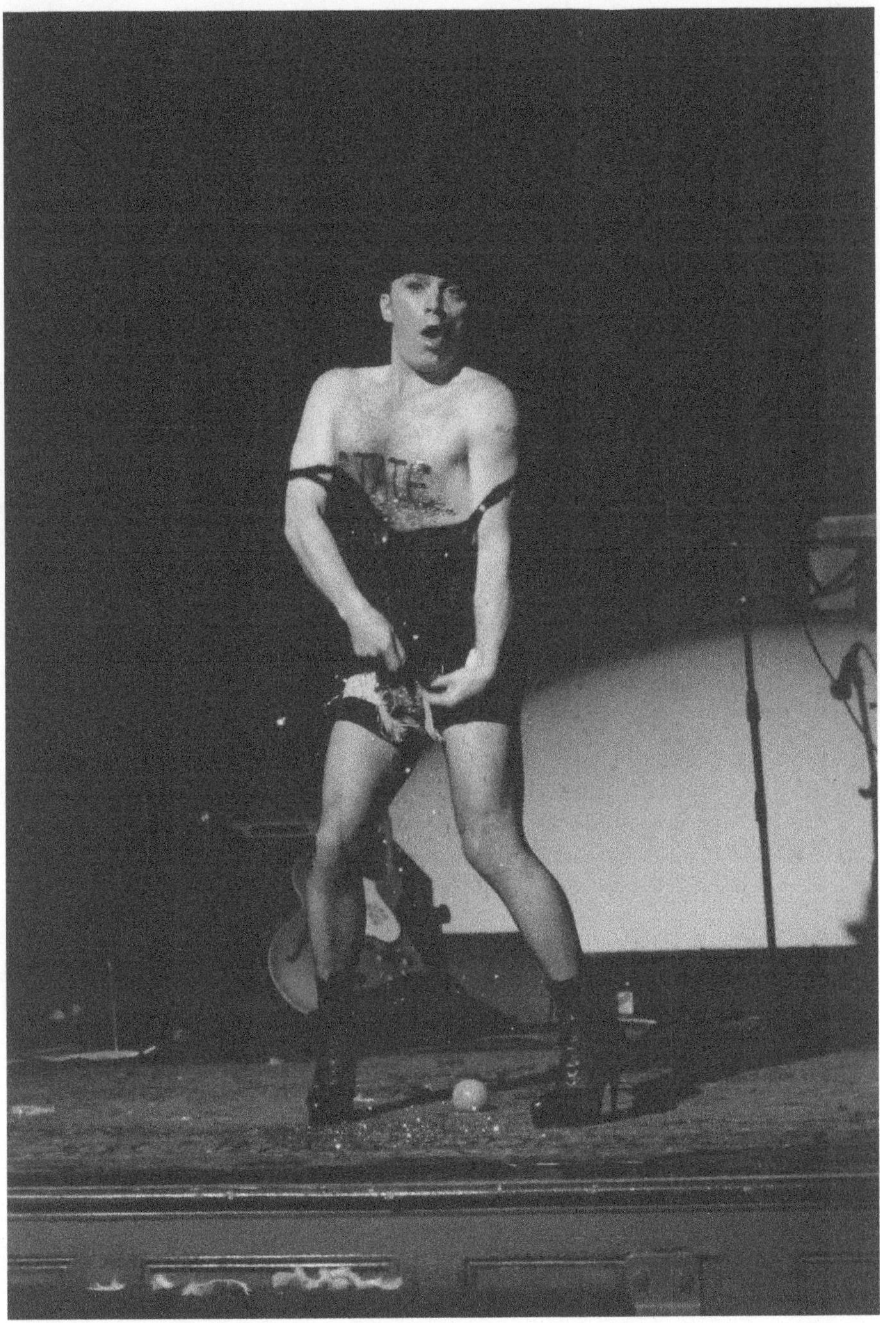

Image 22 "Mr. Sandman Bring Me a Dream," Walter, The Cobden Club, London (2003), credit Sarah Ainslie.

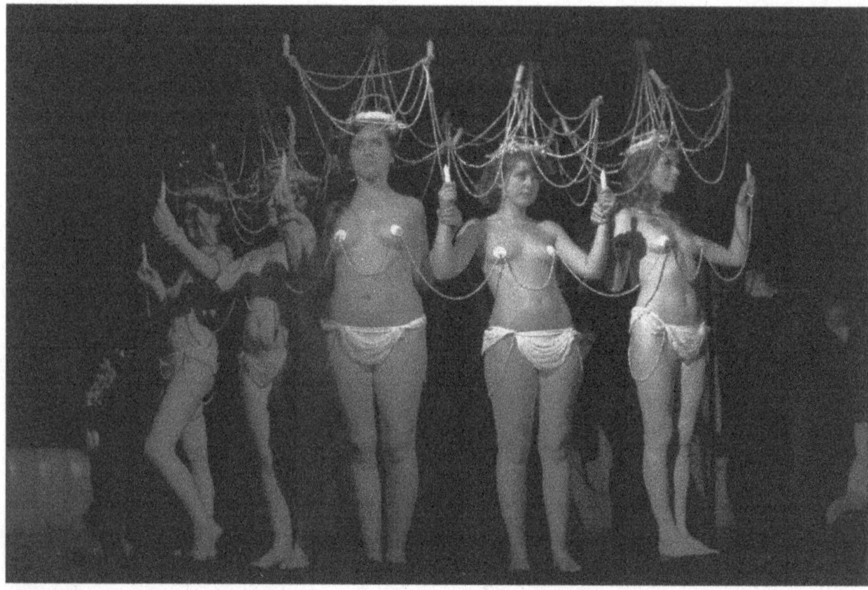

Image 23 "Phantasmagorical" (left to right: Shimrit Elisar, Miss Lily Dumont, Lara Clifton, Tamara Tyrer, Miss Lily White), Cafe de Paris, London (2004), credit Sarah Ainslie.

Tyrer: This is our take on the living chandelier tableau vivant. I had researched this tableau from historical photos and books. The music was "Aquarium" from Saint-Saens' Carnival of the Animals—a magical classical piece.

Clifton: My step-sister Kirsta McSkimming made these fabulous chandelier headpieces. We were joined together so we had to move in the line as one and hold our tits to keep the tassels from being pulled off. We would get the massive giggles!

Tyrer: We would always do a tableau vivant at each show. We researched old performances from Music Hall, from the turn of the century, or from Paris and Berlin, and re-vision it in our own way. The tableau vivant would be a classical painting or an image I'd seen in a book. And that was the same with our dance troupe, the Whoopee Beaux Belles.

Clifton: They had a different remit, didn't they? The Whoopee Beaux Belles were a subverted showgirl troupe.

Tyrer: Yes, I was fascinated by Busby Berkeley. Sometimes we took inspiration from an old image of chorus girls or a Busby Berkeley film, but we re-envisioned it.

Clifton: We weren't trying to do recreations—we scoped out little bits of history, the kind of images and the aesthetics and the feeling behind the acts, and re-created that into something that was current.

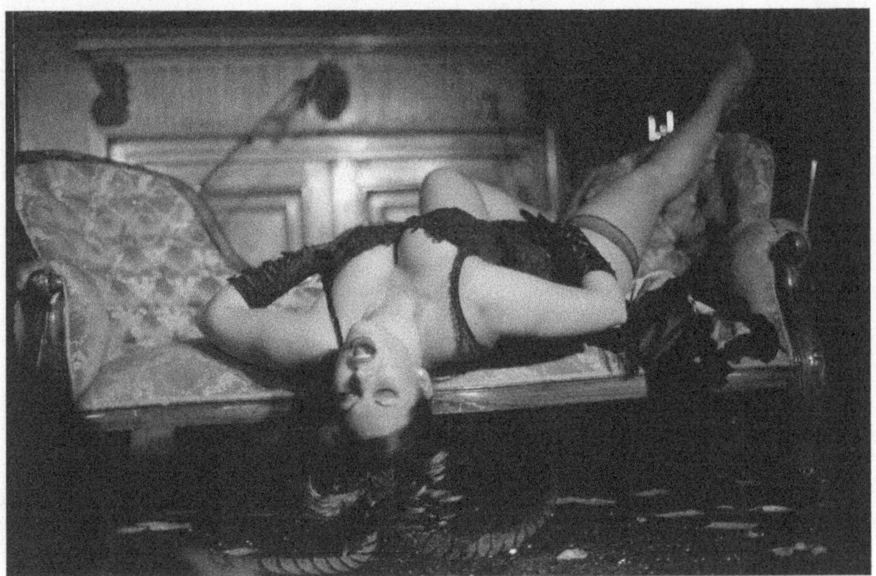

Image 24 "Rancho Notorious," Immodesty Blaize, The Atlantic Bar, London (2004), credit Sarah Ainslie.

Clifton: This picture is from a Western/cowboy-themed night at the Atlantic Bar. People remember it as one of our best, but it was also one of our worst turnouts. That also made it really intimate. This picture shows the sexuality, the intimateness of this exchange—you wouldn't realize that this scene is being played out in a room of 500 people.

Tyrer: We were selling out the Cobden Club, so we found the Atlantic Bar in Piccadilly, an amazing, Art Deco venue with three rooms. But it didn't have a stage. So true to our very ambitious tendencies, we had to bring in a stage and lights.

Clifton: Immodesty evoked that really sassy, old-fashioned burlesque. She was so charismatic and completely owned a room every time she stepped on stage. She quickly became the figurehead of the burgeoning UK neo-burlesque scene.

Tyrer: And she was also really good at making costumes for our themes.

Clifton: When I first met Immodesty, she was also a visual artist. She'd fashioned materials such as lace, beads, and feathers as representations of female genitalia. She was interested in the aesthetics of female desire, the sensual and the ultra-feminine. At that point, Immodesty Blaize was a character for her, and part of her art. But at some point, Immodesty Blaize took over as the main show.

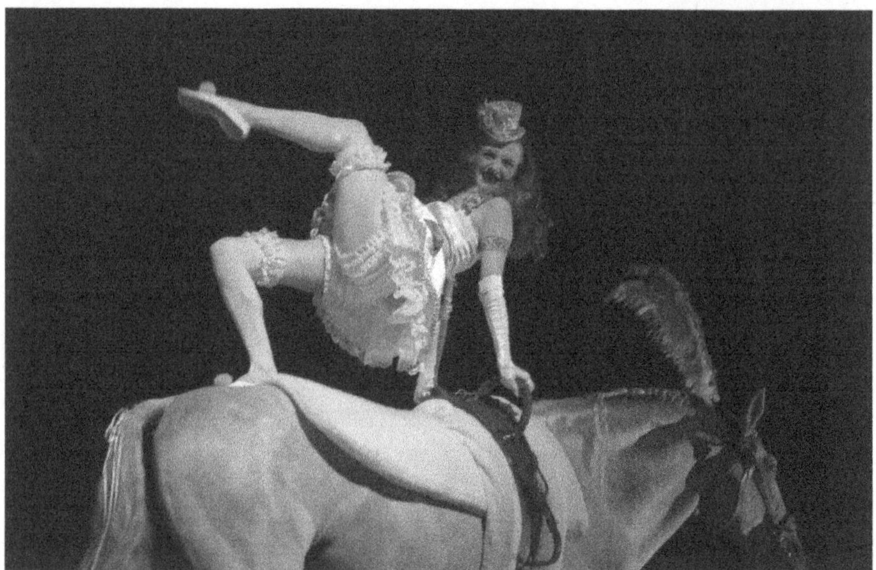

Image 25 "Wink the Other Eye," Miss Lily White, 2005, The Hackney Empire, London, credit Sarah Ainslie.

Clifton: We were getting bigger and bigger all the time. We were going to do a show at the Hackney Empire and we noticed a big door at the back of the stage. We asked what it was for, and they said, "It's a horse door." Lily White had mentioned she wanted to combine her burlesque and equestrian skills one day. So we contacted a place that provided horses for films. This horse, Roman, was lovely.

Tyrer: At the Hackney Empire, we took away the seats so people were still standing even though we were in a theater.

Clifton: Whoopee shows didn't have cabaret seating; they were standing-room only. So it had more in common with nightclubs than the velveteen burlesque clubs that sprung up after. There was this feeling that the audience and the stage were merged. It felt very theatrical but everyone was part of the performance.

Tyrer: We didn't want that kind of stiff atmosphere with the seats.

Clifton: I think that this is what burlesque is about. This is kind of funny, isn't it? Being on a horse. There's a joy there.

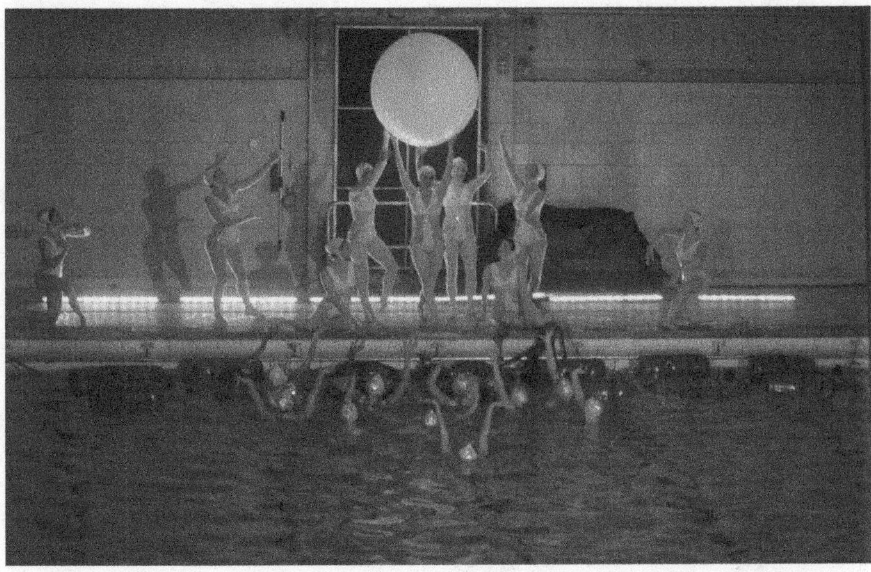

Image 26 "Nymphaeum," The Porchester Baths, London (2006), credit Sarah Ainslie.

Tyrer: "Nymphaeum" was another ambitious plan. I had an obsession with doing a show with synchronized swimmers. We searched for venues and we managed to get quite a bit of funding from the Arts Council. We found a synchronized swimming team and we created this show at the Porchester Baths in West London. That was another immersive theater experience—there was a small swimming pool next to this one that the audience were led around. And we had performers in the foyer.

Clifton: There wasn't any speaking in this show. It was an aesthetic sensory experience attempting to immerse you inside an actual Busby Berkeley film.

Tyrer: We had thirty dancers, including the swimmers, performing around the pool. We taught the dancers to do simple synchronized swimming to re-enact a Busby Berkeley sequence. We also brought in incredible lit fountains that came out of the water.

Tyrer: We were also exploring female mythology. The show was like a performance installation. The audience loved it.

Clifton: The audience came with us on whatever journey we created.

Tyrer: But it's a shame really, that it was just for a few nights and then that was it.

Act III

DIALOGUES

Chapter 15

"What Pleasure Actually Means: An Interview with Intimacy Director Yarit Dor"

by Alexander Millington, with Yarit Dor

Intimacy Direction and Coordination has appeared more frequently since the 2017 MeToo movement, with more credits for the role appearing in theater, film, and television productions. Organizations such as Moving Body Art and Intimacy Directors and Coordinators have been working with production companies and individuals to create intimate scenes for stage and screen in a safe and consenting environment, without stifling the creative vision of the director or the production. Intimacy Direction is built upon The Five Pillars of Safe Intimacy Rehearsal Practices for Stage Performers: Context, Consent, Communication, Choreography, and Closure, and are offered as guidelines to be followed to assist productions in creating a safe working environment for everyone involved in producing and choreographing intimate scenes.[1]

Intimacy specialists Chelsea Pace and Laura Rikard describe theatrical intimacy in their book, *Staging Sex*, as including "the whole spectrum of physical intimacy, including hugs, hand holding, kisses and simulated intercourse."[2] With all these forms of theatrical intimacy, the context of the play can be taken into consideration; is the scene consenting? How much simulation is required? What is the relationship between the characters? And what is the dramaturgical function of the scene? But intimacy can also simply be a look across a room, the touching of hands, familial or platonic. These are all considerations that may be addressed by any director of a performance, but the addition of an intimacy professional in the rehearsal room is to offer an extra safety net. They aim to create the scene fitting within the overall aesthetic of the production while maintaining an environment where the performers are only involved in what is necessary in order to avoid any potential discomfort or triggering. Intimacy Direction is equally about the mental and emotional well-being of the performers and crew involved as it is about the physical well-being and creative vision. Many intimacy professionals compare the role of an Intimacy Director (ID)/Coordinator (IC) to that of a Fight Director/ Coordinator.

Yarit Dor is a world-renowned ID and IC who has written extensively on the subject. She is a co-founder of Moving Body Arts, specializing in a variety of movement disciplines for stage and screen, and has been credited with being the first ID in London's West End, and has been credited with being the first ID in London's West End. Yarit originally came from a movement and fight choreography background but found herself regularly being asked to observe intimate scenes of choreography in rehearsals. Yarit has spoken on the topic of this blending of roles as movement/fight/intimacy choreographer, suggesting that her role is more of a "movement practitioner" as all three roles are "mutually supportive."[3]

> **Millington**: There have been numerous articles published over the last year about Intimacy Direction and Intimacy Coordination, and they jump between the two titles. To start, can you tell me, is there a difference between an ID and IC and if so can you say what the key differences are?
>
> **Dor**: Yes. I think a lot of articles, when they write about the practice they tend to write about it for the screen, which means it is an IC really and sometimes it is mis-written. From my perspective one of the main differences is environment. Intimacy Direction is for live performance, Intimacy Coordination is for screen, television, and media.

The process is very different. In live performance, Intimacy Direction is much more similar to a Movement Director role or a Fight Director role. It is a role that is long standing throughout the rehearsal process; they go into tech, go into dress, go into previews, go into press. If it is a rehearsal process of three to four weeks, you will be there either one session a week or more sessions depending on the level of involvement that the production needs or the actors request, or the director requests. From my perspective, it is the place that allows you to get more into it, to sink your teeth into the role. Anything from giving support, to mitigating communication, to lowering risk factors, to facilitating choreography, consent, agreement, all of those things. You have more time because they see you on a regular basis. Also, for emotional safety, because you see them once a week or more, you can observe how they are doing with the material. Trauma triggers can appear either an hour later, immediately later, a week later, or a couple of weeks later, so in an Intimacy Direction process you have more time to invest in those conversations. If they need modification of the material, you have that time to do it.

With Intimacy Coordination, I would say 70 percent of it is coordination; it is not choreography at all. The facilitation and choreography aspect is only 30 percent, so it is much more of an admin kind of role of consultation; there is a lot of paperwork involved, and it has liability connected to it: from pre-production, production meetings, supplying their protocols, giving them paperwork, chatting with the director, sometimes with the writer or actors, negotiating, and liaising with the departments. To put it in parity with another department it is like the Stunt Coordinator would have to get the equipment, communicate with all departments before a crash mat is brought in or wire work is going to be used, risk assessments and all of that. It is kind of the same for an IC. The equipment such as modesty garments, paddings that are going to be used on the day, all of that is discussed way in advance. We try to do rehearsals before the shoot day as much as possible. Then on set there is a private blocking rehearsal; it is a short rehearsal, not a three-hour session which would be for theater.

> **Millington**: And like you say, you do not get that connection as much as you would with Intimacy Direction; if you are there for weeks and weeks, getting to know them, getting to know any triggers and things like that?
>
> **Dor**: Yes, and after the day, we do offer a check-in chat with them. I think that some ICs call it a "Feedback Session" or "Feedback Meeting." I try and stay away from "Feedback" as a word, because some actors hear it and are like "No, I do not want to have this meeting." But basically, just a very quick conversation to see how they are doing several days later and whether they need any process changes if we have other intimacy scenes coming up soon. So, if there are any triggers there is a bit of time to delegate and refer back to the Producer with some thoughts if they need it. But the process in itself, I would say an IC knows how to adjust the body for camera very quickly. It is a very fast process, especially if using barriers or mats that go between performers; you literally have three seconds to give a note. On set if there is anything that you need to attach to the costume, or if the costume department is not going to use the costume again, you can rip it and slot a barrier in. It is a one-solution moment, whereas on stage you cannot do that. Performers have to be able to perform in the material from beginning to end, hiding external barriers, or working while hiding their modesty garments. It is a much more sustained process, I would say.
>
> **Millington**: And presumably, if you are using modesty garments and things like that, not only have you got to wear it for the whole performance, but you have also got to do it night after night, eight shows a week for however long you are doing a run?
>
> **Dor**: When you look at an intimacy scene on screen, what you see are bits from different takes that were edited together well. But, if you look at one take, not all of it works. Suddenly you see a gap, suddenly they stop performing, suddenly they start laughing. So the editor just takes the best bits of each take and merges it together. Whereas on stage, you can't do that; the actors need to be able to perform the whole thing and feel comfortable. It all has to tell the right story for the play without a stop-start.
>
> **Millington**: You said an ID is present for multiple weeks throughout a production. Is that standard practice at the moment or is that an ideal scenario? I know there are times when an ID can be called last minute if an actor wants one.
>
> **Dor**: A bit of everything. A lot of directors have the awareness nowadays when they see something in the script and they already interview people in their pre-production, or pre-rehearsal period. Sometimes, they do start rehearsing and then the actors request. It also depends on the amount of action; so for example, if the show only has a moment of a kiss, they might

want the ID there for the session that we facilitate the kiss, and then maybe come back to see a run and check in with the artists to see how they are doing. But they might not necessarily want to pay them for a tech rehearsal, a dress, a preview, a press night. I guess it is an ongoing conversation with those performers to see how much support they need. It is similar to a fight; if there was only a push, they would not want to necessarily pay someone to come in for a session. So, it does come down to budget.

Millington: As an intimacy professional how would you define "intimacy" for the stage? Sometimes it is just a kiss, is an ID needed for just a kiss, or a hug, or anything like that? What do you class as "intimacy" and when an ID might be required?

Dor: In my opinion there is "best practice" versus "available practice." "Best practice" is yes, we would want to be in the room when there is a kiss because a kiss is not a simulated action. It is quite vulnerable for most performers to perform. If there is non-contact-based intimacy like attraction, chemistry, I would say, personally, unless the director feels like they are not getting anywhere with their notes or exercises to facilitate non-contact chemistry or attraction between characters, they should consider bringing someone in, but essentially that is acting notes. When an ID does come in to facilitate exercises for that, it does look much like movement and acting exercises. Whereas I think that the minute that there is physical touch and physical intimacy, that is where the question has to be whether an ID needs to come in or not. Context will say a lot because if it is someone sharing news with the other person and they are just placing a hand around a shoulder for example, I think directors and actors have enough capability of negotiating that. I do not think that necessitates an ID.

If the scene turns intimate, the context, the intention of the characters is different; to get attention, to get closer, to profess they are in love, there might be little tweaks that the ID can offer, but we need to consider what is the highest risk. Highest risk is nudity, simulated sex, kissing, making-out, contact with chest or genitals, any sex props that are needed will be quite triggering for people so that needs to be considered. Any moments of simulated sexual assault or sexual violence have to have a Fight Director present, so I would say the most recommended is the higher risk content. There is a kind of middle ground regarding certain moments that might be sensitive to people and that requires a conversation of why does that professional need to be in the room?

I do not agree with some IDs that we are there to facilitate safer practices around derogatory language or race in the rehearsal room, I think that is not an ID job; I think that might be a cultural consultant or drama therapist or psychodramatist. Again, if the context connects to intimacy, then yes. I do not think that we are an umbrella term for all versions of safety in the rehearsal room.

Millington: Is cultural awareness something that an ID should still be aware of, without necessarily being the sole person in the room responsible for it?

Dor: We cannot control the cultural change into consent culture, an equitable culture, just by ourselves. It has to be everyone in the room taking that kind of training and educating themselves. For example, today I chatted with a TV producer who has a montage of different intimacy scenes and a character who is written on all fours. The performers will have to perform simulated vaginal penetration from the back, while using a vibrator. Both characters who are portraying that are people of color, whereas the rest of the characters in the montage performing other sexual positions are white. And the sexual positions in the script for them are not sexual positions that show dominance, that show animalistic nature, that shows any sex props, so for me that was something that I brought up and I said, "I think you need to have a think about this," because it can come across supporting certain stigmas and taboos that we need to consider when we portray intimacy of humans full stop, versus associating something to a particular gender or a particular skin tone.

Millington: So, again, it is not necessarily putting your own thoughts on that but making the director and production team aware of how this *could* be perceived.

Dor: That is why it is important to have EDI (Equality Diversity and Inclusion) training for an ID because they need to be aware that certain choreographic positions that people want to explore might support certain stereotypes within our society, and it is up to us to shift things. But if there is a scene, for example, where a Black character is being tortured by a white character and the context is not intimate, let us say it is violent, slaps or whips or whatever, I do not think that necessitates an ID. It necessitates a Fight Director or Stunt Coordinator, and I would bring a psychologist or trained therapist or a cultural consultant to help that scene.

Millington: ID pre-dates the 2017 MeToo movement, though it is something that has been brought it into the light since the movement. To what extent has the industry's understanding of safe practice developed in response to MeToo?

Dor: Before the MeToo movement, intimacy for stage was being researched and the intimacy choreographer or ID role started to gain attention through the work of Tonia Sina and Adam Noble in the United States. Both come from a stage combat and movement for actors lineage. In the UK, Vanessa Ewan wrote a chapter in her book about transferring stage combat safety concepts to intimacy and movement work. Many of her movement director students at Royal Central of Speech and Drama studying there before MeToo told me about how she incorporated intimacy in the movement classroom way before she wrote her book. Those are just a few of the names out there that started exploring it before the MeToo. So I think these roles would have ultimately emerged by themselves; however, the MeToo gave a massive push and changed working practices quicker. The minute theaters and filming studios had to rewrite their policies, the ID role and IC role fitted in as an added solution and proof for a working culture change.

After MeToo hit the UK, Equity wrote their Agenda for Change mentioning IDs, Intimacy on Set shared their guidelines at the time, and drama schools were implementing safe space policies. HBO pile drived the American version of intimacy coordination onto British sets and shortly all other studios started to follow suit. Suddenly there was a boom of awareness and a search for people doing these roles.

> **Millington**: You have worked with Equity's Intimacy Working Group and co-wrote the guidelines for safe practice in theater productions with regard to intimacy and sex on stage. How responsive do you think the people and the organizations have been to the guidelines now they are in place? Have there been a lot of people acknowledging them and taking them up in their own theaters?
>
> **Dor**: The intimacy for stage guidelines is found on Google search and a link lives on Equity's website. But when we published them in April 2020, Covid was on everyone's mind. Attention to it was dropped and I do think a bigger push and visibility of these was needed. Many theaters in the UK still don't really understand the role of the ID, the level of involvement, and what paperwork they should be requesting or expecting from a trained ID.

I think the intimacy community in the UK was more successful with the BECTU Shooting Intimacy Guidance since TV producers and directors are more active in attaining new knowledge. Whereas in theater I'm still meeting Artistic Directors that get me on a show and admit they never worked with an ID and it was a request of an actor or agent. I can't tell you how often I get the "oh I just want to make sure it is instinctive and not staged." That, of course, then leads us to talk about how consent works and what framework we can use to achieve their vision along with the boundaries of the performers and stage management.

More information about intimacy direction in the UK is needed. I'm currently writing a book and I know the BECTU ICs Branch is looking into adding a sub-branch for IDs.

> **Millington**: How do you work with actors who are not experienced or comfortable with having an IC on set? How do you work with directors who still follow that traditional rehearsal room hierarchy?
>
> **Dor**: As the IC coming in, you are giving a service, so as a service provider you need to have a certain level of flexibility and collaborative intention; however, it is also important that you know what the boundaries of your role are and what you cannot be flexible about, which is safety. Being part of the first generation of UK ICs, I've experienced what many have—the resistance stage and the invitation stage. Some shows like *Adult Material* took me in with open arms and valued my support from the get-go (invitation stage). Whereas other shows were armored for several weeks before they warmed up to the idea that I exist and maybe I am useful after all (resistance stage moving into invitation stage).

Trust is a big part of it. And I get it—why should they trust someone when they've been in the industry for 10+ years already and have directed or acted intimacy scenes without an IC? I can understand them and they are entitled to the status they acquired through years of hard work. I don't want to patronize anyone or shame their practice. The key is how you approach each actor or director and how you try to incorporate their needs in the process. Some actors treat me like a coach and seek out my notes between takes; they are proactive and happy for me to help them tweak their intimacy movements. They know I'm there for them and so they use me as their eyes on the monitor. Others want their independence as actors. After the private blocking rehearsal, they want less coaching and less check-ins since that interrupts their process and how they access emotion. They may need a more "hands-off-approach" with less information stimuli. That process is valid, and it is super-important to respect it if we say that we champion consent.

This similarly happens with directors. Some are super-collaborative to an extent that they want you to stand next to them and they tell you what didn't work and actually ask for your opinion and suggestion. Others want you standing further behind them or even on a different monitor, tucked away in a neighboring tent and welcome your thoughts or suggestions only a couple of times. Others are super-shy and uncomfortable with intimacy, full stop, and they rely on you to empower them that their notes are valid and ask you what they are missing to make it look better.

Some directors are happy for you to rehearse the intimacy a couple of days earlier with the actors even if they themselves cannot make it, whereas others refuse for any pre-shoot day rehearsals to be done without their presence. Every show is different; every director is different, and even if you worked with a director more than once, their practice evolves and they may want to approach it differently.

It is important that no assumptions are made about people, having flexibility with safety, and consent at the helm is the way forward I think.

> **Millington**: Are there more obstacles, do you feel, as an IC on a set working with a director versus working with a theater director on a stage or in a rehearsal room?
>
> **Dor**: All directors are super-creative beings and storytellers. No matter whether in live performance or screen, the biggest obstacle, in my opinion, that differentiates them is the environment and its stress levels.

In theater, the director will have three to five rehearsal weeks to shape the work. They will be dealing with cast difficulties, their own struggles, etc. The stage management team and Assistant Director are a huge support system for the Director. And it is only natural that stress rises in the last week of rehearsals and in tech. Previews is when many directors really get a grasp of what's working and what needs work. Many are in their element when they are in the theater because then they can chisel the piece more because they can see it fully with costume, lights, music, etc., so the stress is still there but morphs a bit.

I do believe that the stresses on set are slightly higher. You know that slogan that "time is money"? That is real, and if you are filming with film, not in digital, then every minute on film is money, literally. I think understanding the psychological effects that a film director is under is key. They work outside of shooting hours as well, meaning sleeping hours are few, they have a huge amount of emails from all departments asking them questions in all hours of the day, they are under pressure from producers and writers to shoot what is scheduled and not miss story beats, they watch the rushes and already think of the editing while also planning ahead and so much more. So sometimes when you see a film director that has a minute of downtime, they are on their phone answering emails. The First AD (Assistant Director) is almost like a Company Stage Manager or Duty Stage Manager, so their job is to manage the set and push the director to go faster so they can stick to the schedule.

Compassion and empathy are so important to foster in our creative spaces. Everyone is struggling in their own way and if we can support each other and understand the other roles around us, that helps immensely.

> **Millington**: What obstacles are still in the way for IDs to create a safe and consenting work environment, particularly within British theater?
>
> **Dor**: First obstacle: in order to create a consent culture, everyone involved in the production has to be educated in the basics of consent and intimacy work in order for the change to happen fully. So how do we make sure that "basics to consent and intimacy work" is available in higher education, in theater spaces, and on set?

Many educational institutions or film production companies ask workers to do online learning in EDI Awareness, Gender Awareness, and Mental Health Awareness before starting their job. Maybe that is the way to go? Doing a "basics to consent and intimacy training" that all students, performers, stage management, producers, and directors take before they start their work on the show or course. How do we provide this training to the industry at a low price or free so it is accessible to everyone?

Second obstacle: where do producers and stage management learn about the role of an ID and how to work with them, such as what paperwork the ID provides? What knowledge and training does an ID need to have, and what training avenues are there at a high standard? What are the going accepted rates for their work? Where can producers find them? What are the basic terms of their service?

Third obstacle: budgeting for an ID on the show. Avoiding last minute hire in the midst of rehearsals which then affects production budget.

Fourth obstacle: looking at the bigger picture, intimacy, fights, and well-being go hand in hand. What is the full duty of care chain on the show? From production mandatory training to mental health resources to Dramatherapist, ID and Fight Director, etc., all these create a framework for safer practices which then allow braver storytelling.

Millington: When you have check-ins with actors, you prefer to say "check-in" rather than a "feedback session," and when you are choreographing a scene, you will use physiological or biological terms. How important is the language that you use?

Dor: Language is key, and it has to be a collaborative process and take people's needs into account. Working language needs to be agreeable with everyone. Session number one is a good time to discuss "how are we going to call X," "what are we as a company comfortable using in our working language vs script language?" "This script has specific actions, what language do we, as a company, want to use for them?" Because not everyone likes, for example, the word "making out." Some prefer "nogging," although it is more slangish. Some may want to call it "they go into more engaged contact." Our process has to be trauma informed and part of that is giving people choice and agency in the space. The boundary is that all language needs to be respectful and clear. Using the word "boobs" might be disrespectful and loaded for some people. Some may want to call it "chest tissue," or just say "front ribcage." It is important to give the company responsibility over their practice so they can develop it further outside of the intimacy rehearsals and use it throughout the rehearsal process. I stay away from being "language police" or forcing a sanitized version because nothing is really sanitized; language is subjective and often affected by culture or place. Even use of tone or pitch changes the meaning and the impact of words. So we accept that it won't be perfect; it won't work for everyone at all times, but we collaborate and raise our awareness together.

For example, I worked with a transgender performer for whom "breast" was not ok for them. Although it is an anatomical term, they were like, "ooh, not sure." So I said, "What would you like to call it?" We can even call it "a purple." I do not mind as long as we both know what we mean and we are comfortable with using that term. It is not triggering anyone then; we are creating a safer process. For me, I immediately go into more anatomical language, but still only anatomical to an extent. I would not say "sit on your ischial tuberosity," because no one would understand what I mean. So it needs to be something that is still accessible. Sometimes you will find that you need to follow it up with another word that describes the same thing, so if they do not know what to offer, you then can give them two options.

Millington: It is having that open conversation so that everyone is aware of what it can be called, what everyone is comfortable with it actually being called, and how you are going to use that moving forward. Like you said, even if you give it a different name, like a purple, as long as everyone is aware of that and everyone is comfortable with it.

Dor: When you look at the play *Closer*, there is a moment in which Clive asks Anna how Dan's genitals were, and that scene has very strong abusive language.[4] When performing the play, actors will need to use that language; they cannot shy away from it. But they can signpost, or notify, the company when they want to use the play/script language. For example: signpost "ok, for a second, if everyone is ok, I am gonna jump into the language of the script, how are we feeling about that?" If they say yes, then you give the nod with the language of the script. When you reach the end of the section, then you go "ok, I am going to go back to our working language, how are we doing?" So then you are not saying the script is wrong or bad, but you know, that signposting is a tool that we are using. Signposting to tap into script language and to tap out of it and back into rehearsal language is crucial as a safety tool that allows separating the reality and life of the play from our own. On *A Strange Loop*, I came in to see them in week 1 to introduce some consent and intimacy rehearsal tools.[5] One of these was language. This musical uses strong, derogatory language in much of its libretto and songs. The main intimacy in the "Inwood Daddy" song has a cascade of strong language so "placeholder language" to substitute words in the script was extremely useful for them and afterwards chose to use it in non-intimacy scenes too. When working on the intimacy choreography for "Inwood Daddy," we all practiced working language vs script language and used placeholder language instead of difficult words in the script. Each time I came back for another intimacy session I saw that they slowly decided as a company to gradually stop using placeholder language when performing the libretto and songs in order to get used to the actual script language. It was their decision as a group as to when and which words and they checked in with the people in the room and theater before doing so. It was beautiful to see how they created a safer and braver process as a company. I merely offered some tools around language boundaries but they were the ones that shaped their rehearsals and their path of settling into the script. Intimacy practice is not hand-holding people through it, I don't want them dependent on me because that is a power dynamic. It is empowering them with tools that they can use. They take what is useful for them and make it their own. That is beautiful to watch!

Millington: I once worked on a production where there are three monologues discussing intimate and sexual acts, similar to Anna Jordan's *Freak*.[6] Do you feel an ID might still be required in a performance where the discussion of sex and intimacy is there, but it is not actually depicted, or would that then come back more to the facilitation about the language and consent rather than the choreography and the movement?

Dor: That is a very good question and I do not know whether I have the answer without giving that question to the performer. Knowing you as a very conscientious director, you would create a safer rehearsal process for that performer. So I think it is more of a question beyond the tools that we are using if there is anything that you need that an ID could provide? It might be that they just need a third person that is not connected so much to the production to bring stuff up to. My initial instinct is I would hold back whether that needs an ID and first open the discussion with the performer.

Millington: It is about assessing if they are comfortable with the language, about what is being discussed and how they are going to perform it and the movement that might go with some of that performance, but it does not have any interaction with other performers.

Dor: Yes, and I propose adding a Plan B which they can perform should they feel unsafe. I think it is a conversation with the performer and there is nothing wrong in bringing in someone the minute that there is a need for someone. I think my fear is that people will latch onto an ID just because they are fearful that their Director's not going to be safe, and yet they have not met the Director, they have not started rehearsal, and the Director still needs to gather everything and hold everything and find their own process that is safe for themselves as well.

Millington: Is it ever appropriate for the play's Director to also serve as ID or should those roles be separated?

Dor: The double role in shows is dependent on the amount of power the role has and where in the hierarchy does it exist. The Director is above the creatives; they are almost the point of the pyramid and they have the overall vision of each scene and the show as a whole. The creative needs the Director to steer them. An ID is a creative that balances safety and artistry with safety being the priority. If a performer says to me "I do not know, I am not comfortable with this," then as an ID my safety and consent button goes off and I start thinking of counter offers that can honor their boundary and still tell the story. I need the Director to confirm whether the counter offers could tell the story in a way that fits the show. The Director is my artistic compass really. If a Director is also an ID on the same show, they will hold the power of a creative plus the "boss power" or "hire-fire power." That endangers the performer's ability to confide in the ID role which should advocate for them. Plus, I think the Director will get super-frustrated when their vision and cast boundaries are at odds. Sometimes you need the person in the middle to help solve it.

There are many IDs that are also Fight Directors or Movement Directors on the same theater show. It is less common on film sets that this would happen. This double role gives them more presence in the rehearsal process but these roles are in the same level of hierarchy since they are all creatives. Doing two creative roles can help establish a safety framework that can work in both fight scenes and intimacy scenes for example. Whereas when these are done by separate creatives, each might have a different approach to safety, consent, and touch within their work. So it has a useful aspect to it as long as the individual is conscious that more presence in rehearsals sometimes gives more reverence and power to that creative. Awareness is key.

Millington: Is there anything you wanted to say about some of the work that either still needs doing or what you would like to achieve?

Dor: I think the activist in me wants to see more mainstream plays about everyone and everyone's intimacy. We are missing stories about intimate relationships and stories exploring pleasure. All people become vulnerable and learn about themselves through intimate and sexual connection. Let us not leave people out or revert to taboos or stigmas. Whether we like it or not, our choices and how we stage intimacy matters for through art we educate others about life and therefore about sex, love, toxic relationships, care, passion, harm, and obsession. I think how intimacy is portrayed is connected to how humanity is portrayed in a vulnerable way and for certain humans to not be portrayed as vulnerable, kind, connected, appreciative humans that enjoy action rather than not enjoy it, what actions lead to, pleasure and what pleasure actually means. Depiction of intimate connection should not be owned by a white body, or a slim, muscular body or an able body or a tall body or a young body. Perfection does not exist so we can enjoy the imperfections of intimate relationships and the complexities of consent and ecstasy. I think it's about time; don't you?

Notes

1   "What Is an Intimacy Director or Coordinator," Intimacy Directors & Coordinators, https://www.idcprofessionals.com/blog/what-is-an-intimacy-director-or-coordinator/.

2   Chelsea Pace and Laura Rikard, *Staging Sex* (New York: Routledge, 2020), 73.

3   Yarit Dor, "Yarit Dor 'I Don't Like to be Boxed In—I Don't Want to be Just a Fight Director," Interview by Rosemary Waugh, *The Stage*, October 28, 2019, https://www.thestage.co.uk/features/yarit-dor-i-dont-like-to-be-boxed-in–i-dont-want-to-be-just-a-fight-director.

4   Patrick Marber, "Closer," in *Patrick Marber Plays: 1* (London: Methuen, 2004), 177–298.

5   Michael R. Jackson, *A Strange Loop*, Directed by Stephen Brackett (London: The Barbican Centre, June 17–September 9, 2023).

6   Alexander Millington, *Three Way* (London: Playdead Press, 2021); Anna Jordan, *Freak* (London: Nick Hern Books, 2014).

Bibliography

Dor, Yarit. "Yarit Dor 'I Don't Like to be Boxed In—I Don't Want to be Just a Fight Director." Interview by Rosemary Waugh. *The Stage*. October 28, 2019. Accessed September 2023. https://www.thestage.co.uk/features/yarit-dor-i-dont-like-to-be-boxed-in–i-dont-want-to-be-just-a-fight-director.

Jackson, R. Michael. *A Strange Loop*. Directed by Stephen Brackett. London: The Barbican Centre, June 17–September 9, 2023.

Jordan, Anna. *Freak*. London: Nick Hern Books, 2014.

Marber, Patrick. "Closer." In *Patrick Marber Plays: 1*, 177–298. London: Methuen, 2004.

Millington, Alexander. *Three Way*. London: Playdead Press, 2021.

Pace, Chelsea and Laura Rikard. *Staging Sex*. New York: Routledge, 2020.

"What Is an Intimacy Director and Coordinator." Intimacy Director & Coordinators. Accessed September 2023. https://www.idcprofessionals.com/blog/what-is-an-intimacy-director-or-coordinator/.

Chapter 16

"FEELING LIBERATION: QUEER GESTURES TOWARD A WORLD WITHOUT RAPE IN JADELYNN ST DRE'S 'CHOREOGRAPHIES OF DISCLOSURE'"

by Julia Havard and Jadelynn St Dre

The following is an excerpt from an interview between scholar-performer Julia Havard (ze/zir) and artist, performer, and organizer Jadelynn St Dre (she/her), who have built a relationship through community collaboration, conspiring, and dreaming together. Central to this discussion is the exhibition "Choreographies of Disclosure: What the Mind Forgets," conceived of and curated by St Dre, and shown at Pro Arts Gallery (Oakland, 2019). The project engaged queer and transgender survivors of sexual violence in community-building and art-making processes, involving visual art, performance, music, dance, poetry, video, and voguing. The project was a tender, intimate artistic investigation, both into how the traumatized body is perceived and how the somatic expressions of an individual who has experienced assault are interpreted.

Content note: This interview explicitly and intentionally discusses sexual violence and the aftermath of trauma as well as its framing in an artistic medium. We understand that you, readers, are the experts of your own bodyminds and experiences.[1] We invite you to take care of yourselves and enter and exit our conversation in ways that feel appropriate for you.

The bolded text at the beginning and close of the interview are excerpts from "Choreographies of Disclosure." These snippets of text were transcribed from St Dre's interviews with queer and trans-people who experienced sexual violence. Recording and interpreting both gestures and spoken words, St Dre created these poetic choreographies, which were then consented to by the participants. These choreographic texts, which comprised the core of the project, were projected on the gallery wall during the exhibition's residency, and played in recordings read by each survivor-participant, which accompanied responsive art works, as described in the interview below.

many quick gestures in succession
IN. OUT. SWOOPING through bouncing fingers first pointing toward you, then at me,
I have to remind myself

right hand comes to scratch left shoulder

That I am talking about myself

**right hand up to shoulder level, bent at the wrist, palm down
and then up to scratch the soft spot behind your right ear
(*twitchtwitch*).**

to keep myself here. with you.

Memories

   **Your "s" drags long and finishes with that
slight smile**

a memory

   Said like a preparation

     like a

       trigger warning

a memory

**A story to tell someone as you're riding down the street,
voice strained yet full of breath.**

*Millions of memories,
everywhere.*[2]

Havard: Where did the seed for this idea originate?

St Dre: The project was conceived in 2016. One of the questions circulating in my brain at the time was related to my own stories of violence: Is there something about that first moment of assault, which for me was when I was four, that somehow left a sort of residual pattern on my body that then could be recognized by other people that wanted to harm me, and that's why it kept happening? Almost like if you touched a piece of tissue paper with your finger, and you could see the residue from your hand. Was there something about that first touch that left an imprint that then was recognizable? Was there something about *me*?

I wondered—if I watched myself in the act of telling these assaults, what insights might I find? So I set up an experiment. I brought in a guy that was working with me at a restaurant, who I truly liked and trusted enough but didn't know very well. He was a cis-straight guy, and I was like, "Come to my studio and sit down, and I'm going to tell you about every single sexual assault that's ever happened to me. I'm going to record myself while I'm doing it. I want to see what my body does while I'm talking about it, because I have no awareness of it." That is where this project started.

Havard: It brings up a lot for me, listening to this origin point. I've had those same questions about myself as someone who's had multiple experiences of sexual violence: "is there something about me?" which always has felt like a shameful question.

St Dre: I hear you.

Havard: It sounds like you're saying, "Okay, that question exists. Let's see what the aesthetics of the telling and of my body in remembering are."

Because gesture, I don't think, is separable from aesthetics. You're bringing something to the surface that's been buried and doing that in a non-narrative way, which I think is actually really radical.

St Dre: Yes. The title "Choreographies of Disclosure: What the Mind Forgets" considers gesture as an entry into the ways that people who have experienced sexual violence tell their stories. "What the Mind Forgets" references the saying "What the mind forgets, the body remembers." Often, survivors of violence are unable to remember aspects of what happened cognitively, although they may experience somatic memory through startle responses, sensory activation, or other physical reactions, which can be disorienting and cause the trauma to be exacerbated.

Havard: Is this why you decided to focus specifically on choreography as the modality for this piece?

St Dre: I wanted to use choreography to uplift gesture as a primary means for communication that is to be trusted just as much as we trust words, which are just expressions of the memories and sensory stimuli that we have access to. I wanted the primary mode of expression to be gesture, to create a different template for how we tell our stories, especially when our stories include trauma.

I really related to what you just shared, when you said, "What are the aesthetics of telling and also the body remembering?" I think that's what's really complicated about the disclosure of trauma. An undeniable component of many sexual assaults is the unstated imperative, "don't tell anyone." So silence becomes a companion phenomenon to sexual assault.

Havard: That's so true.

St Dre: Although it started from these origin points that so many of us experience—why did this happen to me, am I implicated, can people tell I have experienced this—this first experiment grew into a method that sought to affirm and uplift the stories of other survivors in my communities who are so often silent and pathologized, specifically queer and trans-folks and BIPOC (Black, Indigenous, People of Color). I was interested in exposing the dissonance that gets in the way, not just of telling the specifics of what happened, but of being able to express, to be in grief or be enraged, or to feel righteous in the telling of our stories and how they relate to who we are.

After that initial experiment, I devised the method for the larger project. I am queer and biracial, one parent white and one Mestizo, and most of my community are LGBTQIA2s+ (Lesbian, Gay, Bisexual, Trans, Queer, Intersex, Asexual, Two-Spirit, Plus) folk and BIPOC. We've been historically absent from the larger narrative around sexual violence in the mainstream movement—not because we're not here. We're absent because of systematic erasure. The particular ways that we experience this kind of violence and the intersections at which we experience it are not highlighted or affirmed, and thus we are denied reflection and site-specific care. Because we are oppressed not just because of who we are but also because

of who we love, who we do or do not want to fuck or because any aspect of
our desire or lack of desire falls outside of the "norm." Sex is weaponized
against us constantly as a means to keep us small, silent, and invisible—to
erase us. This project was created as a place for us to speak our traumas not
just through our words but through our bodies, our gestures, our rhythms
and tones of voice. Through speaking to each other in these ways, we
were then able to be reflected, understood, and seen, which then inspired
dancing, laughing, celebration, dreaming, visioning.

Havard: Already it's clear that relationship-building is at the core of this
project.

St Dre: Absolutely. The folks that I invited in to work with me are all artists
themselves and members of my community. For the survivor collaborators,
I worked with Vanessa Rochelle Lewis, foundress of the performance and
education initiative Reclaim Ugly, who is also an incredible poet. I invited
in Reaa Puri who is a spectacular filmmaker, and one of the foundresses
of Breaktide Productions. I also invited in Jo Howard who is a brilliant
filmmaker and phenomenal pole dancer. These are all dear beloved ones
that I had worked with on direct actions in the past.

I invited each of them to share aspects of their stories with me, and this
invitation was very open. They chose the location and the manner in which
they told me. While they all used words, Jo shared precious objects with me
that he took out from a cigar box, tenderly showing me each piece over the
course of our conversation. Reaa did a film of herself engaging in different
aspects of meditation and breathwork, and then talked me through the
different things that she was experiencing during filming. Vanessa and I
had a conversation in one of her best friend's living rooms. I made it clear:
I didn't need all the details of their stories. We actually don't need all the
details of what happened to someone in order to access empathy, in order
to access truth and understanding.

These interviews took place over the course of six months. I met with
some of them only once, some multiple times, and each time I had their
consent to video and audio record the interview. After completing these
interviews, I created transcripts, recording what was said, as well as
physical expression, somatic rhythms, patterns, and qualities of movement.
I have pages and pages of this huge notebook describing gesture, like,
"Left hand raises and touches back of neck." Then I inserted my own
interpretations of what the gesture may have wanted to express in written
word—gesture and the lens through which it is interpreted. Then I
inoculated that with bits of verbal information, ways that the person would
describe their experience or feelings in their own words. These comprised
the different "choreographic transcripts," including my own. There were
four, which were then given to Bay Area artists to create a response work.

I want to stop here and highlight the fact that the people who were
involved and had experienced assault had complete control over this entire
situation. At any point they wanted to stop, we would stop. Every edit,

every transcript, everything that I wrote, I gave to them and asked their permission to use it. And when it came to choosing an artist, I gave each of them a collection of artists from which they could choose to create the response work.

Havard: It seems like you constructed a process that was deeply consensual over time, which is also undoing this construct of the singular legalistic moment of consent.

St Dre: That was the intent.

Havard: Also, when you talk about gesture versus interpretation, I'm reminded of a conversation in disability culture circles around audio description, that goes, "Okay, are we describing the anatomical way that the body is moving or are we describing the quality of the movement? Can you ever take away the interpretive quality of that description?" You're doing something really different with the relationship between text and body that opens up questions of sensory access to choreography, which seems relevant in the context of both trauma and disability.

St Dre: Yes! That connection feels so clear. The work emphasized the question of access in many ways—who can tell their stories and why? Who is moved to listen and why? And how do we listen?

This is connected to the next phase of the work: the artist responses. My choreographic transcript was responded to by Lydia Greer, an extraordinary filmmaker and shadow puppeteer. Vanessa Rochelle Lewis worked with the visionary textile artist Angela Hennessy. Jo worked with brilliant photographer Quinn Peck. And Reaa Puri worked with Eliza Barrios, an incredible filmmaker and conceptual performance artist of immense depth and skill. The artists took these transcripts, read them, and created an artistic work in the method of their choosing in response to those transcripts. The only request in this process was that they be willing and open to have the work edited in any way the person whose story they were working with wanted. The artist would come up with a draft, the draft was given to the survivor collaborator, that person would then give feedback, and edits would be made.

This resulted in five different completed response works by these artists. Lydia Greer created a short film that was a montage of different archival clips from US government rape crisis films, horror films, and photography from the book, *Invention of Hysteria*, creating a potent commentary on unsatisfactory archetypes of trauma and traumatic gesture. Eliza Barrios created two works—a short film that was a collection of closeups of gesturing hands and bodies, and also a virtual reality component, where you put on an oculus, are transported to the middle of a tree, and listen to Reaa speak her choreographic text as you look around a park. These works spoke to fragmentation, remembrance, and the nonlinear quality of surviving trauma. Quinn Peck created a series of photographs that were based on scars that he found in nature and also autobiographical photos of himself, which included his top surgery scars, referencing the myriad

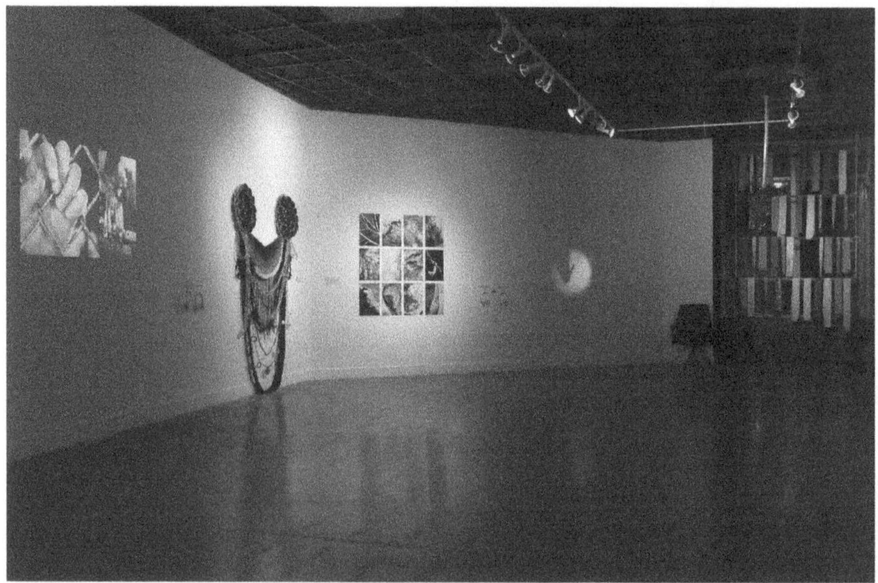

Image 27 Response works, artists listed left to right: *Hysteria* by Lydia Greer inspired by the choreographic text of Jadelynn St Dre, 2016–18; *Persistent Moons: Bodies of Survival* by Angela Hennessy inspired by the choreographic text of Vanessa Rochelle Lewis, 2019; *A Collection of Scars* by Quinn Peck inspired by the choreographic text of Jo Howard, 2018; *Interstice* by Eliza Barrios inspired by the choreographic text of Reaa Puri, 2018–19; Community Textiles by LGBTQIA2s+ residents of the Bay Area, credit Leslie St Dre, 2019.

survival strategies which exist in nature and in us all. Angela Hennessy created a large, ornate sculpture out of pieces of hair, including her own and Vanessa's, and copper and gold leaf, creating a form that could bear the weight of bodies in grief, bodies that survive.

These five response works, along with projected excerpts of the choreographic transcripts, composed the exhibition. Next to each response work were headphones through which people could listen to each survivor speaking the words of their own transcript. Anchoring the exhibition was a musical piece by LeahAnn Mitchell, also known as La Femme Bear, which she wrote in response to all of the works as a whole, her raw and powerful voice singing to our collective coping, and a mural by Leslie Dreyer that honored the collective identities of all who participated and the ways that LGBTQIA2s+ communities hold each other even as the world threatens to tear us apart.

This is a very long description to say that this project was a really sophisticated call and response. The method was very complex and required a lot of time, space, tenderness, and relationship-generating, which I was happy to do because what if our stories were held with that degree of tenderness always? What would it be like to have someone reflect your story to you in a way that was in your control, where you could recognize yourself? The complexity of the method is also why it took a year of organizing and then three years of incubation and development.

Havard: Thank you for tracking through all of those pieces. Hearing them all together, I keep thinking about what you were saying about choreography as entry. As dancers, we think about choreography as layers of movement construction. In this piece, I also see the many layers of movement, each piece with its own movement qualities, and then the tracking of this movement via text in the choreographic transcripts.

Regarding what you just said about how relationship is the methodology in terms of call and response, I was wondering if you could say more about your own position as a trauma therapist, sex therapist, and activist, and how that unique set of skills positioned you in this specific way to do this facilitation work.

St Dre: Caring about people's stories and building relationships is at the heart of how we manifest liberation, which is reflected abundantly in the work of so many incredible organizers and political thinkers in the past and present. We manifest liberation through interdependence, through deeply investing in each other. Relationship as a component of this project was always essential because it's the political ethic in how I was taught to organize, and that's also how I do my work as a clinician, as a support person.

Practically every person I have ever encountered that has experienced sexual violence, before they tell any aspect of their story, wonders: "How is this going to be received?" "Am I going to be believed?" That emphasis on connection, affinity, and audience and how we subsequently change or edit our stories is already in the room.

The other component that's really important that *Choreographies* wanted to emphasize is, how do we listen? What is our responsibility as individuals, not only to provide an actively listening ear but to pre-emptively set the stage for true listening, which includes an awareness of our own biases and the practice of radical empathy?

In *Choreographies*, we are creating the context for sparks of relationship, and within that context, seeing what sparks turn into flame. We are setting the conditions for queer and trans- survivors to receive the kind of witnessing, care, and empathy that allows for vulnerability.

Havard: This really resonates because you and I began our relationship through organizing the Survivors' Symposium at UC Berkeley, which aimed in part to create a space where that context for survivor-centered relationship-building could exist. There's so much detailed thought in this project around every level of how the relationships are held and that work of holding. I'm wondering what the impact was on you, of holding all of these stories and also all of these processes.

St Dre: I want to start by saying I did not organize this project perfectly.
  I hope that this project has other iterations, and there are things that I
  will hold in a different way because of what I've learned, a process that is
  hopefully a part of every project's growth. Some of the project's limitations
  were due to mistakes or other miscommunications, but some were
  definitely because I did not allow myself the same degree of care for my
  story that I facilitated for other people's.

  I'll give a personal example since I don't have others' consent for a
  community one. Lydia, who is white, created a response work to my story.
  The work was brilliant, and I truly treasure it. However, a question I asked
  myself after the project was, "Why did I not find another mixed person or
  another Latine person to respond to my story?"

  That was such a consideration for me in regards to the survivors of
  color, making sure that the artists that they had to choose from were
  artists of color, or that trans-folks could have a trans-person respond
  to their story, but, for me, I didn't even consider that. Because the
  histories of sexual assault and intergenerational trauma in my family are
  predominantly on the Latine side, it felt like a real missed opportunity for
  me to experience reflection in a different way, even though having Lydia's
  response is irreplaceable.

Havard: Right. As a femme who does a lot of care labor, asking for what you
  need, can be so difficult.

St Dre: Even knowing what we need or stopping to consider what we might
  need …

Havard: Part of self-care is pausing long enough to examine what your needs
  even are.

St Dre: Oh I love this. That can be so difficult for trauma survivors, to
  feel like we even have the right. My experiences of violence, over time
  and throughout my childhood, set the conditions for hypervigilance,
  compartmentalization, and dissociation to be huge survival skills that
  I now flex in the world. And you know what, I'm grateful for them and
  all of the ways they have helped me stay alive. We treat survival skills
  as pathology, as opposed to incredible skills that we've developed that
  deserve our gratitude and honor, in addition to our attention if they're not
  working for us anymore, so that we can turn down their intensity or find
  ways to transition them to a space where they're better able to support us,
  especially if they are impacting our ability to live fulfilling, present lives.

  Going through this process for me, while liberating, was also complex.
  In truth, I forgot myself in the process. I forgot that my story was a part
  of this—that I am a survivor too. What I described is very common for
  many survivors who do this kind of supportive work. Why do we so often
  annihilate ourselves in order to do the work of support? There is a true
  need to find other templates.

Havard: Yes. Seeing survivor skills as resources is really impactful and also
  undoes some of the pathologization of the ways that survivors have learned

to move through the world. I appreciate that you're not just making a work about survivors; you're in the work, you're inseparable from it, which I think is a very queer methodology of art-making. You change because of it.

St Dre: It speaks to a larger issue with anti-violence work: what is the importance, when we are people that have experienced violence, of having community? Not only facilitating it for the people that we're supporting, but building community around ourselves, having co-conspirators whose sole purpose is to hold you in a space of mutual, interdependent, accountable care. Where not only are you putting your energy outward caring for others, but you're also considering how you need to be replenished and experience healing in the process, as well.

And Restorative and Transformative Justice really makes the point over and over again of the necessity of community, underscoring too how we must consider the ways that people who cause harm are supported as well, so that the cycles of harm may truly be broken.

Havard: Okay, relatedly, I want to talk more about listening as a part of your methodology. It seems like you're thinking about listening as a practice invoking action, rather than listening as something passive. What work does listening do not only for the creators of this piece but for the audience?

St Dre: As listeners, we miss so much nearly all of the time. We will deny and ignore so much of what people are communicating physically and sensorily because of how deeply we prioritize verbal speech. We can't forget that somatics actually precede verbal language, if we have access to verbal language at all. The things that my body does in response to stimuli, in the act of listening, are at the root of the words that eventually come out of my mouth in response. That's why gesture is the primary conduit through which this project communicates. When we think about listening, we're not only talking about words or other forms of audible language, we're talking about making room for the entirety of the body and all the ways it communicates. In prioritizing gesture, we are making way for the roots of understanding.

Using the anti-violence movement as an example, we're also challenging the assumptions we make about what is understandable. For example, this idea of enthusiastic consent. I understand why it is used as a teaching tool. But, as many brilliant people have pointed out, what is enthusiasm? We have Disability Justice to credit for uplifting this, and questioning the way we listen is absolutely a Disability Justice issue. Whose expressions of enthusiasm are "readable" in a moment of vulnerability and emotion, activation, or somatic overwhelm? How can assumptions about the ways in which different people have access to or use different parts of their body or different modes of speech create a slippery slope that can sometimes lead to shame, silencing, or victim-blaming? Culturally, we prioritize gesture when it keeps people oppressed, but we prioritize language when it's on that person to then express and substantiate themself.

Being able to relate and empathize is absolutely critical for action and for movement. Think about mirror neurons and how amazing it is that when someone yawns, I often yawn after. Does that not translate to: If I see a person in a place where they are expressing pain or trauma, could my body not resonate with that and reflect it? What if they are expressing transformation and restoration? Would my mirror neurons not pick that up and would that not seed transformation and restoration in my body as well?

For example, if we're doing body scanning and I say, "Well in this situation, I was starting to feel afraid, and I had this heavy pit in the base of my stomach." Does that stomach clench not matter? Does that stomach clench not have so much information about the way that we relate to one another and about how we can then move more closely toward the eventual end of sexual violence as we know it, an eventual consistent, true, and radical form of site-specific consent?

Havard: Wow, yes, what if your stomach could listen to another stomach? I think in this responsiveness between bodies, listening with your whole body or listening with our broken bodies to each other's broken bodies, there's something really imperfect that also reminds me of the words left out of the title of this project, "the body remembers." There's a lot of space where language could be or may be even the memory of language. The language exists between the lines, but perhaps the body inhabits that space instead.

It's actually quite common in formal dance spaces and in improvisational dance to listen with a part of your body to someone else's body, and to allow the movement of someone else's body to inform your movement. When you're dancing in unison, there's this experience of feeling your body dance the other bodies and feeling those bodies dancing you. I keep coming back to some tools of formal choreography that actually seem deeply in line with some of this, like what is the potentially transformative work beyond discourse?

St Dre: Dance and Movement Therapy is predicated on some of that awareness. My question is, when we think about any sort of art form that has been institutionalized, when is it dance? When do we call it dance, and when do we call it listening, to reference the example that you just gave? Because then I'm thinking about partner dance. I used to do salsa and Lindy Hop swing …

Havard: Of course you did.

St Dre: Oh, it was so fun. When you're listening to someone else's body and when you have a partner that you're really vibing with, you get that seamless, responsive quality to your energy. Does it carry when you go out afterwards to get a meal? Would it carry in a moment where your partner experienced harm? Would you still be dancing, then, or would you still be listening?

Havard: This is helping me understand that you actually are not talking about choreography metaphorically. You are extending the word, literally, beyond a formal dance setting. I think that's really important for how we think about choreography, because there's this presumption in dance spaces that the body means something different in the studio, like maybe you don't need consent in the same way you would outside of the rehearsal room. What if the type of embodied listening that happens in a moment of particularly well-facilitated sexual consent translated to movement on a stage; what that would do for the violence that does happen in formal performance spaces?

I want to talk about what's left behind after the exhibit. When you gave a guest lecture in my class "Writing Sex in Media and Performance," you brought in the headdress you created for the final performance that had the words of people who had seen the exhibition inscribed throughout. The students, as they passed it around, could unroll these scrolls that were records of the exhibition and LGBTQIA2s+ viewers' reactions to it. The students reflected back that being able to interact with that piece of the performance was really impactful, which shows this power of the haptic in experiencing performance.

What's the pedagogical use of what's left behind in not only creating an archive of the exhibition, but also moving toward the goal of feeling liberation?

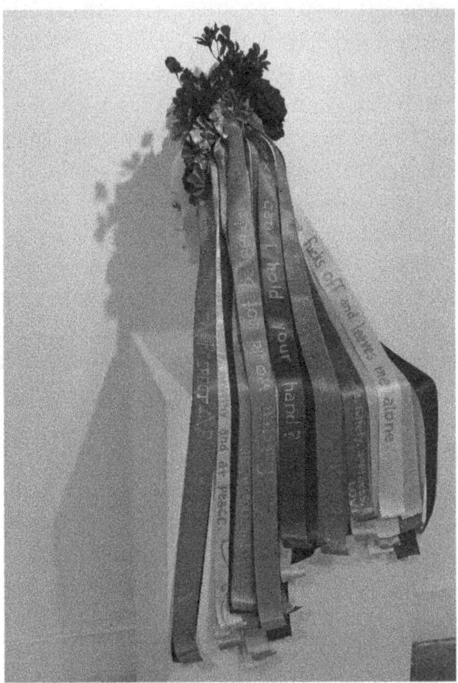

Image 28 Colorful ribbon scrolls with visions of a world without rape unfurl from the headdress, perched on a pedestal, vibrant and majestic with its crown of flowers. Created by Jadelynn St Dre, Cassandra Clark, LGBTQIA2s+ residents of the Bay Area, 2019, credit Leslie St Dre, 2019.

St Dre: I am obsessed with ephemera. I think every performance work
I've ever done has left something behind. I feel like any type of artistic
work wants to create a lasting impression: something that asks people
to continue to think, a provocation. That's how we often move people to
action, when something sticks with them that they feel they have
to understand further; then that person goes to experience other art and
learn from other voices, constantly sourcing information. Getting to an
opinion is never the point. Getting to a constant reflexive state of thinking
through and taking action is the point. Ephemera reverberates and allows
access to embodied elements of performance work, even after they have
ended.

The headdress, as a part of the performance, sought to engage the
viewers in visioning as a tangible action. Throughout the course of the
exhibition, there was a corner where members of the LGBTQIA2s+
community were invited, as they viewed the exhibition, to write their
vision of a world without sexual assault on these textiles.

Whenever I would go to the gallery, I would find new scrolls that
people would place on the hanging fabric ladder by the window. It was
incredible, this constant reflection of the work we were doing. For the
final performance, a fantastic costume artist named Cassandra Clark and I
built this headdress I conceived of, styled after a traditional Mexican floral
headdress based off of Baile Folklórico, connected to my cultural ancestry.
We took the statements on the scrolls, re-wrote them by hand, and rolled
the scrolls onto the headdress so that they clustered around my head.
In the final performance, it was used as a performance prop, essentially,
or agitator is a better word.

Havard: I love the substitution of agitator for prop.

St Dre: The final performance was the culmination of the exhibit. Azin Seraj, a
gifted filmmaker, created an opening video work for the closing night that
was rich, ephemeral, and longing. LeahAnn Mitchell, the extraordinary
musician I mentioned earlier, sang an excerpt of the song she had written
to anchor the exhibition. Jo Howard, Vanessa Rochelle Lewis, and Reaa
Puri all performed pieces as well—Vanessa a piece of her transformative
original poetry *Love Spirituals for Faeries with Broken Wings*, Reaa a tender
invitation to breath and ritual, and Jo a sensual dance he choreographed
that incited us all into connection and joy. Bay Area inspiration, organizer,
and artist Kin Folkz, who also led a community talk back for the exhibit,
designed the sound for the performance and also brought in The Haus of
Devine to do a final, phenomenal vogue performance which closed the
show.

I collaborated with Ori Doria-Quesada, who is an incredible physical
performer and acrobat. We created the performance component in which
the headdress was unraveled, during which I recited a poem I had written
while walking a straight line as Ori spun and tumbled around me. The
performance gesture with the headdress began in silence. Ori unraveled

and read the first scroll to start, and then I walked around the audience space, holding out my hand as an invitation. Anyone that wanted to could put their hand in mine, which created this moment of direct connection and consent for the audience, in which they chose whether or not to engage with the piece, to be close to my body. If someone grabbed my hand, I then bent my head down and they unfurled the scroll visions and read them aloud. The readings themselves brought laughter, sighs, murmurs of affirmation, and tears.

We had audience voices speaking these collected visions, collected over the course of the exhibition, of what a world without sexual violence could look like. Those visions are particularly important to name into space so that they can be witnessed because the realness is that LGBTQIA2s+ folk, we need vision to survive. Most of us grew up having to imagine that people like us even existed, that a world could exist in which we would be welcome, where we wouldn't be harmed, where we would be accepted and embraced.

Havard: I think you're right that queer and trans-gestures hold a different analysis. You've raised the question in our previous conversations, "What visionary potentials do queer and BIPOC stories and bodies incite?" This exhibition, in answer to this question, brought together a group of people that wouldn't have been brought together otherwise, and then you facilitated this process that had all of these ripples of healing.

St Dre: This space was created for and by queer and trans-folk that had experienced sexual assault, unapologetically. However, it was also a space that wanted cisgender heterosexual folk and white folk to enter and hear these stories because of the need for conspirators. My work really wants to invite people in not only as witnesses, but also to ask people, "Where are you implicated in this? Where are you complicit in the messaging around sexual violence? Whose voices are you uplifting, and are you aware of the particular ways that LGBTQIA2s+ folk are impacted by sexual assault?" Inviting them into that conversation with a degree of directness and clarity but also tenderness I think set the conditions for some real learning to happen in that space as well, because the space wanted to be celebratory of our community's incredible vision and survival, and also wanted to ask the question—why does this space not already exist in abundance? And for the folks that are not part of these communities, what are you doing that perpetuates our invisibilization?

The naming of identity was essential here. This project, although we emphasized the voices of BIPOC folk, also included white people. Leslie Dreyer's gorgeous wall mural really demonstrates how we were strategic in the way we chose to talk about the identities that were in the room. They crafted these intersecting triangles, referencing triangles as a symbol of oppression and reclamation for queer folk, within which were these fractaled shapes that included aspects of each participant's identity that they consented to share. They included things like racial and cultural identities, gender, nationality, as well as things like "BlackMagical Butch-ish Femme," "Shapeshifter," and "Grump." Instead of every wall tag listing identities, we chose to name identities collaboratively, artistically. We wanted to suggest that the survivors' and artists' self-identification in their stories and in the artwork is more integral to the viewing experience than the curatorial objectification of naming identities in a list on a wall tag.

When you look at Angela Hennessy's piece that is literally crafted out of her own and Vanessa's hair on the wall, or you look at Quinn Peck's piece that depicts scars of nature alongside his own top surgery scars, you get who these people are without having to do the identity politic of listing everything out.

Wall tags provide context in institutional art spaces, but they're also an anthropological tool, naming and categorizing things. So in thinking about how to present identity that was part of the dissonance that was present.

Havard: There are ways that you held this space based on your skills and identities that very few other people could. That you saw so many different sides and held so many different lenses around systems of oppression reminds me of a methodology of "mestiza consciousness," as Gloria Anzaldúa puts it in *Borderlands/ La Frontera: The New Mestiza*. There's a way that you really build bridges that I think is central to seeing the body and self in its fullness.

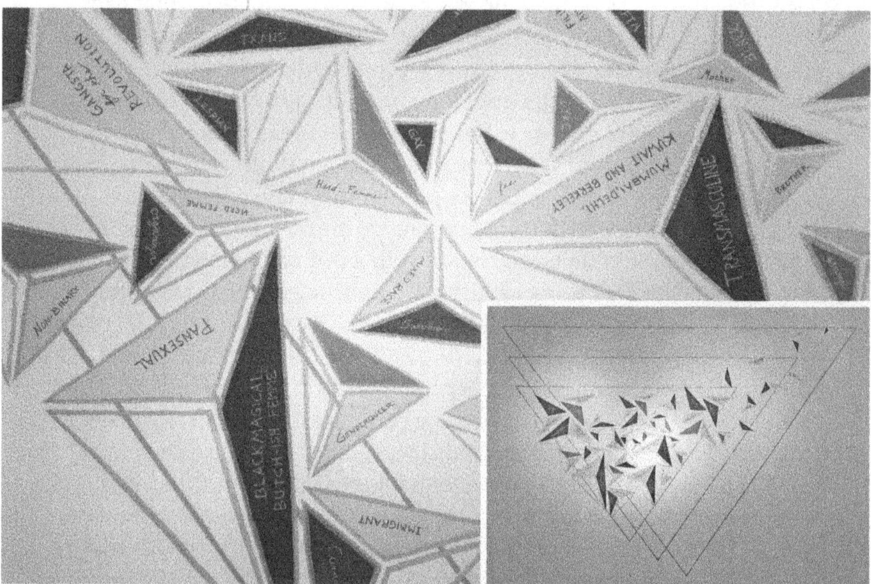

Image 29 Mural with accumulation of identities of the artists involved in Choreographies written into triangles that are arranged geometrically and then splinter apart across the wall. Mural. *Our Collective Identity*, Leslie Dreyer, 2018. Close-up detail and full shot, credit Leslie St Dre, 2019.

St Dre: That was really touching, what you said. I don't know that I had named it as "mestiza consciousness" but that feels right on. It is very connected to being liminal beings who live in that liminal space. I do think that there's something special about that ability to bridge, and in it is another call to action.

I want to come back to your question about feeling liberation. When I'm thinking about something like the end of sexual violence, which for most people feels so unachievable, who else would we go to but LGBTQIA2s+ folks, and especially BIPOC folk in those communities, to seed these visions—the folks that already depend on vision creation to survive and who disproportionately experience higher degrees of violence as well? The headdress wanted to continue to exist after the exhibition was over, but it also wanted to uplift and make the point of the enduring transformative potential of LGBTQIA2s+ folk and specifically Black, Indigenous, folk of color's brilliance to be architects of the path that moves us forward toward liberation from the ever-present threat of sexual violence.

As a teaching tool, continuing to have these visions spoken into space creates that echo or ripple that allows people to access these visions of better futures. That is both for people outside of the community who may or may not have encountered our communities speaking our truths, but also for folks in our communities, to see ourselves reflected and represented. These visions existing in the world counter isolation and create more space for people to know that they are not completely alone in their experiences, which is literally lifesaving.

Havard: Thank you for breaking that down. That was very moving.

St Dre: What I really want to say is that, Julia, you and I, these are our stories. This project is for us. This project belongs to all of us in the LGBTQIA2s+ communities who have experienced sexual violence and survived. That's why I dream that it will continue in the future, in different contexts and iterations. It feels really wonderful to talk it through with you, and again, I'm so grateful.

Havard: I'm grateful for your work! When I attended the exhibition, I had the feeling that this is a space that feels like the source of something … We can't abolish rape until we imagine a world without rape.

I'm tired, but I also have to do this. **Red flush along collar bone, traveling down between chest.**

    I don't entirely trust that others are going to get it right.
Right elbow bends bicep, lifts arm with palm open toward face.
Relating back to self-care—love myself or whatever,
this
weird hybrid of a body that I have.
                    The weight of scars
                      Raw
          Craving

**Short laugh followed by clenched jaw and the pull of brow, eyes pressed,
nose surrounded by lifted cheek.**
I'm struggling.
**That stone
Spinning
Spin spin
Spin
Spinning**
　　　　A slow investment in me.
I don't have forever, but also, I do.

*I think a lot of us—we know how to do that pretty easily now,
this particular ritual.*

　　　We tell our stories in ritual, in fire, in flame, in water soaked roots.

Like taking a shower or bath,

you can't just take a bath once, and you're done.

　　We don't know how to be awake in the world.

　　Once that's in order, everything else is just dominoes.

If we just start at that point

　　　　—exhale.[3]

Notes

1　In this context, we mean bodymind as Margaret Price understands it in the 2015
piece, "The Bodymind Problem and the Possibilities of Pain," as a strategy of working
against the falsity of mind-body dualism while acknowledging the ways that mental
and physical processes inform each other and often *are* each other (269).
2　Choreographic Transcript from "Choreographies of Disclosure."
3　Choreographic Transcript from "Choreographies of Disclosure."

Bibliography

Anzaldúa, Gloria. *Borderlands/La Frontera: The New Mestiza*. San Francisco: Aunt Lute
　　Books, 1987.
Price, Margaret. "The Bodymind Problem and the Possibilities of Pain." *Hypatia* 30, no. 1
　　(Winter 2015): 268–84.

Chapter 17

"THE QUEEN OF FILTH: ROSE WOOD COMES CLEAN WITH JOE E. JEFFREYS"

by Joe E. Jeffreys, with Rose Wood

Rose Wood is hardcore. On stages worldwide for over twenty years, Rose has offered short narrative theatrical performances that often incorporate actual bodily penetration and defecation. There are few out there like this gob-smacking trans artist.

I have known Rose for over a dozen years and witnessed and videotaped many of their anarchies. For this interview we chatted in their apartment at New York City's Chelsea Hotel where they are one of the last remaining permanent residents. Wearing a t-shirt of their own design with the word "other" stenciled across the chest, we spoke about what inspires them to create, about the purposes and uses of censorship, and what exactly is sex on stage.

Jeffreys: How do you describe yourself?

Wood: People ask me how I identify, what are my pronouns, etc. My response is that I'm an artist. I don't care how you refer to me—I know who I am and what someone calls me will not change that. If you see a man, a woman, a multiple gender, then call it as you see it.

The art of performance has been a discovery process for me, allowing me to develop and access different parts of myself and develop different talents and abilities. I was first able to explore my gender issues through performance. I would describe myself as transgender—I've had nine surgeries including breast implants and facial surgery—but it's something I had to go through to be comfortable in my skin rather than an identity. I'm not a fan of the politics that go along with all of that stuff, but onstage I'm certainly a gender outlaw, gender non-conformer, gender problem.

It also brought up my interest in theater and in storytelling and actually having an impact on people rather than just entertaining them. From there, especially during the Covid pandemic, I've moved more specifically into theater because my greatest impact is not shock and body tricks. The theater is the most potent part and I'm currently working to develop that aspect even further.

The director of the Berlin Film Festival came to a show of mine and said to me, "Well, you know, Rose, in Berlin, people fuck on stage." I replied that making love on the stage is nice, but doesn't necessarily make you an artist. Making good theater on the stage is the work of an artist. He liked that a lot.

The problem is that when sex is entertainment, if it becomes truly erotic people go into their own arousal space and they cease to connect to the people around them. It becomes an internal experience rather than a connective experience. The ideal to create an erotic mood in the room without bringing people into that space, but still allowing them to connect to other people in the room.

A big question for me is what's the motive for having a sexual act on the stage? Are you showcasing a desirable body to create desire, like showing food to a hungry dog? Everybody's seen that and it doesn't really qualify as theater; at best it's entertainment. Another reason for doing something sexual on the stage is intent to arouse the audience but then there's the problem that you will ultimately lose the audience.

There's a prevailing belief that if sex is shown onstage it's for the purpose of titillation. Sex though has other inferences. When sex comes into a discussion, it's presumed to be for adults, as it is part of the adult experience. Children dance and sing as do adults so these things are not particular to the adult experience. Sex is part of adult life. There are other things that are particularly adult such as a 9–5 job, divorce, marriage, and retirement. Putting adult subjects on stage allows you to create a portrait of adult life.

Jeffreys: Doesn't the idea of stage immediately assume a performer and observer relationship? A kind of awareness that you are being observed.

Wood: What inevitably becomes an issue is what kind of stage is it? I worked in the early 2000s in escort bars and there was no stage per se. There were boxes which were elevated little mini stages, which were to arouse and to entertain and to solicit prostitution. That was the purpose of those boxes. Then there are burlesque stages and vaudeville stages where there's a level of informality and the intent is to entertain. Then there's a theater stage where the intent is not as much to entertain but to enlighten or to share insight on the human experience. So each stage has a different motive that's attached to it.

Jeffreys: Or different expectations.

Wood: Exactly. So when you go into a strip club, you don't expect theater; you're looking for entertainment, you're looking for titillation. In an escort bar you're looking exclusively for interactive entertainment. During a theater show, you aren't expecting someone in the cast to start selling their sexual services to you unless it fits with the narrative. The setting both informs and creates expectation.

Jeffreys: But all of them still do have that audience/performer relationship contract, whereas that contract is flexible in these ways that you're saying.

Tell me about your signature act—the Bottle Act.

Wood: I was working in an escort bar and the customers believe you are there to solicit. So I'm dancing on a block and a man comes to give me money and I turn so that he could put it in my stocking and he, without asking, very suddenly shoved dollar bills in my rectum. The room caught that. Things kind of came to a stop and the music kept playing but everybody was waiting to see what I would do. I had the choice of getting angry and trying to get him thrown out. There wasn't any security though. I could have been ashamed, and walked off with hurt feelings. Instead, I chose to own it. I pulled each dollar out very slowly, unfolded it and put it in my stocking one after the other. It was 2 or 3 dollars. I resumed dancing and could feel that everyone in the room was relieved and happy. It was a big thing for me: a moment of shame could become a moment of success. I then memorialized that in a performance, which became a theatrical performance.

Jeffreys: So, your Bottle Act memorializes a specific experience you had. Isn't there also a history of bottle numbers where a performer comes out on stage and sticks a bottle up their rectum?

Wood: There are often times sex shows where somebody will squirt milk from their nipples, shoot a ping pong ball with their vagina, stick a large bottle up their rectum and do tricks, stunts. A famous stunt is where a woman will put a pen in her vagina and write on something. They're just tricks though. That's not theater. It's a different thing from theater. There's a long history of sex tricks. The Amsterdam Museum of Sex presents sex tricks but that falls in the category of entertainment.

Jeffreys: Why do you say it's not theater?

Wood: Because it doesn't give insight into human nature. It's kind of "Ha-ha!" I can do this.

Jeffreys: It's isolated. A concrete event versus something in a context.

Wood: Yeah, there is no story. The key is story.

In my Bottle Act, my character is clearly the lowest status in the room. Her attire is tawdry and she's trying to sell her services and there are no takers. She is naked and insulted. She doesn't like what she's doing. She finds a used condom in her rectum which is just an example of an unpleasant reality of her life. With the only thing that she has, her whiskey bottle, she puts it down and she sits on it and she lifts it up and flips off the audience. The message of this is that she's saying, "fuck you" some more. There's a switch in power in the room because suddenly she's more intimidating and more dangerous and more captivating than everyone else in the room. So the whole power dynamic flips with her kind of admission and acceptance of her lowest status and her strength. She turns the bottle into a weapon.

Jeffreys: At the end of your Bottle Act, the thing that always gets the audience going after they see you sit down on the bottle and stand up picking it right up with you then pulling it out of your rectum is taking a big swig out of the bottle and spewing it all over them. That's the ultimate climax of the number. There's always a strong reaction to that final moment.

Wood: There's this unmistakable understanding that she knows her power and that she has her dignity and that any lack she has does not in her mind make her less than anyone.

Jeffreys: Does that character have a name?

Wood: No. Just I call her the bottle lady. She recurs. She has other performances that she does. She's always resentful.

Jeffreys: Can you talk about what inspires you to create? When did you start performing?

Wood: I actually started performing when I was ten years old. I was doing magic from the time I was eight or nine years old.

Jeffreys: You're still doing magic. A different kind, perhaps, but still magic in ways both mundane and profound.

Wood: I got put into a cabaret show at a local community center. I showed a woman there my magic stuff and she helped me create two acts that I did in an adult's cabaret show. And I was in school plays and then I was still doing card magic and working as a gambling spotter in my late teens and into my early twenties. Then I let go of that. Casino life was not for me.

Years went by. I realized that I was not going to turn into a potbelly stove and still had plenty of life in my body, and could go back to show biz. And so I did and I have been performing now for about twenty-three years and it has been very successful. I've done 6,700 shows for The Box alone, as well as other shows and traveling the world performing.

Jeffreys: Was it erotic performing that you went straight into in your forties or did that only come about when you were hired by The Box?[1]

Wood: I started in burlesque and dancing in transsexual bars. There was an erotic component because burlesque is about the tease. It was good training for me to be on stage and to learn and relearn stage skills. But ultimately I found that I was stuck because it's really about the ladies and the men. Boylesque was a separate thing. There was nothing really for trans-people. There's a little history of it but it's marginal.

I was doing drag but I wasn't really connected to the drag performance community. I didn't want to lip sync and I wasn't a singer or a comic. But I was having a measure of success with burlesque. I won an award for "Most Exotic Move" at the Burlesque Hall of Fame competitions in 2006. Alongside creating more classical numbers, I also made a series of pieces that included full nudity and insertion. My work began to be less welcome in the burlesque community.

The turning point was when The Box opened in 2007. They didn't want burlesque. They wanted theater. So I showed them a variety of things. The Bottle Act for them was theater. They thought that they wanted to have an erotic show but the problem was that the audience that they had was sophisticated and the erotic pieces were not landing at all.

The Box is a very expensive club. Customers weren't going to pay a lot of money to see someone shake their boobs because you could see that in a strip club or a burlesque show. We even went so far as to have people having sex on stage. The audience was amazingly uninterested because they knew exactly what it was and where it was going. They would rather just do it themselves, which they felt free to do. People were having sex in the room. Sex on stage was not something to buy an expensive bottle of champagne for.

The owner realized that though he wasn't fond of what I was doing he liked the effect. It created a comradery in the room of people saying, "I've never seen anything like that." They were talking to each other and they were a little bit shocked, a little bit offended, but in a way that created connection between people. When something is successful, they say, "More please" and as I continued to make more, it became something that people came to see. They said, "Well, we heard we're going to be shocked."

So the real question is, can you deliver? And I could deliver.

I started to create a context for seeing things that were extreme, excessive, or crazy. People began to come for it. The Box was getting twenty to thirty calls a week, "How dare you! How could you do that?" The general manager was having a wonderful time saying, "Well, you know, it's theater. What we do is simulated. You didn't actually get hit with a piece of excrement. That was a brownie." And so people brought back their friends to have that experience and to watch their responses. It created a whole context for doing performances.

The challenge was that there were people who had just heard about it and sometimes these tales got out of control. So what do you do? I mean you don't want to not meet their expectations. Somehow my own inclination and my skill at delivering this kind of material grew, so it became increasingly intense and shocking. As my work developed, something opened up for me. My theatrical mind began to blossom.

Jeffreys: How many numbers would you say you've created at The Box?

Wood: I've probably created about seventy acts. Some of them are problematic, difficult, only for the holidays, etc. I've pared down to about thirty-five good, solid pieces.

Jeffreys: Is there anything that you're always aiming for when you're creating a new number? There's some element, some feeling, something you're trying to communicate?

Wood: On the one hand, I want to tell a story. I don't want the trick or the sensational moments to be the only reason for the number. It's not shock for shock's sake. The interesting thing really is the character's mind. What's behind what you're seeing? That's the most fascinating part. The true reveal is not the body. The true reveal is the mental and emotional nature of the character.

Jeffreys: Yes, because frequently you come out on stage and you're completely taken everything off in the first fifteen seconds. So strip is clearly not the act. The question becomes where does it go from there?

Wood: I do a number where the character starts naked, duct taped to a chair, and clearly has been badly abused. There's blood. There's cuts. There's black and blue marks. A beer bottle's been taped up in my rectum. My genitals are stretched and taped to my leg. It's somebody who's been held hostage and beaten and it is intended to be disturbing. And then near the end the character finally gets the hood off and you see that they've been hit in the mouth with enough force to knock out a number of teeth. They had been bound and hit in a very sensitive part of the body with a fist or bottle. Seeking a little relief, they pick up a nearby mirror that has a pile of cocaine on it. As they bend over the mirror to snort the cocaine, they see their face in the mirror, bloodied and cut. The damage is more compelling than the drugs, and as they hold the mirror vertically to get a better look, the drugs fall to the floor. They use the mirror to voyeuristically survey their damaged body and, in the process, see the bottle that had been stuck inside them hanging from the tape on their body. Suddenly, the horror of what they see turns to arousal and they fellate the bottle, reinsert it, and kiss their image in the mirror. And so you see that the person was probably in some way complicit in this act, this violent scene that took place. That is what it took to turn them on. So for me, there's a fully naked body, something stuck in the rectum, genital taping, bloody mouth, and missing teeth, but the real shocker is that they liked it. The heart of the number is that something which is awful to us is someone else's turn-on.

Jeffreys: What I find interesting is that it's a reversal.

Wood: It's a reversal. You think it's going one way but then it flips and that becomes something that's erotic. Now for the person I'm portraying, that's a sexual experience. Is that sex or am I showing the emotional pathology of this character?

I'm using my openings, my orifices. I'm using my rectum, my mouth. I fellate the bottle because I'm turned on by it even with my damaged mouth. I'm continuing to get off from this. Now, I'm portraying this, it's not my own version of a fun sexual experience. So is that sex on stage?

And the difference between a trick, you know, squirting, I can squirt excrement out of my rear end about six to ten feet. That's a trick that by itself has no story. It's "Ha-ha!" Look at me.

Jeffreys: It needs a narrative context, a tent of a beginning, middle and end.

Wood: Right and any single one of those things without a story and a meaning that has theatrical things to it, like a reversal, a build, a theatrical arc, becomes just a trick.

Jeffreys: Talk a little bit about the role of humor in your work. Your work is funny. It is sexual slapstick. But it does take a while for audiences to see it that way, if ever.

Wood: My humor on stage is that of a clown. I take something that people do and exaggerate it. So I'm treating my body with a callousness that normally they might not have. If a man is masturbating, but then suddenly does it at five times the speed, it's funny. If a woman is rubbing herself and suddenly it becomes so fast that she goes out of control, it's funny. If you stand on a toilet seat that's not a normal thing to do. But if you're pregnant and in high heels and you stand on a toilet seat where there's such a high risk of falling, it's heightened stakes and unexpected solutions. Humor can soften things. Humor can allow you to continue. But the problem that I don't like with a lot of humor is that it lets you off the hook emotionally. If something is too jokey, you can dismiss it without confronting it. So that balance has to be carefully monitored.

Jeffreys: Has The Box ever faced censorship issues that you can talk about? And what happened with the club in Las Vegas you worked at that actually went to trial?

Wood: The Box in NYC has definitely had some censorship issues. I was pushing the envelope, and the owners were not yet sure that we could defend the extreme things I was doing. There was a period where the club was having issues with different regulatory agencies, and, as a result, we had a steady flow of inspectors coming through. The owners were concerned that the inspectors might not appreciate what I was doing onstage. Inspectors aren't culture people; they are bureaucrats. During this time, a lot of my pieces were pulled from the show, and temporarily replaced with more tame numbers.

In a bar where you serve alcohol, you're not allowed to show genitals or female nipples. However, though The Box served alcohol, they were licensed as a theater by the local community board, so there was some slack in that rule. Another big factor was the political climate. I was approached by a group of people who worked with a First Amendment organization. At that time, the city had worked hard to close down porn stores, porn theaters, and gay bars. Under the war cry of morality, zoning changed. The argument was that these places lowered property values, so it was helpful to be rid of them. They'd pushed as hard as they could and were aware that there could be potential community backlash if they went further. If there had been fifty other extreme performers like myself, they'd have censored us, but since it was really just me, there wasn't enough of a need. Coming after just me might have set off a big First Amendment case, and turning my case into a cause célèbre. Bad for NYC Police business. They left me alone.

The Box opened a venue in Las Vegas in 2011 called The Act. It was going to be a cleaner show, no nudity. It was owned by a very conservative landlord, Sheldon Adelson, a member of the GOP.

The club wasn't working. The primary problem was the location. Nearly all tourists in Vegas go to the club that's in their hotel. The Act was located in a shopping mall. It had a little fan base but wasn't making nearly enough money to justify staying open. Clearly it needed to shut down, but how would you do that? The investors just wanted to lock the doors and put a sign in front saying "CLOSED." However, when you are a famous club owner/creator, that's not the way you want to leave. He decided that the club would be shut down because it was too extreme for Las Vegas.

They brought me over. They had me do my bottle act, and I did that nightly for two weeks. Adelson's daughter came to see it. Week 3 they planned to do something so flagrantly in violation of all of the laws that we'd definitely get closed down. In spite of its reputation as Sin City, Las Vegas has more restrictions than almost any city in America.

They staged the whole evening. I did my Toilet number. It's a brutal, cold, unpleasant number. I refer to it as my "Queen of Filth" act. The entertainment comes from watching the responses of the audience members. To be witnesses to the violation, the entertainment director of The Act invited club owners and entertainment directors from the mega clubs in the area to come see something they'd never seen before. At the time, I wasn't aware of their plans.

The show goes on. Then suddenly it's time for me to do my number and I do my number. And as opposed to applause, it was very restrained and very quiet after. The curtain just closed. I went back to my room. I heard nothing. That was it. I continued my run for another week and did not do the toilet number again. I did the Bottle Act and another number where it was simulated oral sex.

Then The Act's entertainment director drove me to the airport and said, "Rose, you didn't know this, but that particular night was the funniest night of my life." Very few people know what actually happened. There were about eight tables with three to four powerful men at each. Well, when I did the toilet number, they were overwhelmed. At most of the tables, one of the men vomited on the table right in front of the other men. This created a problem. If anyone heard that Mr. So and So vomited on a table, they'd be shamed. With only three or four guys at each table, the person who vomited would know that one of them told the story would find out who told and take revenge.

It was supposed to be a night where something so outrageous happened, that they had to close the club. After my performance, they all got together and checked in with one another. "Look, no matter what way we go with this, we're wrong. We're wrong for being here, we're wrong for taking part in this. The best solution is—let's all agree that this never happened."

Jeffreys: How then does the club get taken to court in Vegas?

Wood: Just my bottle number and the other number were enough to receive warning that their content was in violation of the laws. Simulating drug use and simulating sexual content were not allowed. There were numbers where the girl dancers pretended to do oral sex on one of the girls. Just purely pretend; they were fully clothed. I was pretending to do oral sex on one of the women who was wearing a bathing suit. There was simulated cocaine use with these huge mirrors with piles of powder and oversized straws. It was clearly a vaudeville version of a cocaine party. That was enough to get it to court in Vegas because that was a violation. And the finale was described in court: "and we saw someone who had the genitalia of both sexes sit on a Jack Daniels bottle, and lift it off the ground without help from their hands." The judge said, "I've heard enough."

Jeffreys: What was the final outcome of the trial?

Wood: The club was closed.

Jeffreys: Aren't there other clubs in Vegas doing the same type of things?

Wood: The rules are very strictly enforced in Las Vegas and no one dares to push back. There's plenty of prostitution and drugs, but they are handled very discreetly. A lot of clubs come and go. This was just planning, a tactical error. It wasn't that it wasn't a good club. It was a lovely club. This is part of the club world, it's part of theater world. It's the right show in the wrong place and at the wrong time.

I've been used in this way several times. A NYC club promoter hired me to do a performance at Splash Bar, my "Walk on the Wild Side" number and it went over fabulously. After my act, he rushed me out the door. The former owner of the club stopped me as I was leaving, handed me a $100 tip, and said, "I couldn't love this more." The promoter said, "Now, now, now, now, now time to go." And I ran.

I found out the party was shut down because my number was considered obscene. What I did went too far. It broke all their rules. Now it appeared that Rose broke their rules but I had been hired by somebody who knew exactly what I was going to do with the intent that I break all their rules. The party was not making enough money but the promoter didn't want to be seen as a failure. Best to go out for being notorious, for being too wild. The promoter's wild party was shut down because Rose broke the rules. This kind of press enhances the promoter's reputation.

Jeffreys: If you have to quickly tell somebody what it is you do, maybe even just a phrase, what do you say?

Wood: I have two phrases. One is the Queen of Filth and the other is the Mother of all Motherfuckers. The Queen of Filth is my own. Just a quick story of where that comes from—at a certain point my work became increasingly extreme and I started to get a bigger response than other performers I was on a bill with. It started to skew the show a little bit. Some performers, who were my friends, went to the owner of one of the clubs and said, "You know, Rose is kind of tipping the show here. This is not really good for the show." And the owner said, "Well, everybody seems to like that stuff." "Well, yeah but it makes it less of a show and more of a Rose thing." I got cut from the show without an explanation.

Then people started requesting what I did and the owner told the performers who had made this complaint. And they said, "Well, you know, Rose didn't invent this stuff. We can do it too." He said, "Oh, okay, go ahead. Do some of it." It turned out that they couldn't, or that they didn't really go there. I didn't know any of this but a friend of mine who was part of the scene said, "Rose, this is what's happened. Your friends kind of went behind your back and did this." I said, "Well, gee, you know, like, what do you think I should do?" And, he said, "You've gotta show them who's the Queen of Filth."

I thought, "Oh!" So I came up with the toilet number. The motivation was simply: to make something that goes so far and is so brutal, not just with what the audience sees but the character and the story and the intent behind it. And I made the number and I brought it to The Box and it debuted on one of the owner's birthdays. And they said, "Rose you've broken through to another level." So that became my "I'm the queen of filth piece."

Looking back, I realized that the performers who said I skewed the show, they were right. I was angry at that moment, but I really needed to have an avenue for me to explore the extreme side of what I do.

Jeffreys: So Queen of Filth, the toilet number has come up a few times. For people who have not had the pleasure of seeing it, can you describe it?

Wood: It's a character who's transsexual. They're angry at the audience for even being there. There is a toilet on stage and the character plays with excrement from the toilet. They remove clothing, smear excrement on their body, and then masturbate with it. Then they take a plunger and use it to play with the excrement and then put it down on the stage. The character takes a long look at the audience, and then sits on the plunger. They go up and down penetrating themselves with the plunger sixteen times, and pull it out from their rectum and deep throat it, cleaning it off. They turn their back to the audience, put one foot on the toilet, take a toilet brush, and open it into a long thing. You see the bristles and they insert the bristles and repeatedly penetrate themselves with that. They flip off the audience as the curtain closes.

Jeffreys: What's the music for that number?

Wood: "Fuck the Pain Away" by Peaches.

Jeffreys: And the sixteen times is because?

Wood: The number of times that she says, "Fuck the pain away."

Jeffreys: What about the Motherfucker of all Motherfuckers? Where does that come from?

Wood: Raven O came up with that name. People refer to me as the Mother of The Box. Just by my nature, I'm maternal. There are a lot of kids there and I'm an old bag and maternal. They need a little schooling. They need a little discipline. They respect me just because I'm so—for one I'm old. Clearly, I have my own issues and I'm so extreme that I'm an anti-authority. I'm not like their mother or their priest or whatever. I have a nice relationship with the family of performers.

Jeffreys: Is there any number that you've wanted to do on stage that you just think this can't be performed?

Wood: During a period in 2007 in the Middle East, there was a purge of gay men. Anyone accused of or reputed to be gay could be grabbed by a group of military men at night and their rectums were glued shut with a powerful glue. They were beaten, given a strong laxative, and left to die painfully in the street. The hospitals weren't allowed to take them. This torture murder was a message to other gay men. I was so deeply horrified by this that I conceived of a number as a protest.

I created the performance and shared it with some friends. They told me that they thought I'd get shot, The Box burned down, and that I'd need to find another way to say it. I had made the Toilet number and this issue was very present for me. Around that period, a Black man, Abner Louima had been arrested for no apparent reason, and in the Police station, an officer sodomized him with a plunger. The Toilet number connected so closely with this incident that I decided I'd need to create a separate piece.

It was clear that I'd have to look for another way to express my rage. My gut reaction had been that whatever Holy man found justification in a sacred text, a holy text, to torture and murder that way, should have the pages of that text shoved up his ass one at a time. I decided to use a secular Holy person symbolically, namely Anna Wintour, the high priestess of the religion of Fashion, and *Vogue* magazine was her sacred text.

I had her acting out a kink secretly in the bathroom. She shits herself in the women's room when no one's looking and shoves the pages of her own magazine up her butt with the plunger and then pulls up her underwear, adjusts her dress, and goes back out into the room like nothing happened. In the process she gets shit on her hand and rather than wipe it off, she holds out her hand for someone to help her down from the stage. Someone graciously takes her hand to help her, only to find that she has contaminated them with her shit.

Before this she was kinky but this is the true reveal, showing the malice of the Holy Person. The number shows my desire to expose the minds of the "holy ones" who murder men because of their sexuality, without pointing a finger at them specifically. For me this performance takes on the quality of a ritual done in memory of the men lost to this vile mentality. She's passed on her illness, her shit. That shit I have on my hand is fake (it was hidden in my purse) because I wouldn't get shit on the hand of someone helping me down the stairs. That's where the story is more important than having all of the shit be real. That's the mind of that character. I found another way to tell the story and while no one would understand that that is exactly what the story is, it becomes for me a kind of ritual where I am remembering the purpose of this number. It's actually a violent number. I often go into shock when I do it.

Jeffreys: Can you talk about some of the physical preparations that you may have to do for some of these numbers on a nightly basis and how some of this work has affected your body over six thousand performances.

Wood: To do what I do requires extensive physical maintenance. For one, I have to keep everything clean. Things are coming and going from my rectum and they have to be clean. Care has to be taken that no one comes in contact with them because it's effectively hazardous material. It's one thing if it's between consenting adults; it's another thing when it's become part of work. Everything is done with great care. I also have to watch my diet and time my eating very carefully because I do defecate on stage live, not in every piece, but it's something that I have to be able to do when requested.

I have developed a body timing. I use a laxative and suppository and know exactly how much time I have before I will defecate. There's a lot of discipline and timing involved in everything that I consume: food, supplements, liquids, etc. For example, I'll use chlorophyll supplements to keep my stool from smelling. I want to minimize the unpleasantness for the people working on stage. Some of the acts where I am penetrating myself in a violent or aggressive way, I have to be stretched and prepared and relaxed prior or I will cause damage or go into shock. I'm trying to tell the story, not to make it an erotic act. My body has to be well warmed up to avoid muscle spasms. I have a series of drills that I run to get all my systems tuned up as high as possible.

Jeffreys: So lastly, what do you think your impact is/has been? What will your legacy be?

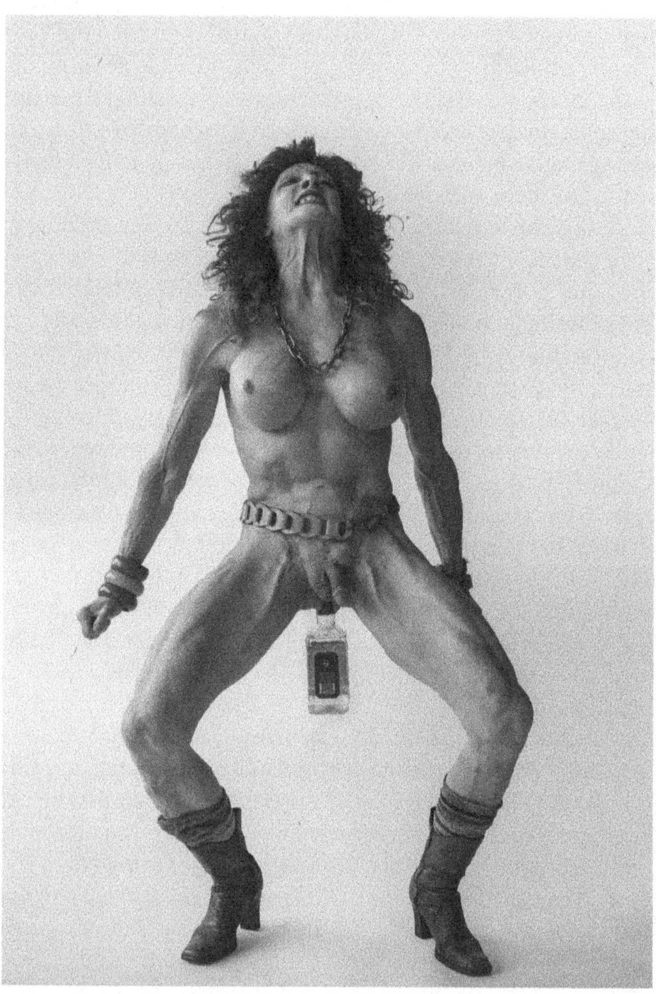

Image 30 Rose Wood, credit Eli Schmidt.

Wood: I have a humorous image that in fifty years outside of The Box in the park across the street there'll be a statue of a transsexual peeing like in Belgium, the Manneken Pis, you know, the little boy who peed on the fire. Something like that bronze of him.

But one of the big issues I have is that so much entertainment is in the middle. I see no real edge. I'm not seeing the edgy, the subversive, the things that make you want to talk about what your night was. I feel there's a hunger for real experience. It's something people really want. They really want to have an experience. They want to be able to say that something really, truly wild happened. They don't want to be injured but they really want the danger. They really want to experience the edges of human experience. They want to see something really crazy. That's just not out there. I would rather people be overwhelmed but have an experience that will touch them.

When you see a tightrope walker, you know they could fall and die but you also know they're highly trained. They're pushing their game both for you and for themselves. Chances are they will make it but the risk is there. In my case, I know what I'm doing, and though some of the things I do are edgy, I think everybody has the feeling that I'm going to be okay. The safety paired with danger gives it the excitement of circus, and allows them to experience it as theater. Risk and danger are part of my work. A lot of circus relies on and is about risk and danger. The problem is that in a circus you are simply seeing a trick or daredevil stunt. It has nothing to do with your darker psychological tendencies, gives no insight into your nature and is not part of a story. I will do something dangerous as part of a story. The story includes things that are specific to your life as an adult human being who has an adult body and does adult things from sex to drugs to the abuse of other people's bodies to whatever else. We don't want to harm ourselves or others onstage, but it can be helpful to use the fullest range of bodily expression as it is helpful for a painter to have different colors. By touching the audience on multiple levels, it's possible to have a much deeper impact, and this should not be confused with someone simply doing a trick or attempting to arouse you.

Note

1   The Box is an exclusive late night New York City nightclub with a no-hold-barred reputation, celebrity and moneyed clientele, and wild variety show with several unique sets each night.

NOTES ON CONTRIBUTORS

Sarah Ainslie is a freelance photographer whose work is inspired by living and working in London's East End: documenting the working lives of women in the area, Shoreditch at night, Strip Pubs in the East End, Smithfield Market, Brick Lane, and Arsenal Football supporters. She also facilitates community projects.

Carolina Are is a researcher with a PhD in digital criminology currently working as an Innovation Fellow at Northumbria University's Centre for Digital Citizens. Her research focuses on platforms' censorship of nudity, sex, and sex work. She's also a pole dance performer, instructor, activist, and creator at @bloggeronpole.

Anna Brooke is a teacher, healing arts practitioner, and author of *Stripped Down: How Burlesque Led Me Home* (2020). She is also known as Rev. Legs Malone, a burlesque performer, producer, educator, and advocate for all things striptease.

Alison J Carr is an artist, mentor, and scholar. She works visually and creates performances, examining bodies on display and the contexts they perform in. Routledge published her book, *Viewing Pleasure and Being A Showgirl: How Do I Look?*, in 2018, and her novella, *The Night*, was published in 2023.

Stacey Clare is a stripper, writer, activist, theater-maker, and co-founding member of the East London Strippers Collective (ELSC). Author of *The Ethical Stripper* 2022 and co-creator of Edinburgh Fringe show *Ask A Stripper*, Stacey continues to draw from her experience working in the sex industry to write and perform in Scotland.

Lara Clifton After leaving a job as a runner to become an exotic dancer, Lara met Tamara Tyrer in Miss Lara Clifton's Academy of Burlesque. Together they created the Whoopee Club which successfully rocked London until 2009. She is now full-time impressaria of Screaming Alley, a radical cabaret production company in Ramsgate, UK.

Julie Cook lives and works in Ynysybwl, South Wales. Her work is photography based with an emphasis on artists' books. Her research engages with issues of voyeurism in public and private space. Much of the work is collaborative in the making and often in its outcomes. She contributed to *Another Country: British Documentary Photography Since 1945* (2022).

DawN Crandell (aka Miss AuroraBoobRealis) is an interdisciplinary performing artist creating work in the space where burlesque, dance, poetry, theater, and drag meet. She is a co-founder of Boombox Burlesque: A Hip Hop Burlesque Festival, brASS: Brown RadicalAss Burlesque, and, back in 2007, Brown Girls Burlesque.

Yarit Dor, a pioneering certified Intimacy Director/Coordinator since 2018, was the first intimacy director to work in London's West End (*Death of a Salesman*) and is a contributor to many UK union guidelines. Intimacy direction credits include shows at West End, National Theatre, Shakespeare's Globe, Royal Court, Young Vic, and Rambert Dance.

Julia Havard is a genderful disabled white queer artist, access-worker, and researcher based in Philadelphia, PA. Ze received zir PhD in Performance Studies from the University of California Berkeley. Zir scholarly and performance work explores sexual culture, aesthetics, and dance as sites of world-building. www.juliahavard.net

Ash Hudson-Myers is a researcher, some-times lecturer, and full-time cryptid. Their research interests include theatrical depictions of illness, and sex as performance. Their work also explores ideas surrounding sex, sexuality, and queer studies more broadly. They cannot be found anywhere.

Toussaint Jeanlouis is a performer, actor, singer, dancer, personal trainer, and teacher.

Joe E. Jeffreys is a drag historian. He has published on the subject in encyclopedias, academic journals, and essay anthologies. His drag happy video work has screened internationally at festivals, galleries, and museums including the Tate Modern. He teaches at New York University and The New School. https://vimeo.com/joejeffreys.

Ra Malika Imhotep, PhD (Ra/They/Them/doll) is an ancestor-accountable cultural worker currently serving as an Assistant Professor of Global African Diaspora Studies at Spelman College. They are an organizer, curator, Black feminist performance artist and a published poet.

Erin Rachel Kaplan is Assistant Professor of Critical Theory, Dramatic Literature, & Practice at California State University, Sacramento. Her research has been published in *Theatre Topics, Theatre Annual, The Journal of American Drama & Theatre,* and more. She holds a PhD in Theatre & Performance Studies with a graduate certificate in Women & Gender Studies from the University of Colorado Boulder.

Sharon Kivland is an artist and writer, an editor, and a publisher.

Ella-Gabriel Mason is an artist and educator based in Philadelphia, PA. Their research focuses on how marginalized populations use dance and performance skills to navigate tight places. They are an adjunct instructor at Temple

University. See more of their performance, installation, and video work at www. moriahellamason.com.

Julia Matias holds a PhD from the University of Toronto, focusing on feminist research-creation in neo-burlesque. A Curatorial Research Fellow at the Trans-Feminist & Queer Digital Praxis Workshop, she's a passionate advocate of praxis-informed research and a practicing neo-burlesque artist, having performed and taught internationally.

Alexander Millington is Creative Director of Split Infinitive Theatre and Lecturer in Performing Arts. His practice-based research explores acts of intimacy and sexual behavior in contemporary British playwriting and performance. Published scripts include *Three Way*, *I Heart Michael Ball*, and *A Caravan Named Desire* with Playdead Press.

Lynn Sally is a scholar and performing artist. Her second book, *Neo-Burlesque: Striptease as Transformation*, was published by Rutgers University Press (2022). She produces and performs as Dr. Lucky, the World's Premiere Ph(Double)D. www.lynnsally.com.

Jadelynn St Dre is an organizer, educator, trauma therapist, and performance artist whose work centers on sexual violence, embodied pleasure, and LGBTQIA2s+ liberation. Her works, produced both nationally and internationally, include a detailed chapter about the *Choreographies* project in the upcoming publication *I Don't Know but Together We Do!* (Autonomous Press).

Zahra Stardust is an artist, scholar, writer, and mermaid. She is interested in queer birthing, somatic sex education, grief work, neurodivergence, intimacy coordination, and maximalist fashion. Her book *Indie Porn* will be published by Duke University Press in 2024.

Tamara Tyrer is a film and performance artist. Tyrer is an Associate Lecturer at Central St Martins and she has a PhD in moving image and female subjectivity. Tyrer's work has been shown at The National Gallery, The Lethaby Gallery, The Blackpool Tower Ballroom, and The V&A, amongst others.

Emily Underwood-Lee is Professor of Performance Studies at the University of South Wales. Her research is concerned with stories of the maternal, gender, health/ illness, and contemporary feminist performance practice. Recent publications include *Maternal Performance: Feminist Relations* (Palgrave 2021) and *Mothering Performance: Maternal Action* (Routledge 2022).

Marissa Vigneault is Associate Professor of Art History at Utah State University. Her widely published research examines the ongoing influence of feminist politics on artistic production, and the role of technology in shaping and affirming one's gender and sexuality via visual representation.

Rose Wood is a full-time performer/performance artist/visual artist. Working exclusively since 2007 for The Box, a high-end club/theater in NYC and London, Rose splits time between the two cities. Outsiders, outliers, and queer creatures are the characters in Rose's world, revealing concealed truths about the human condition... 7,500 performances and counting.

Index